John Lewis Geiger

A Peep at Mexico:

Narrative of a Journey Across the Republic From the Pacific of the Gulf...

John Lewis Geiger

A Peep at Mexico:
Narrative of a Journey Across the Republic From the Pacific of the Gulf...

ISBN/EAN: 9783744799867

Printed in Europe, USA, Canada, Australia, Japan

Cover: Foto ©Andreas Hilbeck / pixelio.de

More available books at **www.hansebooks.com**

A PEEP AT MEXICO:

*NARRATIVE OF A JOURNEY
ACROSS THE REPUBLIC FROM THE PACIFIC
TO THE GULF
IN DECEMBER 1873 AND JANUARY 1874.*

BY

JOHN LEWIS GEIGER, F.R.G.S.

ILLUSTRATED BY
Four Maps and Forty-five Photographs.

LONDON:
TRÜBNER & CO., 57 & 59 LUDGATE HILL.
1874.
[All rights reserved.]

PREFACE.

MEXICO, the first European colony on the North American Continent, has for the last three centuries, and especially in modern times, been a favourite resort of travellers and naturalists, and its capital, as well as the country between it and the eastern coast, have been frequently and ably described.

The portion westward of the metropolis, however, has not been so often visited, and information concerning it is comparatively scarce.

I have therefore ventured to offer the following pages to the reader, in the hope that some novel facts may be gleaned from them, especially as my journey afforded me an insight into the country under exceptionally favourable circumstances.

The photographs accompanying this volume will, I trust, prove acceptable as an aid towards the better appreciation of scenes of which my imperfect description may have failed to convey a correct idea.

Twenty-three of their number are reductions from negatives taken by me on the route (many representing views probably never previously photographed); the others are copies from photographs either prepared specially for me, or personally selected on the spot.

The short time spent by me in the Republic necessarily precludes the remotest claim to completeness for these pages: they simply contain the record of such facts as came under my notice, nor have. I entertained a more ambitious aim than to connect the isolated links of travel and enjoyment.
J. L. G.

London, *August* 29, 1874.

CONTENTS.

CHAPTER I.
FROM SAN FRANCISCO TO MANZANILLO.

Departure from San Francisco—A misnomer—San Diego—Its bay and its condition—The Lower Californian coast—Dolphins and flying-fishes—Cape St Lucas—American cousins of the Needles—Within the tropics—Mazatlan—Distance lends enchantment to the view—A dangerous pier—Dull streets—A sea of fire—Arrival at Manzanillo—Strange scenes—An airy bed—A chilly soldier—The Laguna de Cuyutlan—Short streets and small houses—The *plaza*—*Agua fresca*—A picturesque view—The harbour—German merchants—*Calentura*—Water-carriers, . . . 1–19

CHAPTER II.
FROM MANZANILLO TO COLIMA.

Early departures—A changeable lake—A curious steamer—Departure from Manzanillo—Uncomfortable thoughts—The Laguna de Cuyutlancillo—Cuyutlancillo—A straggling party—*Mozos* and their attire—Tropical forest—*Organo* cactus—Magnificent birds—An Indian village—The Rio de la Armeria—*Frijoles*—*Tortillas*—A small bill—Saddle-mules *versus* waggons—Hacienda de la Calera—*Agua de Coco*—A dark walk—The Via de Colima—Entrance into Colima—*Fonda* Hidalgo, . . . 20–40

CHAPTER III.
COLIMA.

A pleasant change—Situation of Colima—Climate—Fever—Streets and houses—The *plaza*—Its four sides—The *Plaza Nueva*—The

Rio de Colima—Baths—Wonderful gardens—A *vuelta* on the *plaza*—Appearance of the people—Their dress—*Charro*—*Modes de Colima*—The theatre—The market—Cotton factories—Clever artisans—Position and productions of the State of Colima—Produce for home consumption and export—Import trade—Mexican promotion—Respectable Governors, ... 41-64

CHAPTER IV.

COLIMA TO SAYULA.

Preparations for departure—Cheerful intelligence—Start from Colima—*Ranchos* and their crops—Small-pox—*Barrancas*—Barranca de Tonila—Tonila—Abundance of food—The standard *menu*—The Volcan de Colima—The Pico Helado—*Pedregales*—Enter the State of Jalisco—Hacienda San Marcos—A fine view—Barranca de Beltran—Luxuriant plants and magnificent birds—*Mulas de cargo*—Barranca de Vueltas—The *pueblo* of the *hacienda* labourers—Hacienda del Platanar—Strange scene—The escort—A dangerous forest—Evil and remedy united—Indulgent authorities—Barranca de Atenquique—A country restaurant—*Nopales*—*Maguey*—Its uses—*Pulque*—*Mezcal* and *Tequile*—Arrival at Zapotlan—Its inhabitants—Corrupt priests—The hotel—The *plaza*—Fighting-cocks—A comfortable priest—Situation of Zapotlan—Its climate—Its manufactures and products—Mineral wealth—Departure from Zapotlan—A brigand punished—Graves by the roadside—Brigands and brigandage—The summit of the pass—A magnificent view—Arrival at Sayula, ... 65-99

CHAPTER V.

SAYULA TO GUADALAJARA.

A family likeness—Sayula—Its climate—An extensive vista—An attempt at swindling—First experience of a *diligencia*—Departure from Sayula—Closely packed—Cavalry escort—Lago de Sayula—La Cofradia—Carbonate of soda or *tequesquite*—A cotton-tree—Cebollas—Mexican *diligencias*—*Cocheros* and their assistants—Laguna de Zacoalco—A horrible road—Mismanagement of public works—Pozos—An extensive plateau—Santa Ana Acatlan—Santa Cruz and Christmas processions—The valley of Guadalajara—Mexican waggons and carts—Travelling *Indios*—A small but dangerous *barranca*—An agreeable change—Arrival at Guadalajara—Comfortable quarters, ... 100-120

CHAPTER VI.

GUADALAJARA.

The State of Jalisco—Situation of its capital—Its climate—Streets and houses—Architecture—Wretched outlying quarters—The *plaza*—The cathedral—The *palacio*—The *portales*—*Dulces*—Native toys—Clay images—*Cajones*—Composition of the population—Cotton factories and paper-mill—The Salto factory—Brigands and *plagiarios*—A picnic interrupted—Brave men—Insecurity of the city—Juan Panadero—A happy editor—Voz de Jalisco, the priest's paper—A violent pamphlet—Hospital de San Miguel de Belen—A morbid taste—The department for the lunatics—The schools—The Cimenterio de Belen—*Gavetas*—The burial-place of the poor—The Hospicio de Guadalajara—A town of charities—The *cuna*—Customs encouraging immorality—The schools—Superior embroidery—Trades for youths—The church and a doll-show—Girl's school of San Diego—The *teatro*, a Roman ruin—Fine interior—A Mexican Italian-opera troupe—Bull-fights, and the bull-arena—An enthusiastic audience—The *paseo*—The *alameda*—A Guadalajaran Rotten Row—Walks in the *portales*—Evening *vueltas* on the plaza—A practical arrangement—Female seclusion—Serenades without music—A simple pulley—Middle-age habits retained—Strange contrasts, ... 121–163

CHAPTER VII.

FROM GUADALAJARA TO GUANAJUATO.

Departure from Guadalajara—San Pedro—A poor district—Beggars—The valley of the Lerma—Lago de Chapala—Puente de Tololotlan—Zapotlanejo—A joke—Puente de Calderon—Tepatitlan—Sterile country—La Venta de Pegueros—A forced halt—San Juan de los Lagos—Its saint and its fair—*Organo* fences—Lagos—A clean *diputado*—*Arboles del Peru* or Peruvian pepper-trees—Enter the State of Guanajuato—Leon—Silao—Rugged country—Marfil—Arrival at Guanajuato, ... 164–188

CHAPTER VIII.

GUANAJUATO.

From bad to good—Site of Guanajuato—*Jardin de la Union*—New theatre—Superior administration—Foreign residents—Fine country houses—*Loza*—The *presas*—*El Cantador*—A Sunday afternoon there—Riders—Mineral wealth—*La Valenciana* mine—A pestilential road—A valuable village—A monster shaft—Mining operations—Other mines—Yield of precious metals—*Conductas*—The *Castillo de Granaditas*—*Trajes del pais*—Silver figures—Situation of Guanajuato, ... 189‑212

CHAPTER IX.

FROM GUANAJUATO TO THE CAPITAL.

Departure from Guanajuato—Irapuato—Improvement in the country—Salamanca—Celaya—Artificial irrigation—The *Plaza*—*Baños*—Apaseo—Indian village—Enter the State of Querétaro—Arrival at the State capital—Superior hotel—Aspect of the town—Its manufactures—Situation and population—A hard day—*Questa China*—An oasis in the desert—San Juan del Rio—Enter the State of Mexico—The watershed—Arrival at Tula—Our clerical fellow-passenger—Venta del Refugio—A sermon—Traffic on the road—Huehuetoca—A finely balanced coach—Cuautitlan—Wide and shady roads—Tlalnepantla—The valley of Mexico—Irrigation—Modern Aztecs—Approach the capital—Arrival in the city of Mexico, ... 213‑245

CHAPTER X.

IN THE CAPITAL.

Hotel Iturbide—Arrived in the *tierra fria*—*Plaza mayor*—The Cathedral—The *Sagrario*—The *Palacio del Gobierno*—*Portales de Mercaderes*—*Casa de Cabildo*—*Lonja*—*Portales de las flores*—View from Cathedral tower—The *Alameda*—Statue of Charles IV.—The *Paseo de Bucareli*—The Tacubaya tramway—Tacubaya—*Plagiarios*—The *plagio* of Señor Cervantes—The Tlalpam Railway—Chapultepec—*Ahuehuetes*—Spanish moss—Puente de Alvarado—Aqueduct of San Cosme—Fuente de Tlaxpana—Tree of the *noche triste*—Tacuba—The *teocalli*—Trivoli de San Cosme—Guadalupe—A stone frigate—*Paseo de la Viga*—The canal—*Indios*—Guatemozin's bust—*Garita de la Viga*—Floating gardens—The Roldan market—Santo Anita—Ixtacalco—A strange burial-ground—The calendar stone—Aztec war-god—Sacrificial stone—The Museum—The Academy of San Carlos—Cimenterio de San Fernando—The *Cinco de Mayo*—Theatres—Situation of the city of Mexico—Its buildings and streets—Climate—The people—Foreigners, ... 246‑294

CONTENTS.

CHAPTER XI.

ON SOCIETY AND POLITICS.

General ignorance about Mexico—Causes of the civil wars—Laws of Reform—The Intervention—Maximilian's death—Measures against the priests and religious societies—Custom-house malpractices—Inheritance from the Spaniards—Population of the Republic—Creoles—*Mestizos*—Indians—Climate and productiveness of the country—The future, ... 295-322

CHAPTER XII.

FROM MEXICO TO THE GULF.

Departure from the capital—*Buena vista* station—The Mexico and Vera Cruz Railway—A cold night—Apizaco and the branch line to Puebla—Pico de Orizaba—Boca del Monte—Maltrata—Escorts—Barranca del Infiernillo—Arrival at Orizaba—Fertility around the town—Cotton factory—Resume journey—Barranca de Metlac—Córdoba—Atoyác—Chiquihuite Falls—Luxuriant vegetation of *tierra caliente*—Barrenness of the country near the coast—Arrival at Vera Cruz—Hotel de las Diligencias—Peculiar hotel arrangements—The *norte*—Baths—Embarkation on board the *Floride* and departure, ... 323-353

LIST OF PHOTOGRAPHS.

———o———

THE photographs in this volume have been prepared partly from the author's negatives, partly from photographic prints by Messrs Spencer, Sawyer, Bird & Co., Ealing Dean, Middlesex. They are printed by the mechanical autotype process in permanent pigments.

MEXICAN EAGLE, PHOTOGRAPHED FROM A SILK EMBROIDERY WORKED IN COLOURS BY AN INMATE OF THE HOSPICIO DE GUADALAJARA, *Frontispiece.*

	TO FACE PAGE
SAN FRANCISCO AND THE GOLDEN GATE,	3
MAZATLAN; THE BEACH,	9
CHIEF STREET IN MAZATLAN,	10
MANZANILLO; THE BAY,	15
MANZANILLO; LAGUNA DE CUYUTLAN IN BACKGROUND,	17
SHORE OF LAGUNA DE CUYUTLAN, MANZANILLO,	19
STREET IN COLIMA,	43
RUINED CATHEDRAL AND STATE PRISON ON THE EAST SIDE OF THE PLAZA DE ARMAS, COLIMA,	45
PLAZA DE ARMAS, COLIMA; NORTH SIDE,	46
DO. DO. SOUTH SIDE,	47
DO. DO. WEST SIDE,	47
THE RIO DE COLIMA AFTER THE RAINY SEASON,	48
STREET IN THE SUBURBS OF COLIMA,	50
VIEW TAKEN FROM AN AZOTEA, COLIMA,	64
STREET IN SAYULA,	100
DO. DO.	102
PART OF ESCORT IN THE PATIO OF THE FONDA, SAYULA,	104
THE CATHEDRAL, GUADALAJARA,	124
INTERIOR OF CATHEDRAL, GUADALAJARA,	126
STREET IN GUADALAJARA, LEADING TO THE HOSPICIO,	142
BULL-ARENA, HOSPICIO IN BACKGROUND, GUADALAJARA,	151

	TO FACE PAGE
BULL-ARENA, GUADALAJARA,	152
FOUNTAIN IN THE ALAMEDA, GUADALAJARA,	156
WALK IN THE ALAMEDA, GUADALAJARA,	157
THE PASEO, GUADALAJARA,	158
VIEW TAKEN FROM AN AZOTEA, GUADALAJARA,	161
GUANAJUATO; NORTH-WEST PART,	191
CHIEF STREET IN GUANAJUATO, WITH CATHEDRAL,	194
THE CATHEDRAL, CITY OF MEXICO,	243
THE PALACIO, CITY OF MEXICO,	249
PORTALES MERCADERES, MEXICO,	250
PLAZA MAYOR, MEXICO,	251
ENTRANCE TO CHAPULTEPEC,	260
CASTLE OF CHAPULTEPEC, NEAR MEXICO,	262
TREE OF THE "NOCHE TRISTE" AT POPOTLA, NEAR MEXICO,	268
CHURCH OF GUADALUPE, NEAR CITY OF MEXICO,	272
TOLTEC CALENDAR STONE, CITY OF MEXICO,	281
VIEW ON THE MEXICAN RAILWAY: THE VALLEY OF MALTRATA AND THE PICO DE ORIZABA,	330
VIEW OF THE RAILWAY SKIRTING THE SIDE OF THE BARRANCA DEL INFIERNILLO,	333
VIEW NEAR ORIZABA,	334
ORIZABA,	336
CURVED RAILWAY BRIDGE OVER THE BARRANCA DE METLAC,	342
THE ATOYÁC RAILWAY BRIDGE,	345
THE ALAMEDA, VERA CRUZ,	353

LIST OF MAPS.

HYPSOMETRICAL MAP OF THE REPUBLIC OF MEXICO,	*After preface.*
MAP OF PORTION OF MEXICO, FROM THE PACIFIC TO GUADALAJARA,	*To face p.* 20
MAP OF PORTION OF MEXICO, FROM GUADALAJARA TO CITY OF MEXICO,	164
MAP OF PORTION OF MEXICO, SHOWING RAILWAY TO VERA CRUZ,	323

A PEEP AT MEXICO.

CHAPTER I.

FROM SAN FRANCISCO TO MANZANILLO.

Departure from San Francisco—A misnomer—San Diego—Its bay and its condition—The Lower Californian coast—Dolphins and flying-fishes—Cape St Lucas—American cousins of the Needles—Within the tropics—Mazatlan—Distance lends enchantment to the view—A dangerous pier—Dull streets—A sea of fire—Arrival at Manzanillo—Strange scenes—An airy bed—A chilly soldier—The Laguna de Cuyutlan—Short streets and small houses—The *plaza*—*Agua fresca*—A picturesque view—The harbour—German merchants—*Calentura*—Water-carriers.

IT was on Thursday, December the 4th, 1873, that I quitted San Francisco, and embarked on board the Pacific mail-steamer *Montana*, bound for the Mexican coast and Panama.

The glorious weather I had enjoyed during my stay in California had given way for the last two days to gusts of wind and drizzling rain; the hitherto splendidly clear sky was now covered with black, heavy clouds, and the streets of San Francisco had for the moment lost their cheerfulness and fascination.

I looked upon wind and weather, however, without any feeling of discomfort, for was I not on my way to the tropics, where the rains were over? and what cared I for Scotch mist, leaden sky, and muddy streets, when a few days would bring me to palms and brilliant sunshine?

At twelve o'clock, the time appointed for starting, the steamer is unmoored, her huge paddle-wheels revolve astern, and the heavy ship gently backs towards the centre of the bay; the signal-gun is fired; and now good-bye to San Francisco, young and prosperous metropolis of the Pacific,—good-bye to the beautiful Golden State, and its warm-hearted, hospitable people.

The *Montana* proceeds slowly down the spacious bay, past numerous wharves crowded with craft of all shapes and sizes, and flying the flags of all nations. We gradually begin to lose sight of the city's tall buildings, and gliding by the isolated houses and villas along the shore, we are soon abreast of Alcatraz Island, which occupies the

SAN FRANCISCO AND THE GOLDEN GATE

very centre of the channel, and is entirely covered by its red-brick fort. After passing the bare brown hills of Angel Island, a mile away on our right, the shores of the bay rapidly approach one another, and we steam briskly through the gap left by two rocky promontories—the celebrated Golden Gate, that threshold to the wonderland of twenty years ago, that goal on which the hopes of all adventurers and treasure-seekers were then centered.

We had scarcely left Fort Point, with its graceful lighthouse and extensive fortifications, and were just nearing Point Bonita on the other side, when for awhile the rain ceased and through a break in the clouds the sun sent forth his piercing rays over the troubled waters, seeming to transform the surf that dashed against the craggy coast into showers of diamonds, and casting a magic lustre over the grand and impressive scene.

On the outlying rocks huge seals and thousands of sea-fowl, by their barking and screeching, seemed most thoroughly to enjoy the tumult of the waves, whilst black-fish and porpoises appeared near the sides of the steamer, and flocks of gulls were following in her wake.

Two miles to our left, we caught sight of the Cliff House and Seal Rocks, bright with many a pleasant reminiscence of happy hours, and before us lay for thousands of miles the broad expanse of the Pacific.

Yet what a sad misnomer this proved to-day! Half a gale blowing from the south caused the waters to be anything but *peaceful*, and recalled to memory the normal condition of the Bay of Biscay rather than that of an ocean which owes its name to a reputation for tranquillity.

After crossing the bar, the steamer's head was turned southward, and away we went against sea and wind, the *Montana* pitching and rolling to such a degree as to compel the majority of the passengers to seek the privacy of their cabins.

For the next fifty-two hours we sailed along the Californian coast, at a distance of about fifteen miles; and at five o'clock in the afternoon of December 6th reached San Diego, the southernmost town belonging to the United States on the Pacific, and within a few miles of the Mexican frontier.

San Diego Bay is full of shoals and sandbanks,

and the channel leading to the harbour most tortuous and intricate. The steamer was moored to the head of a pier which traverses the shallow approach to the land for about half a mile. The town itself, situate in a barren, desert-like country, is almost entirely composed of wooden houses, and is the exact type of what Americans would call a new Western town. Unlike most of these, however, San Diego is not in a very flourishing condition, and is said to be losing in importance and population. There are, notwithstanding, some who have faith in the future of the place, who still believe in a speedy completion of the Texas Pacific Railway, which intends making its terminus here, and regard matters in a more cheerful light.

Next morning, at eight o'clock, we resumed our voyage, and for the following three days coasted along Lower California, at times out of sight of land, but mostly at distances from eight to fifteen miles from the shore. It is difficult to imagine anything more desolate than the appearance of this coast. It presents a continuous line of rugged mountains of a reddish-brown colour, without a tree or a shrub, or indeed any green thing; more forbidding in its awful, arid solitude than any wilderness, more dreary and monotonous than the prairie or the ocean. It was quite a relief to turn the eye away from shore towards the sea, which, in this latitude, is by no means inanimate. Dolphins were seen blowing jets of water high up into the air, black-fish and porpoises gambolled in all directions, whilst from the bows of the steamer we watched the graceful flying-fishes rising in crowds out of the water, and in long, sweeping circles endeavouring to escape from the mysterious monster, which, although harmless, frightened them doubtless more than the largest whale.

In the morning of December the 10th we arrived at Cape St Lucas, where we remained for a short time in order to send a boat ashore with a passenger and the mail-bags. This cape, the southernmost part of the Lower Californian peninsula, is a series of detached rocks, precipitous masses of various sizes and grotesque shapes, hollowed into countless small bays and caves, where hundreds of seals and sea-fowl have taken up their abode.

The so-called town consists of but three houses and a few huts standing on a decline that, between cliffs and hills, slopes gently down to the beach. The only vegetation apparent is huge cacti, which densely cover the surrounding hills, and here and there a palm near the houses; but, despite the seeming barrenness of the land, there is much in this cosy, isolated little place that imparts to it that peculiar charm inseparable from a tropical landscape.

Proceeding on our voyage, we observed three large rocks rising in succession from the sea, and vividly suggestive of the Isle of Wight Needles; and then rounding another headland, the steamer changed her course to almost due east, on her way across the entrance of the Gulf of California in the direction of Mazatlan.

We were now within the tropics, a circumstance of which every turn reminded us. It was not only the increased temperature that told of our progress south; the very air seemed changed, and appeared as if tinged with a purple hue, giving exquisite softness to the jagged outlines of the copper-coloured rocks on the sterile coast, and a deeper, clearer blue to the waters of the sea. The gulls that had followed the ship in crowds ever since we left San Francisco were now growing scarcer and scarcer, and where hundreds had two days ago gathered, amidst their shrill notes, the smallest trifle that fell from the steamer, only three or four might now be seen flapping their wings lazily in the hot air, and refreshing themselves by an occasional bath, for the fatigues of this their foreign trip.

Shortly after our departure from Cape St Lucas, we lost sight of land until early next morning, when Mazatlan became visible, snugly situate at the foot of rocks and hills, and on the shore of a small circular bay. Viewed from the sea, the town is most picturesque in its aspect. The low, white, flat-roofed houses, overshadowed by tall palms, and surrounded by giant-leaved bananas, impart to it a truly tropical character, and awaken a longing to go ashore, in order to examine more closely a scene to which distance can lend such enchantment. The experiment of course proved disappointing.

After the *Montana* had anchored, a quarter of an

MAZATLAN. THE BEACH.

hour's row brought me to the pier, which juts out about a hundred feet from the land.

This was the first time that I had set foot on Mexican soil, and I silently asked myself if the ground I trod was, in its nature, emblematic of the whole country. This pier did not possess a single entire plank; it was rotten and decayed from beginning to end, and unless the eye could be riveted on the ground, an immersion in the sea would have been the unavoidable consequence.

The pier was formerly provided with rails, on which horse-cars transported goods from the landing-stage to the opposite custom-house, but for some unknown reason they had been removed; another step, as my informant expressed himself, in the retrogression so potent in this part of the country.

Mazatlan may be described as a collection of straight, narrow streets, paved with pebbles, and lined with low, whitewashed houses. The latter are solidly built of stone or *adobe*,* and, with few exceptions, contain a ground-floor alone. A few

---

* *Adobe* is sun-dried brick, and the most common building material all over Mexico. It is formed in shapes measuring about fifteen by eight inches in length and width, and about three inches in thickness.

more imposing buildings, belonging to the wealthy merchants of the town, are constructed on a plan (as I afterwards discovered) universally adopted in Mexico, viz., round the sides of an interior square yard, on to which all the rooms open. There is great comfort in such an arrangement in a climate where shade in the open air is absolutely indispensable.

There is a small public square (*plaza*) in Mazatlan, lined with orange-trees, and provided with benches, but otherwise unattractive. I also saw a number of spacious gardens, adorned with cocoa-palms, bananas, *zapotes*, and a great variety of other tropical plants; but little care seems to be bestowed on their cultivation, and they appeared wild and slovenly.

The streets of the town are dull in the extreme. There are no vehicles of any kind, and but few pedestrians; a mule-driver beating his heavily-packed animal, or a hawker seated on a doorstep with his few goods spread out on a cloth before him on the pavement, form almost the only occupants. Besides this, the shops lack show-windows, and the houses, with their big iron-barred win-

CHIEF STREET IN MAZATLAN.

dows, are one the image of the other; so that a more tame or colourless effect can be scarcely conceived.

The population, numbering about 20,000, is chiefly due to *Mestizos*,* whose features betoken peculiarities of both component races,—the complexion being a yellow brown, and not unlike that of the Arabs. In the best quarters there reside many descendants of true Spanish blood, whilst in the outskirts, composed of thatched huts, the pure Indians prevail.

In the evening, the *Montana* proceeded on her voyage. The heat was becoming so intense, that people hesitated to retire to their cabins, and the deck was full and gay until a late hour. On that night the sea was illuminated by the most magnificent phosphorescence; the slightest ruffle on its calm surface flashed into a splendid sheet of fire, and where the steamer came in contact with the water, it would glitter with a million sparks, which lingered until a wide and brilliant trail marked the wake of the speeding ship.

The distance between Mazatlan and Manzanillo is

* Half-castes of Spanish and Indian blood.

about three hundred miles, which took the *Montana* thirty hours to accomplish, and at nine o'clock in the evening of Friday, December 12th, I arrived at the latter port. The sky was overcast, and the night gloomy, when I disembarked and was rowed ashore. The hot, heavy air was thick with insects, and appeared almost too dense to breathe; the waters gleamed like liquid fire, as each plash of the oars scintillated with waves of rising light; while from the shore, as yet undiscernible, the breeze wafted notes of music, soft and harmonious. Was this real, or the delusion of a dream, the mockery of inventive imagination?

I had not time to doubt; the boat was steered to a low pier, a plank of which yielded to my tread, and I stood before a wooden shed—the custom-house—which I was invited to enter by dark-complexioned officials with enormous hats.

After the examination of luggage, which proved less severe than I anticipated, a number of porters shouldered boxes and portmanteaus, and we walked towards the only *fonda* (inn) in the place.

Across an open space, where dark women and children were squatting before huts dimly lit by tiny lamps of palm-oil, I came to a narrow street, through which, on account of the crowds that thronged it, it was difficult to advance.

All Manzanillo, it seemed, had turned out to enjoy the comparative coolness of the evening after the scorching heat of the day. There were the tall, mysterious figures of the men, dressed in white, with their wide-brimmed *sombreros*, and knife, sword, or pistol strapped round their waists; the dark-skinned women, whose most substantial garment was the cloth wrapped around their heads, their offspring in their arms; children of every age playing amidst a crowd of dogs and pigs,— all mingling and moving.

At the corner of the street, the company was grouped on doorsteps or squatting on the ground, listening to the melancholy strains of two musicians, who, on a fiddle and a contrabasso, performed a strange and plaintive air, that sounded like a tradition of bygone generations.

What a weird, bewildering scene! It was as if I had entered another world; as if what I heard and saw were scarcely real; as if the towering palm in the background were an optical illusion;

as if the chirping of a million insects, and the hissing of the surf, were the phantoms of a fevered brain, or the visions of a trance.

I was, however, soon convinced of the reality of the situation when the *fonda* was reached, and a low barn-like structure of *adobe*, roofed with straw, pointed out as the sleeping accommodation. I was allotted a small square space partitioned by boards, possessing no window, but provided with a small bed and a rough table. The former consisted of an iron frame, a canvas covering over a network of wire, and a mosquito-curtain, which meagre arrangement I found fully adequate to the requirements of the climate.

The heat of Manzanillo is proverbial, and a story which I heard related about it is too characteristic to be omitted. The legend runs that a soldier stationed here, who had not led the most exemplary of lives, was, when he died, condemned to a region not usually named by polite society. Shortly, however, after his burial, his wife was not a little astonished to see her husband return, and beg her to give him his blanket, as he was afraid of catching cold in his new quarters.

MANZANILLO. THE BAY.

Manzanillo is situate in 19° 6′ 45″ north latitude, and 104° 32′ 10″ longitude west of Greenwich, on a fine circular bay, surrounded on all sides, excepting the narrow entrance from the sea, by a range of hills, clothed from head to foot with the richest and most varied vegetation. On the other side of these hills, and not two hundred yards from the ocean, lies an extensive lake of brackish water, the Laguna de Cuyutlan. The town is built partly along the narrow strip of land between the mountains and the bay, partly on a small open space formed by a gap in the heights, and bordered on one side by the sea, and on the other by the lake. It comprises three or four short, narrow streets, intersecting at right angles the principal thoroughfare, which runs parallel to the shore, and all are neatly paved with small round pebbles. The houses are, with few exceptions, one-storied, and either substantially constructed of *adobe*, or lightly built of wood; all are protected by tiled, sloping roofs, on account of the heavy rains so frequent here in the wet season. There are a goodly collection of neatly-constructed huts, with thickly-thatched roofs, distributed around the town on the slopes, belonging to a community of Indians.

There is an attempt at a *plaza*, if a few benches placed on a small open space planted with half-a-dozen trees, may so be called, but the centre of the square is disfigured by hovels and stalls, where Indian women expose for sale the various fruits of the country, and sugar-cane in pieces. Here can be also purchased, for a very moderate sum, the cooling drinks, termed collectively *agua fresca*, and containing, besides water and sugar, the juice and seed of different fruits.

Ascending one of the hills at the southern end of the beach, a lovely panorama of the little town and all its surroundings may be obtained. To the left stretch the blue waters of the tranquil sea, a portion of which, imprisoned by a huge ring of verdant hills, forms the prettiest bay imaginable. Two large sailing vessels, anchored a short distance from the shore, were discharging cargo into small lighters, and on the beach the sturdy little mules were receiving bales and cases, to be carried into the interior. The streets and houses, viewed from here, add a charming quaint-

ness to the view; their white walls and red-tiled roofs contrasted pleasantly with the deep green of the slopes, while the Indian huts, nestling irregularly amid the luxuriant herbage, imparted a wild individuality to the scene. From the peaks to the right, giant cacti stretch their perpendicular arms far above the trees and shrubs; and beyond, the waters of the Laguna, fringed in the distance by the faint lines of the opposite shore, add a dreamy background to the picture.

The absence of the palm deprives this remarkable view of the element perhaps most conspicuous in a tropical landscape. But for this, a scene more perfect in the richness of its vegetation, more detailed in the harmonious gradations of its perspective, or more delicate with exquisite colouring and alternate lights and shadows, is scarcely conceivable.

The Bay of Manzanillo forms a superior natural harbour. It is almost circular, and about six miles in diameter; its depth allows vessels of whatever tonnage to anchor within a short distance of the shore, while its entrance, about two miles in width, is free from bars or shallows. The town owes its existence entirely to the harbour, and is nothing else but the port for Colima and a few smaller inland cities. Nothing, if we except the rickety pier before mentioned, has been attempted to improve the harbour, or facilitate the process of embarking and disembarking. The consequence is, that merchandise must be transferred to lighters, and finally brought ashore through the surf on the backs of porters.

Three mercantile firms, all composed of Germans (natives of Hamburg), transact the entire trade of the port. They possess tastefully-built houses, with airy rooms and shady verandahs, situate on the beach near the landing-place. Substantial fences enclose yards, warehouses, and stables, the approaches to which are all day thronged with *mozos*,* *arrieros*,† saddle-horses, and pack-mules, imparting to the locality the only appearance of life and prosperity it possesses.

Manzanillo is an unhealthy place, especially at the end of the dry season (March and April), when the lake is almost devoid of moisture, and its bed

---

* *Mozo*, literally, youth, lad, is the name given to all men-servants.
† *Arriero*, muleteer.

SHORE OF LAGUNA DE CUYUTLAN. MANZANILLO

cloaked with putrifying matter. Fever of an intermittent type, termed *calentura*, is then very prevalent, and spares few of the inhabitants. Although rarely fatal it is weakening to a great degree, and its enfeebling effects are only too plainly observable in the emaciated and worn-out appearance of the resident Europeans and the majority of Mexicans. Even now (December), when the rains have ended, the healthiest month commenced, and the Laguna quite full of water, I saw several poor fellows in agonies, and shivering terrifically under their thick blankets, though the thermometer showed 100° in the shade.

Owing to the proximity of the brackish contents of the lake, the water obtained at Manzanillo is most unwholesome, and unfit for drinking purposes. It is, however, procured in tolerably good quality from a small stream at a short distance up-country, whilst the troops of mules and donkeys which carry the liquid into the town, in large earthenware jars set in wooden frames, are associations inalienable from the place.

CHAPTER II.

FROM MANZANILLO TO COLIMA.

Early departures—A changeable lake—A curious steamer—Departure from Manzanillo—Uncomfortable thoughts—The Laguna de Cuyutlancillo—Cuyutlancillo—A straggling party—*Mozos* and their attire—Tropical forest—*Organo* cactus—Magnificent birds—An Indian village—The Rio de la Armeria—*Frijoles*—*Tortillas*—A small bill—Saddle-mules *versus* waggons—Hacienda de la Calera—*Agua de Coco*—A dark walk—The Via de Colima—Entrance into Colima—*Fonda* Hidalgo.

ALL departures in Mexico, curiously enough, take place at unearthly hours. During my entire stay in the country, I never set forth on my journeys at what one could call a convenient time. When on horseback, your servants would impress you with the necessity of starting at five or six o'clock in the morning, in order, as they said, to avoid the heat of the midday sun; but we proceeded on our route, as the result showed, as expeditiously during that time as any other, often reaching our destination at two or three in the afternoon,— a practical comment on the needlessness of their warnings. When travelling in the diligence, no matter what the distance or the time occupied in traversing it, the start was invariably fixed between two and five A.M.

The reason for this I was unable to discover, but having been prepared beforehand for this idiosyncrasy, as common to Mexican travelling agents, I was not surprised to learn that the hour appointed for quitting Manzanillo was half-past three in the morning. This time, however, there did exist good reason, for without departing at that early hour, it would be impossible to reach Colima on the same day.

The distance from the coast to the capital of the state is eighty miles, to accomplish which three different modes of locomotion were to be employed.

A steamer was to convey us thirty-five miles along the Laguna de Cuyutlan, mules the next eight miles, and the rest was to be performed in a waggon. These arrangements were made for us by one of the resident merchants, and, as far as speed was concerned, proved excellent.

Had I arrived here a month earlier, I should have found the little steamer wedged powerlessly in the mud of the lake, instead of afloat as at present, and a ride of forty miles on muleback, or a drive of equal length over horrible roads, instead of an enchanting passage across the Laguna, would have awaited me. Owing to the rapid evaporation of the lake, it is only during about four months of the year that it possesses sufficient water to float the steamer; during the remaining months the Laguna is reduced to a conglomeration of large pools, which are often separated by miles of intervening bed.

It is entirely due to the energy and enterprise of Mr M——, the United States Consul at Colima, that this improved means of communication has been called into being. Two years ago nobody dreamt of it; now, during the few months the steamer runs, it is crowded on every trip with as many bales and cases as the tiny craft will hold. A canal, as the owner of the steamer suggested to me, of about three hundred yards in length at Manzanillo, would not only connect the sea with the lake, and allow merchandise to be taken off the ocean-vessels in boats, which could transport it almost half the distance towards Colima, but would also keep the Laguna constantly full, thus ensuring means of navigation throughout the year, and removing the chief source of fever and other maladies with which Manzanillo is now afflicted; "but," he added with a significant look, "we are in Mexico, and not in the States."

I examined the little steamer on the day before we were to use it, and though paying a full tribute of admiration to the energy that prompted its establishment, and grateful for the good fortune which afforded me such advantages, yet I could not suppress a smile at the first glimpse of a craft, which resembles anything else in the world rather than the purpose for which it is intended. Imagine a small Thames lighter, about thirty-five feet long and ten wide, with a square protuberance on either side, an upper deck supported by slight pillars, about ten feet above the water, with a small cabin and a wheelhouse on the top, and you have a faint idea of the symmetrical proportions of the steamer on the Laguna de Cuyutlan. The engine is, perhaps, the greatest curiosity of all. It was, I believe, formerly employed in driving a small saw-mill at Colima, and has for years boasted the possession of a huge boiler, and tiny cylinders, whilst it still retains its old leather bands to transmit the motion to the paddle-wheels.

In the early morning of December the 14th, all was prepared, and the little engine was fuming and fussing as if about to propel a five-thousand-ton packet across the ocean.

I am uncertain whether it was the hissing noise which gave rise to the thought of a possible explosion, or whether suspicious movements in the water reminded me of its slimy inhabitants, but I must confess that, as in the darkness of night I embarked, and groped blindly over bales, cases, and bundles, I could not repress a shudder when the idea flashed across my mind that it was just in the range of possibility that the funny box might smash, or explode in the middle of the lake, and we, ourselves, provide a dainty breakfast for the thousands of alligators with which it swarms.

The Laguna de Cuyutlan runs north-west and south-east, parallel with the sea-shore, and is only divided from the ocean by a narrow strip of land. Its entire length is about forty miles, and its width varies between four and ten. It is almost completely enclosed by mangrove jungle, which overruns the banks, and creates numerous islets by its growth where the water is shallowest. It is not the large species, with giant stem and monster roots, but a small, shrub-like kind, so closely tangled as almost to form a solid mass; while its sinuous roots by their mutual coils and circles, surpass the strongest wickerwork in consistency.

This jungle extends for miles,—an unbroken wall of sombre foliage; nor is the Laguna often visible to the traveller for the long islands, that by their parallel position enclose narrow and river-like channels. A peculiarity of this jungle is its uniform shape, both in height and width, which recalls our own neat hedgerows so vividly that the English spectator is almost tempted to believe that an army of gardeners have clipped and trimmed it with their careful shears.

There is no variety in the vegetation; mangroves

jealously monopolise all available space. The stagnant waters are covered with a brownish-green slime, which, where intermixed with the fallen branches of a tree, or a collection of withered leaves, forms small floating islands; and the little craft, as she steamed along, cleaved through the thick viscous surface, and disclosed the dark, turbid liquid below.

At intervals, a black uneven line, glimmering above the ooze, would betray the presence of an ugly alligator, whilst a hundred divers, conscious of their agility, and careless of the neighbouring monster, bobbed merrily up and down, as if playing hide and seek with the rest of the world.

Some spots were literally crowded with numerous varieties of ducks and teal, which, though little used to disturbances of this kind, allowed the steamer to approach within a few yards before they sought to escape. Their cackling, too, would often alarm a company of huge white cranes, quietly congregated on a sandbank, and compel them, with one accord, to spread their lazy wings and seek some other fishing-ground.

On the floating islands, proud storks and sedate melancholy herons were engaged in catching and consuming their breakfast, whilst every nook of the mangrove thickets, every shallow in the lake, every log of wood on the water, was tenanted by all manner of birds, including alike the busy wagtail, the grandfatherly pelican, and the stately flamingo. As we cut the placid waters, a brace of neat sand-pipers or a swift kingfisher, scared by the snort of the engine, would suddenly emerge from the margin of the channel, and, darting ahead, be again frightened into the air almost before they had settled.

Soaring in graceful circles far overhead, a variety of hawks view the scene from aloft, ready to pounce upon whatever appears an easy prey, whilst thousands of dark-blue glittering swallows hurry from island to island, feeding plenteously on the myriads of insects that hover above the water.

As the south-east end of the Laguna is approached, the mangrove jungle ceases, and the entire expanse of the lake is seen disclosing the hills that border the waters to the northward, with their robe of clustering oil-palms; while to the rear, range after range of rising mountains are at length crowned by the snow-capped peak of the majestic Volcan de Colima in the far distance.

At 10 A.M. we arrived at Cuyutlancillo, as the landing-place at the extremity of the Laguna is called, representing a large wooden shed on the beach, used as a storehouse for the goods transported by the steamer, and half-a-dozen native huts sparsely distributed over the ground in the vicinity. Here we found *mozos* as well as riding and pack mules in attendance, ready to convey us and our luggage to the Rio de la Armeria. Without much delay, bags and portmanteaus were transferred from the steamer to the pack-saddles, and as the place was intensely hot, without one object of interest to prompt a longer stay, we were ourselves on the saddle and the road before an hour had elapsed. As four mules were required for the luggage, and as our five *mozos* were all mounted, the little caravan comprised twelve animals guarded by eight riders; and as it is a most difficult matter, where no danger is apprehended, to make Mexican servants understand

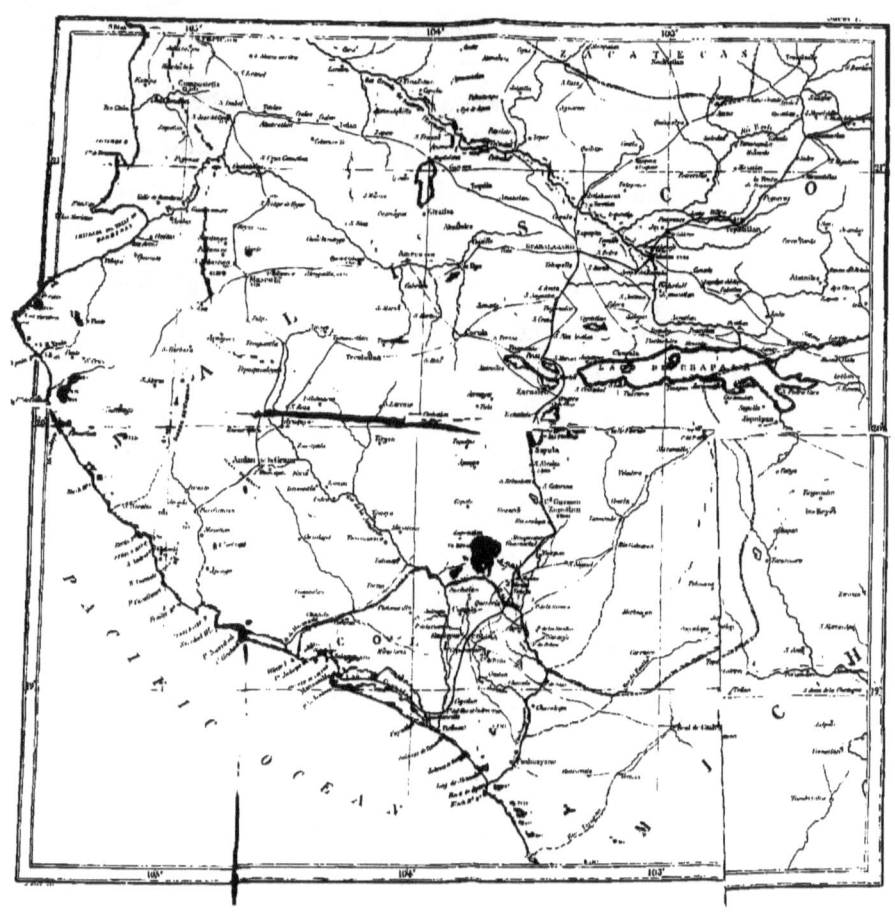

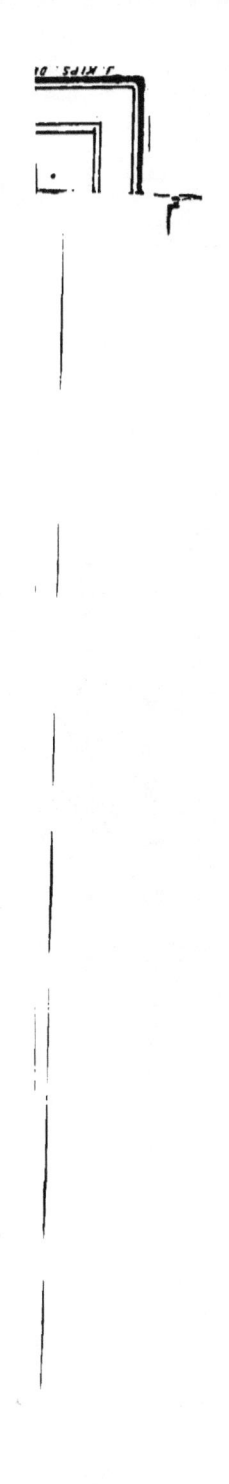

a portion OF MICO

ig the travels of

that they are to keep together, our party was scattered over half-a-mile of the road before we had been ten minutes on the move.

The *mozos* were dressed in the usual costume of their order—white or pale pink cotton jacket and drawers, the latter supplemented by leather trousers slit open on the outside from the knee to the ground; on their heads was the capacious *sombrero*, or wide-brimmed hat, manufactured of palm-leaf straw or felt. Both the latter and the leather trousers are garments admirably adapted to the requirements of the country and climate.

In a land where to ride is almost as usual as to walk, and where at the same time the heat is intense, this open, leather habiliment combines coolness with substantial protection against the hardness of the Mexican saddle, whilst the *sombrero*, although heavy, is a capital guard against the fierce rays of a tropical sun, and renders the use of a sun-shade superfluous.

Boots or shoes are rarely worn by Indians and half-castes; they use compact sandals of strong leather.

From Cuyutlancillo to the Paso del Rio de la

Armeria is about eight miles in distance, and when the river is low enough to permit vehicles to ford over, the entire road from the lake to Colima (fifty-five miles in all) can be traversed on wheels; but at present the Rio is still too high to allow of this. This proved eventually a most fortunate circumstance, as the ride to the river was enjoyable in the extreme, whilst the drive thence to Colima was anything but agreeable.

From the lake a wide path of soft sandy soil winds through forests of impenetrable and most fruitful undergrowth. The trees are not large, but are so interwoven as to form impassable barriers, even apart from the bushes and shrubs that spring from every spot of vacant ground. Hundreds of creepers cling to every trunk, and twine round every branch, connecting by a thousand wiry threads thickets, shrubs, and cacti,— a massive bulwark of profuse vegetation, through which the axe alone can hew a way. The huge *organo* cactus, with its tree-like stem, often two feet in diameter, and ten to fifteen feet high, sends up its stiff, straight branches to a height of thirty or forty feet from the ground, whilst the smaller species mingle in thousands with the shrubs and bushes nearer the earth. Wherever the creepers may have neglected trunk or bough, prolific parasites, gay alike with taper leaf and gorgeous blossom, hasten to perform their part in this fairy work of nature. The flowers have little scent, but their profusion of white, yellow, and red blended with the countless shades of green, charm the eye with tints as various as they are magnificent.

This teeming region of vegetable life is the haunt of birds, which, for brightness of plumage, equal, if not surpass, those on the Laguna. Parrots, resplendent with red and green, flew away screeching as we approached, whilst tiny humming-birds with their golden hues were darting hither and thither, till they disappeared in the bushes. Graceful birds, with glistening feathers of a bluish-black and pointed beak, seemed here as common as our crows, and like them divided their attention between ravenous hunger and timid flight.

This portion of the *tierra caliente* and the Laguna de Cuyutlan is a most fertile field for ornithological research, and I have no hesitation in saying that there exists here many a species as yet undescribed.

As we approached the Rio, the country gradually became more open; we traversed sunny plots of green sward, more similar to a garden or park than to land almost untouched by human hand. Here we saw wild turkeys, a kind of partridge, numbers of buzzards, the now familiar swallows, vultures perched calmly on the very top of the tallest trees, and sentinel hawks which watched the scene from far aloft.

We soon entered a small Indian village, perched on the height that bounds the river, and consisting of a few well-built and neatly-thatched huts ranged on either side of the road.

Before each of these homesteads bananas, oranges, water-melons, and other fruits, were exhibited for sale on a little stand, whilst the inmates, men, women, and children, were grouped under the open verandah, and busied in the sympathetic task of removing another genus of prolific parasite, an occupation not rare among the lower classes of all tropical and semi-tropical countries. Their costume is of the lightest possible description; the upper part of the body is left almost bare, though the immense *sombrero* is never omitted. We passed the village without a halt, and descending the high bank, followed one of the *mozos* through the river, which, however, was so high and rapid that we were thoroughly drenched before the opposite shore was gained.

The Rio de la Armeria, during the dry season, dwindles to a shallow stream hardly more than fifty yards in width, though at this time a large volume of water, filling the entire bed (which was about a hundred and fifty yards wide), came thundering down its rocky course with a seething and impetuous current.

Arrived on the other side, we dismounted at a *hacienda*, where a rude and rickety waggon was waiting to take us on to Colima. Before we proceeded, however, we sat down to a tempting meal of several courses, the last of which was the usual termination to every Mexican repast, the dish of *frijoles*. I had already made their acquaintance at Manzanillo, and until I quitted Mexican soil on the shores of the Atlantic, they continued my tried and trusty companions.

Frijoles are small brown beans, stewed in lard, and palatably seasoned, resembling, in outward appearance more than in taste, the "*fool*" of the Arabs, a mess prepared in a similar manner minus the lard. Unlike the majority of national Mexican dishes, the savoury flavour of *frijoles* is appreciated by the foreigner, who soon accustoms himself to them, either plain or with the addition of grated cheese or *chile*, which latter (pod as well as seeds) is a favourite adjunct to every course served on a Mexican table.

Frijoles are invariably accompanied by *tortillas*, the peculiar native substitute for bread. During my progress across the country, I had frequent opportunities of seeing them prepared. Half-boiled maize, mixed with the requisite quantity of water, is ground between a small sloping slab of stone and a stone-roller (both *metate* and roller are generally made of lava), until the paste has attained the consistency of tough, leathery dough, when it is patted between the hands into thin cakes equal in size to our small plate, and in thickness to ordinary card-board. They are next quickly baked between heated stones, and are then eaten while still hot.

As the Indians, and indeed all the poorer natives, are unacquainted with forks and spoons, a piece of *tortilla* serves them as a substitute, and it is amusing to see the dexterity with which these people eat their *frijoles* with the aid of a spoon, which itself disappears with the last mouthful of beans. Novices, as a rule, find the warm, damp, flabby *tortilla*, insipid and unpalatable, but the veterans are as fond of them as the Indians themselves.

Whilst we were at table, the pack-mules and the attending *mozos* walked into the quadrangle, there to rest awhile, and follow us at their leisure whilst we preceded them in the waggon.

Five dollars was all we paid for dinner supplied to ourselves and the *mozos*, eight persons in all, besides fodder for twelve mules—amazingly cheap when compared with Californian charges.

At two o'clock in the afternoon we resumed our journey, and were soon bumping and jolting over a villainous road, along which the two wretched mules could hardly drag the rumbling vehicle. We much regretted the change. The elastic tread of the nimble saddle-mules had hitherto carried us pleasantly over the execrable paths, and the Mexican saddles, though awkward at first, proved easy in long rides; now, however, we had to endure shocks and shakes, the effects of stones and ruts, which were far from being palliated by the waggon's worn-out springs. If the miserable mules halted for a second, where a bad place had over-taxed their powers, the *cochero* would unmercifully whip the poor little brutes, or throw stones at them, accompanying his active demonstrations with shouts and exclamations flavoured with a selection of expletives, which, although uttered in Spanish, it would be impossible to mention here. The strength and endurance of these little *mulas* is really wonderful. Their outward appearance is so very unfavourable that it seemed impossible for them to draw the waggon over the first mile; but they warmed to their work to such a degree, that, at the conclusion of their twenty miles' stage, they appeared fresher than at starting.

The country through which we travelled was similar to that on the other side of the river. As we progressed the sandy soil vanished, and gravel and rock took its place, whilst the vegetation became more sparse, and Indian villages frequent.

A little further on, the country grew more exposed and cultivated; fields appeared here and there, dotted over with huts, and pleasingly relieved by picturesque plantations of cocoa-palms and bananas.

At five o'clock we came to a *hacienda* called La Calera, where we stopped to procure a change of mules. This *hacienda* is a large building encircled by wooden palings gaudily painted, and surrounded by numerous huts cosily sheltered by shady trees. Whilst a man on horseback was engaged in catching the animals with a *lazo* in the spacious *corral* adjacent to the house, we entered the broad verandah, and were treated to some delicious *agua de coco* by the hospitable manager of the estate. Of all refreshing drinks, none can compare with the milk, or rather water, of the green, unripe cocoa-nut; and parched as we were by heat and dust, the cool, clear liquid, with its slight admixture of carbonic acid, was thoroughly relished.

In the meantime the two mules had been caught and sent forward on the road to be changed a few miles ahead, and resuming our seats in the waggon, we continued on our rough path.

Ever since leaving the Rio de la Armeria we had been gently and gradually ascending, and we now perceived more distinctly the rising nature of the ground. When evening came, we were toiling up hills, overgrown with the richest verdure, and jolting over a tedious road furrowed with ruts and strewn with rock. One height passed, and a steep descent, over a small river or a gulch, would lead us to a renewed incline loftier than that preceding, and as this was repeated for hours, we at last stepped out to lighten the load, and followed the waggon on foot over stones, holes, and waterpools.

Although assured by every one that the road was perfectly safe the whole way from the coast to Colima, we could not forget the many stories we had heard about robbers and kidnappers in Mexico generally.

From the lake to the Rio, we were accompanied by five *mozos* armed with the straight sword of the country, called the *macheta*, and constantly on the look-out; but we were now alone, and were travelling not in the confidence-inspiring daylight, but through a hilly forest in the pitchiest of nights. I confess I could not repress some anxiety as we followed the waggon in utter darkness, and often through narrow defiles of rock; and even Mr L——, who has passed thirty years of his life in the country, was not wholly at his ease. On we tramped, however, patiently and silently, revolver in hand, until all the hills and streams were safely passed, and we were once more seated in the waggon.

We now entered a spacious road, the Via de Colima, which leads for five miles through the splendid valley of Colima up to the town itself.

Whenever we were on higher ground, a few dim lights in the distance would indicate the direction of the city. Again and again the lights disappeared as we descended into hollows, but only to shine out more distinctly as we attained the summit of the next hillock. At length we were past the huts that line both sides of the road, past the long stone fences that encircle plantations and *haciendas*, and finally entered the narrow streets of Colima, whose pebbly pavement caused the waggon to shake and shiver as if it were going to fall to bits. The *cochero* exerted himself to end the day's work with a flourish, and cracked his whip with a vehemence that set the poor mules galloping over the cruel stones as if it were the commencement, and not the close, of their journey. So we threaded street after street, and turned many a sharp corner, where watchmen with large lanterns were keeping guard, as in Europe centuries ago; and finally at ten o'clock halted before the modest house of the *Fonda* Hidalgo, the best inn of the town.

The remarkably stout landlady, after pointing out to us our primitive bedrooms in the immediate vicinity of the stable, prepared a speedy supper, and we sat down to a substantial meal of *frijoles*, and other dishes in which garlic distinctly predominated.

CHAPTER III.

COLIMA.

A pleasant change—Situation of Colima—Climate—Fever—Streets and houses—The *plaza*—Its four sides—The *Plaza Nueva*—The Rio de Colima—Baths—Wonderful gardens—A *vuelta* on the *plaza*—Appearance of the people—Their dress—*Charro*—*Modes de Colima*—The theatre—The market—Cotton factories—Clever artisans—Position and productions of the State of Colima—Produce for home consumption and export—Import trade—Mexican promotion—Respectable Governors.

THE morning after our arrival (15th of December) we were most kindly invited to exchange the indifferent quarters in the *fonda* for others in the luxurious house of some German merchants—an invitation which we were only too glad to accept, and we soon found ourselves in the enjoyment of the most perfect accommodation imaginable in this part of the globe.

My stay in Colima extended over five days, and as this time was assiduously employed in exploring the town and its vicinity, very little was, I think, left unseen.

Colima marks the site of an Indian town

before the conquest, in north lat. 19° 11,' and long. 103° 46' 30" west of Greenwich, on the river of the same name, and in a fine valley of great extent, entirely surrounded by mountains, amongst which the lofty Volcan de Colima towers royally above all others on the northern horizon.

The town numbers 25,000 inhabitants, the great majority of whom are Indians and *mestizos*, whose claim to an admixture of Spanish blood seems very remote. Situate as it is at an elevation of about 1500 feet above the level of the sea, its climate is superior to that of the coast, and the temperature somewhat lower. The heat, however, in the middle of the day, is such as to render a walk no painless task; and the streets are generally deserted from an hour after sunrise until towards sunset.

Calentura, although much less prevalent than in Manzanillo, is not uncommon, and a prolonged residence in the city acts in a most detrimental manner on the health of Europeans and North Americans, as, I am sorry to say, I found ample means of judging.

The town is laid out in long, straight streets,

about thirty feet wide, paved with large round pebbles (*cobble-stones*, as they say in the States), and lined with solidly-built brick or *adobe* houses. In the better quarters the latter are plastered over, whitewashed, and often ornamented with a few lines or arabesques of motley patterns, not dissimilar from the coloured walls of Southern Italy. The buildings generally contain the ground-floor alone, and are flat-roofed. The better class possess lofty and spacious rooms, all opening on to a verandah which runs round the four sides of an interior square yard, the plan already noticed at Mazatlan.

This open verandah serves as sitting-room, and the table is frequently laid there in preference to the inner apartments; at night a portion of it forms the sleeping-place for the servants, and it is altogether the most important part of the edifice, especially in the *tierra caliente*. Banana plants, coffee and orange trees, as well as shrubs and flowers, convert the inner yard into a fragrant garden, and often a plashing fountain imparts coolness and freshness to the air. Towards the street the buildings, however beautiful within, present a dull and monotonous appearance, the exterior including but a large gateway with heavy, antique locks, and a row of iron-barred windows, whilst from the flat roofs jut forth horizontally a number of iron pipes, sometimes grotesquely ornamented, and intended to drain the water from the *azotea*.*

As the style of architecture is usually the same, the streets for the most part resemble one another; and as they are all of one width, with no shop-windows to act as sign-posts, it is a difficult matter for the stranger to find his way.

The almost total absence of carriages and waggons renders Colima peculiarly quiet; and when once the sun has fairly risen above the horizon, the streets would be entirely deserted, were it not for a few mules marching on under their heavy loads of long *alfalfa* grass, maize-straw, pottery or water-jars, or an occasional train of *mulas de cargo* conveying merchandise into the town, and escorted by *arrieros* on horseback.

In the early morning the streets are lively, and crowded with natives on their way to or

* *Azotea*, literally *platform*, is the name given to the flat roofs in Mexico.

RUINED CATHEDRAL AND STATE PRISON ON THE EAST SIDE OF THE PLAZA DE ARMAS, COLIMA.

from market, *mozos* carrying loads from one house to another, water-carriers laden with the day's supply, and a hundred more incidentals of domestic life. In the evening, a great portion of the population walk out, mostly towards the public square or garden, where they enjoy the customary *vuelta*.

The public square, or *Plaza de Armas*, or simply the *Plaza*, is here, as in every other Mexican town, the centre of out-door life. It is an open space of about eighty yards square. On the eastern side stand the remains of an old cathedral, which could never, even previous to the ravages of ruin, have been a comely structure; and next to it rises a long, two-storied pile, which, far advanced on the road to destruction, retains but few remnants of its original plaster and whitewash, and with its gaping patches of brick and stone looks as if it had never been completed. Some of the windows are entirely or partly blocked with rough masonry, whilst the others are mere apertures in the wall, alike destitute of glass or iron.

This is at once the chief guard-house, the State prison, and the office of the *Mayoria de*

Plaza. In the large square gateway a number of soldiers, whose dark complexions denote them to be Indians, clad in uniforms of white canvas, are always loitering, whilst all through the day a couple of buglers will issue forth, and shock the ear with terribly discordant blasts from instruments which evidently never were attuned to one another.

The northern side of the *Plaza* displays the finest buildings in Colima; a row of houses in the Moorish style, two-storied, with the upper floor erected over the pavement so as to form a covered pathway, gracefully arched, from one end of the square to the other. The upper part of these houses is used for private residences, whilst the ground-floor is employed as shops, the best in the town. The two remaining sides of the *Plaza* are lined with buildings of an inferior type, strangely contrasting with those just mentioned. In the centre of the square a large circular fountain furnishes the neighbourhood with a plentiful supply of water, whilst at the edges of the quadrangle runs a broad walk planted with orange and lime trees, and provided at short intervals with clumsy benches of *adobe*, stuccoed and

PLAZA DE ARMAS. COLIMA. NORTH SIDE

PLAZA DE ARMAS, COLIMA, SOUTH SIDE

painted pink. These benches, however, are so high that only giants can sit on them if they would rest both their bodies and their feet at the same time.

The *Alameda* on the *Plaza Nueva* is a small but shady and pleasant public garden. It covers scarcely more ground than the *plaza*, is surrounded by high walls, furnished with iron gates. The interior is richly wooded with different trees, among which palms, oleander, orange, and lemon are the most conspicuous, whilst bananas with their enormous leaves, and loads of fruit hanging in thick, heavy clusters, render the scene truly tropical.

Walks tastefully laid out, and well kept, meet at a pretty fountain, whose ample basin harbours two giant cranes, and many other waterbirds. A portion of the *Alameda* is reserved and apportioned, in small square plots, to private people as separate gardens for themselves. A number of these are most daintily arranged, fenced round with a neat paling of wood, and possessing besides many curious plants, little jets of water, decorations of figures and shells, and snug seats under branching trees.

Through the city runs the Rio de Colima, a small stream at this time of year, divided into several shallow and narrow arms flowing over a wide bed. In the middle of the rainy season this becomes brimful; at the time of my visit, however (December), there was only sufficient water to supply the numerous baths erected along its course, and the temporary laundry establishments.

The baths embrace numbers of small square basins through which the stream is led. They are partitioned by solid stone walls, and left open at the top.

The views along the river bed are extremely picturesque. Gardens and plantations on either side brighten the landscape with palms and bananas, whilst huts, baths, and thickets of green in the very watercourse, diversify its outlines.

Owing to the attention and kindness of my amiable hosts, my sojourn in Colima passed most pleasantly. Excursions into the neighbourhood, as well as rides through the suburbs, were undertaken every morning at sunrise, when the coolness of the atmosphere and the freshness of the surroundings enhanced a hundred times the natural beauties of this favoured spot. A plunge into a spacious swimming bath, specially reserved for the use of the foreign residents,

THE RIO DE COLIMA AFTER THE RAINY SEASON

inaugurated the day; and before long a visit was generally paid to one of the magnificent fruit-gardens in the immediate vicinity of the town.

Pen and fancy are alike baffled by the prodigal wealth of vegetable life that greets the eye on its first glance at these gardens; impenetrable tracts of trees and shrubs, uncurbed in their lavish freedom, vast fortresses of vegetation through which the sun's rays fail to pierce, seem as wild as they are wonderful; a closer inspection, however, finds these forests crossed and recrossed by narrow paths and small ditches, and reveals a method amid all this apparent confusion. Blossoms of splendid hue on one tree, fruit in extravagant abundance on another, leaves of every sort and shape, verdure in all its grotesquely curved forms, cacti and creepers trailing like serpents on the ground;—what a strange epitome of tropical luxuriance!

The mere endeavour to enumerate *all* the various plants and fruits cultivated in these gardens would be presumptuous; a few, however, I noted down at the time.

Besides the familiar cocoa-palm, the different kinds of plantains or bananas, and the many varieties of orange, lemon, and lime trees, there are cacao-trees, which rejoice in the native name of Cacahoaquahuitl (*Theobroma cacao*), with their fruit, the main substance of chocolate, growing out of the trunk, the coffee-shrub (*Coffea Arabica*), the zapote (*Casimiroa edulis*), the guava or guayava (*Psidium guaiava*), the mango (*Mangifera Indica*), the mamey (*Lucuma mammosa*), the granadita or granadilla de China (*Passiflora quadrangularis*), the chirimoya or chirimolla (*Anona cherimolia*), the pine-apple or piña (*Ananassa sativa*), the aguacate (*Persea gratissima*).

These gardens belong to wealthy citizens, and are under the charge of managers, who sell their produce for the owners, or are rather supposed to do so. The contents of a green cocoa-nut opened at the lodge, was the usual and invigorating conclusion of a walk round these marvellous plantations.

In the evening, after dinner, it is the custom to take the air on the *plaza*. Every other day a military band stations itself in the centre of the square near the fountain, and performs there between the hours of seven and nine, whilst all the world and his wife are engaged in mild exercise or

STREET IN THE SUBURBS OF CULIMA

cool repose on the stone benches. The *plaza* thus affords a favourable opportunity for observing its visitors in the silvery light of the evening moon.

I had heard much when in the United States, and especially in California, about the beauty of Mexican women; but this praise proved the exaggeration not unfrequently bestowed on strange and unknown objects, the mere remoteness of which, both as regards distance and knowledge, endows them with qualities they in nowise possess. As far as Colima is concerned, I did not meet with a single face that could be called beautiful, or even pretty; and my subsequent experience of the Republic offered no inducement to improve my original opinion. Nine-tenths of the population are Indians, either pure-blooded or with an admixture, more or less remote, of European blood, their colour ranging between a dark coppery-brown and a pale yellow. Whilst the men are generally well-made, somewhat tall and muscular, the women, as a rule, are small and slight. They almost always possess large black eyes, remarkably white, regular teeth, and luxuriant, straight, jet-black hair. But here all their beauty ends, and ill-shaped noses, large mouths, and often prominent cheek-bones, destroy all the advantages derived from their other perfections. I do not, of course, here include the descendants of pure Spanish blood, who naturally rank in this respect with their European kinsmen.

The climate of Colima, and the *tierra caliente* generally, renders very light clothing a necessity.

The white or pink cotton trousers and jacket of the men of the lower orders have already been mentioned; the women of the same class wear an ordinary gown of light texture, as a rule gaudy in its colour, whilst from the waist upwards they confine themselves to the *camisa* of thin white cotton, which exposes as much as it conceals. It is only when going away from home for some distance that they wear the *rebozo* folded round head and shoulders, a large head-cloth, often of a dark blue material with very thin white stripes.

The men of the better classes, which in proportion to the entire population are inconsiderable, dress either in the European style, or in *charro*, as the natives designate the old Mexican costume. The latter, for ordinary wear, is gradually becoming obsolete, but is generally used for riding. It consists of leather trousers, slit open from the knee downwards on the outside of both legs, and disclosing the white drawers worn underneath, and a short jacket of cloth or leather faced with braiding. Mexican beaux delight in a gorgeous display of silver buttons, buckles, and lacing both on trousers and jacket, which, with the silver plating of the heavy Mexican saddle, appear pompous and showy. As all their horses, however, are small, rider, saddle, and steed seem sadly out of proportion.

For riding, large sixteenth-century boots of light brown leather are often preferred to the *chaparerras*, as the leather trousers are denominated; and huge spurs, such as belong to the stage in the performance of a Shakesperian play, are rarely omitted. The *sombrero*, blazing at times with rich gold or silver trimmings, heads every description of Mexican costume.

The ladies of Colima are not distinguished for the good taste exhibited in their dress, and although the newest Paris fashions can hardly be expected to penetrate into this out-of-the-way corner of the world, yet, where nature has created such perfect combinations of colour and form, one might hope to see more perception on their part with regard to personal attire. They use the most decided and conspicuous colours, sometimes in the most atrocious mixtures. Thus the dress of bright scarlet is often relieved by a sash of glaring yellow, or a gown as green as grass will be set off by deep-blue trimmings. A lady in a dress of intermediate hue is a rarity; it is sure to be either a very pronounced blue, or a very pronounced green, or a very pronounced red; and there are few who, disdaining show, adopt a suit of modest black.

But it must be remembered that I have only been speaking of extraordinary and holiday costumes; at ordinary times, printed muslin or cotton dresses, out of which, as a rule, all colour has been washed, lend to the belles of Colima an almost menial appearance. Gloves are almost entirely dispensed with, and instead of hat or bonnet, the *rebozo*, or the more refined Spanish *mantilla*, droops over head and shoulders. Dresses, as well as other items of ladies' attire, appear to be ill-made, and render their otherwise shapely figures unsightly; add to this a naturally awkward and rather waddling gait, and the exterior of Colima's daughters cannot be called graceful.

One evening we visited the theatre. A troupe that had been previously performing in the South and Central American coast towns was to act some Spanish piece; and as the performances take place only twice a week, all Colima was astir not to miss the fun.

Shape and purpose are the sole points in which this theatre resembles a civilised playhouse, otherwise it is the most singular building of its kind. Its construction is of the rudest possible description, and the interior, with its rough poles and planks, is ludicrously suggestive of a builder's scaffolding. Two common poles, coupled half-way with coarse ropes, form the pillars supporting the tiers, which latter, as indeed everything else, are rudely constructed of rough deal boards. Beyond a little whitewash, no attempt is made to disguise the *matière première*, and the wood is often left as the tree grew it.

The ceiling is of canvas tightly fastened to the

sides, and the chandelier a wooden frame of two squares, lined with small tin pots filled with palm-oil.

The whole arrangement savoured of a large booth at a fair or race-meeting at home; indeed, I have seen better structures of a temporary kind than the *teatro* in Colima, which is of the same capacity as the St James's in London, and adapted for as many people. There are two tiers above the ground-floor; on the latter (the bare earth), rude benches arranged in rows, with a gangway down the middle, occupy the portion generally allotted to stalls and pit. The box-tiers on the ground and first floors are open galleries, separated by wooden railings, about a foot high, into partitions, presenting towards the front a rude wooden balustrade, so low that the spectators seemed in constant danger of an airy passage into the pit. The tier on the second floor forms the gallery. The planks which compose the floor of the latter are not even uniformly adjusted, and there is no railing of any kind. The audience comprehended all the various elements of this odd population, from the foreign merchants with their families down to the yellow *mestizo* and brown Indian. The gods, nearly all Indians, were seated on the edge of the boards, their white-trousered legs dangling in the air, and all but touching the heads of the people in the boxes beneath, whilst the women were standing or squatting about in all directions. The box-tiers were filled with ladies attired in the most gairish of colours, and looking like so many parrots; whilst the pit was occupied by men dressed in *charro*, or the more sober costume of Europe. It was indeed a remarkable medley of motley garbs and quaint figures.

The acting, considering the house, was tolerably fair; but it was impossible, on account of the intense heat, to see it out, and I was thankful when the rag of a white canvas curtain, with a paper angel pasted on the middle, closed upon the first act, and allowed me to escape into the cool night air.

Near the *plaza* is the market, which is held in a small place furnished with a number of stalls. The principal dealers occupy the latter, whilst a large proportion of produce is displayed on the ground in the neighbouring streets, under the shade of large square pieces of matting suspended on centre poles, like huge umbrellas. The articles offered for sale are of the most varied nature.

Besides the butcher's assortment of fresh and dried meats, and the baker's stock of small flat rolls and multifarious *pan dulce* (sweet biscuits or small cakes), there are all the numberless fruits of this prolific region — sugar-cane entire or in pieces, water-melons, yams, and countless other vegetables, amongst which *chile* and three or four species of beans are the most plentifully represented. Maize, rice, coffee, and tobacco are displayed in great abundance; whilst in another direction the brown earthenware of the country, large *sombreros* made of coarse straw, and an odd mixture of common German and Birmingham knick-knacks, are exhibited. Some half-dozen stalls are reserved for saddlery and other leather goods of native workmanship, as well as *sarapes, fajas,** and *rebozos*. These goods are hawked all day on the square and adjacent streets by itinerant dealers, who, as a rule, select a bench in the *plaza* for the depository of their wares when tired.

* *Fajas* are long narrow cloths used to secure the trousers round the waist; they are generally of a red colour.

Maize and rice straw, alfalfa grass, small lots of cotton, as well as of charcoal, take up a considerable space of the market, whilst every vacant corner is devoted to a vendor of *dulces* (sweetmeats) or *agua fresca*. Sunday is the chief market-day, and from sunrise to about eight o'clock no more animated and picturesque scene than is here presented can be conceived. The people from the surrounding country, pure Indians for the most part, come to town for the occasion, bringing their produce for sale, and buying supplies with the proceeds. Nor can the chattering, laughing, and eager bargaining of the whole assemblage be equalled by any but negroes under similar circumstances, as notorious in the markets of Havana and other cities in the West Indies. The diversity of physiognomies, however, as well as of costume and colour, renders the market in Colima, and those of Mexico generally, superior in interest, both human and artistic.

There are three cotton factories near Colima, the owners and managers of which are all foreigners. The largest of these establishments is the San Cuyatano mill, which, at the time of my visit, was not working on account of financial difficulties with which its administrators were hampered. The Atrevida and the Armonia are smaller factories. I only visited the latter, a well-arranged and neatly-kept place, possessing fine English machinery of quite modern date. These manufactories produce coarse yarns, and a common kind of grey shirting known as *manta*. The cotton consumed is nearly all grown in the State of Colima, and the hands employed are Indian and half-caste women and girls, who, I am told, are most efficient at their work.

The native population are clever at every sort of handiwork. I had occasion to admire the expeditious skill of a native tailor, bootmaker, and saddler. A day and a half before my departure I had ordered a *charro* jacket, a pair of high riding-boots, and a revolver-belt; and true to the minute I received each article, well finished and fitting admirably. As a stranger I was charged full Californian prices, but a resident would doubtless have been supplied cheaply.

The State of Colima is one of the smallest in the Republic, and originally was included in the State of Jalisco. It covers an area of about 2500 square miles, and numbers about 60,000 inhabitants.

Its geographical position, north and south of the 19th degree of north latitude, and its gradual ascent from the sea-shore towards the great central plateau of Mexico to an altitude of about 3000 feet, together with its rich soil and plentiful supplies of water, adapt it for every kind of tropical and semi-tropical produce. Rice, sugar-cane, indigo, maize, and cotton are cultivated in splendid quality, not to mention the great quantities of fruits and vegetables. The coffee indigenous to Colima is noted throughout Mexico for its excellence, and I am assured on good authority that it rivals the best Mocha.

Owing to a deplorable absence of enterprise and energy among its inhabitants, the state still remains in a most primitive, and, as far as the rural parts are affected, most uncivilised condition. This indolent indifference is due, in great measure, to the existing insecurity created by the never-ending *pronunciamientos*, the chronic disease of Old Spain, and of all nations impregnated with her blood. *Pronunciamientos* imply *guerrilla* bands, which, under the plea of fighting for one party or the other, infest the roads, and appropriate whatever they can purloin; and even when the revolutions are quelled, the nature of the country encourages not a few *guerrilleros* to persevere in their misdeeds with impunity. The uncertainty both of life and property hitherto has, as might be anticipated, rendered any real progress impossible, and it is not surprising that, under the circumstances, no proprietor is forthcoming to cultivate the ground on a large scale, and derive those benefits from the land and climate which their peculiarities undoubtedly warrant. If the country were once intersected by good roads, the evil would in a great measure be alleviated, since the authorities (such as they are) could be enabled to maintain a stricter supervision on the one hand, and, on the other, the transport of produce and wares would be rendered less expensive and difficult; but good or even tolerable highways are perfectly unknown, not only in the State of Colima, but in Mexico generally; and the construction of railways, although repeatedly proposed and agitated, is for various reasons a matter reserved for the future. It thus happens that the crops raised are hardly more than is required for the consumption of the state itself, and in some degree for that of its neighbours. As for exportation, it is limited almost entirely to produce requiring no cultivation, and what is grown in the vicinity of the coast, such as fine woods and cocoa-nut-oil. Other products—such as sugar, cotton, and indigo—on account of the small quantities shipped, scarcely deserve as yet the name of exports.

If ever the present evils, the offshoots of deficient communication, brigandage, and mal-administration, be removed, it would be an easy matter to increase the productivity of the State of Colima to more than ten times its present yield.

The import trade is entirely in the hands of German merchants, and they supply both the state and its capital with all the foreign goods required. The latter, to the extent of two-thirds of the entire importation, are manufactured in England.

Owing to the absence for the last year or so of any serious revolution, this part of the country is at present considered fairly safe, but its internal condition has as yet derived no benefit from the temporary tranquillity. The inhabitants are so used to *pronunciamientos* and civil strife, that a year's quiet simply leads them to apprehend a new outbreak the sooner, and it will require a prolonged period of peace before the public mind can be thoroughly reassured. This will appear the more comprehensible when it is known that success as a leader of *guerrilleros*, a term which is here always synonymous with brigands, is, as a rule, rewarded by elevation to office of high rank, either civil or military; and many a general or judge could, in company with the present Governor of the State of Colima, recall a not distant period replete with reminiscences of a wild and lawless life.

VIEW TAKEN FROM AN AZOTEA, COLIMA

CHAPTER IV.

COLIMA TO SAYULA.

Preparations for departure—Cheerful intelligence—Start from Colima—*Ranchos* and their crops—Smallpox—*Barrancas*—Barranca de Tonila—Tonila—Abundance of food—The standard *menu*—The Volcan de Colima—The Pico Helado—*Pedregales*—Enter the State of Jalisco—Hacienda San Marcos—A fine view—Barranca de Beltran—Luxuriant plants and magnificent birds—*Mulas de cargo* —Barranca de Vueltas—The *pueblo* of the *hacienda* labourers—Hacienda del Platanar—Strange scene—The escort—A dangerous forest—Evil and remedy united—Indulgent authorities—Barranca de Atenquique—A country restaurant—*Nopales*—*Maguey*—Its uses —*Pulque*—*Mexcal* and *Tequile*—Arrival at Zapotlan—Its inhabitants—Corrupt priests—The hotel—The *plaza*—Fighting-cocks—A comfortable priest—Situation of Zapotlan—Its climate—Its manufactures and products—Mineral wealth—Departure from Zapotlan—A brigand punished—Graves by the roadside—Brigands and brigandage—The summit of the pass—A magnificent view—Arrival at Sayula.

WHILST a journey of less than a hundred miles in Europe or the United States requires nothing more than a portmanteau, a railway ticket, and a few hours' travel, such an undertaking in Mexico is connected with precautions much more formidable, and the time employed in reaching your destination is counted by days instead of hours. For two days previous to the departure of my two travelling companions and myself from Colima, the preparations for the journey, the state of the roads, what escorts we should require, and a number of minor details connected with *mozos*, saddles, and pack-mules, monopolised all our attention, and engrossed our conversation. The evening before we left, after having selected from numerous saddle-mules those that were suitable, and the final instructions being given, our arrangements were somewhat upset by a communication received from the German Consul (on account of the temporary absence of the United States Consul, the only foreign representative in the place) to the effect that great caution was necessary on our second day's march, owing to the presence of a band of thirty brigands in that part of the route. The letter closed with the cheering news that this band had in the last few days despatched several travellers into the "better land beyond," as the Consul expressed himself. As I had no wish to make the acquaintance of that "better land," at least until I had completed my travels through that worse land Mexico, and as my travelling companions shared that opinion, messages were at once despatched requesting a strong escort to be sent from Zapotlan to meet us.

At length, at seven o'clock in the morning of Saturday, December 20th, after having lost two cool hours of daylight through every species of delay, we bid farewell to the hospitable house of the Messrs A. O. & Co., accompanied for two miles by two kind friends, who had been unceasing in their attentions during our stay in their city. Our small caravan consisted, besides ourselves, of six mounted *mozos* (partly armed with revolvers, partly with *machetas*) and four pack-mules—an inclusive total of nine men and thirteen animals. The choice of our friends assured us of the trustworthiness of the men, and inspired us with some confidence

As soon as we had ridden through the straight narrow streets of the city, we emerged into a wide road hedged off on both sides by low stone walls from the adjoining *ranchos*. Even from its remnant it is evident that this road must once have been well constructed, but, like every other public work in the country, it has since its completion, years and years ago, been left much worn and never repaired; it may be thus easily imagined what constant use and heavy rains have now spared of the original smooth surface and partial stone paving. As we proceeded northward the country gradually and gently ascended, and before we had advanced many miles, we missed the familiar cocoa-palms—unable as they are to flourish at this increased elevation—not to meet with them again until the shores of the Gulf were reached; but the hardier bananas still followed us in our wanderings through village and plantation. Through the low walls, constructed of large stones, boulders, and pieces of lava, with which the neighbourhood abounds, we caught glimpses of rich rice-fields as well as acres of maize, sugar-cane, cotton, and tobacco; but only a small proportion of the enclosed land was cultivated, and large tracts of ground, covered with rank vegetation, separated the comparatively small plots under cultivation.

We now and then swerved from the road to avoid a bend; our way then led over tolerably even paths, through wild country overgrown with trees, shrubs, creepers, and cacti, inhabited by hundreds of pretty birds, and apparently unchanged by the touch of man.

I had heard at Colima that smallpox was alarmingly prevalent among the Indian population in the suburbs and vicinity of the city. As we passed their hamlets at a distance of from eight to ten miles away from the town, evidences of the disease were perceptible before many a hut along the road, where dead children were laid out in rough coffins decked with poor and scanty drapery, while their sorrowing relations were huddled round crucifix and lighted candle. About twelve miles out of Colima the road crosses numerous streamlets and valleys, which increased in size and depth as we proceeded and approached the hills. About six miles before Tonila (our first halting-place, and eighteen miles distant from Colima) we came to the Barranca del Arenal, the first of many precipitous ravines to be traversed by us in the next fifty miles of our journey. *Barranca* is the name given in Mexico to all deep valleys, ravines, or gulches with steep sides, or as people in the United States would say, to all "cañons" of any importance. The word is intended more especially to denominate chasms formed by the action, during ages, of a strong flow of water on soft and gravelly soil. Where the ground is fertile, and water abundant, the multifarious foliage spread over the steeps of the *barrancas*, and along the margin of the stream, is most luxuriant; whilst in higher altitudes, where the nature of the soil is unfavourable to vegetation, and the country sterile, *barrancas* with bare, sandy sides are not uncommon. Before reaching the Barranca de Tonila, on the edge of which is the picturesque little town of the same name, we passed over not a few small gulches, the babbling brooks of which threaded through beautiful and bushy thickets, and gushed in miniature cascades, when some chance rock in their course endeavoured, though in vain, to check the flow of their restless, limpid waters. This *barranca* region is one of surpassing loveliness, and although lacking grandeur of formation, it is rich in every attribute required to render a landscape fascinating: hill and dale, gaunt rock and rugged watercourse, and all the reciprocal charms of torrent, leafage, and mountain in the back ground, under the transparent splendours of a tropical sky.

We arrived at Tonila shortly after noon, and were quickly served with a meal of many courses. Even in the smallest Mexican village, and where the *fonda* is sometimes nothing but a native hut, good food is to be found in abundance; and those who do not object to a copious use of garlic, and an application at times of slightly rancid oil instead of butter, will do remarkably well, in spite of a somewhat stereotyped bill of fare. They will be able to enjoy thick rice-soup, eggs cooked in various ways, ragouts and stews of chicken, mutton, veal, and pork, as well as round slices of beef resembling an Albert biscuit in size, and a wafer in consistency, served almost raw, and intended for beef-steak.

As we still had a long journey before us, we did not stop any longer in the tumble-down *fonda* than was absolutely necessary, and at two o'clock the little caravan was again on the move.

From Colima to Tonila our route lay almost due north, only bearing a little to the eastward to avoid collision with the grand Volcan de Colima, at whose foot, at a distance of barely ten miles, Tonila is situate. The majestic mountain crest, with its veil of thin, white, misty smoke, had fronted us all through the day—a magnificent background to all the exquisite landscapes that were succeeding each other like dissolving views. The vapour arises from a small crater, not at the top, but about half-way up the eastern side of the mountain. This crater was formed about five years ago, when a violent eruption of short duration completely caked the neighbouring land with lava and scoriæ, but it now continues in the quietest manner to limit its influence to its own immediate vicinity. About five miles due north of the Volcan de Colima another grand peak rears its giant head towards the sky; this is an extinct volcano, and named Pico Helado, or Frozen Peak, from the fact that more snow is to be found on its summit than on that of the Pico de Fuego (as the active volcano is often called), owing to the absence of subterranean heat. The height of these mountains is about 11,000 feet above the level of the sea, and about 8000 above the country from which they rise.

On leaving Tonila, our route continued in a due northerly direction along the eastern side of these giants, and so near to them that we were able to distinguish the numerous ravines and gulches on their slopes. They are densely wooded, and shrubs and trees venture within a few hundred feet of their summits. The path over which we rode was hard and terribly broken, being composed of lava in layers vomited forth in the far ages by the volcanoes, and the road was one hopeless mass of ruts, holes, and loose stones. These lava formations are frequent on Mexican roads, and travellers, *arrieros*, and diligence-drivers alike cordially abominate the horrible *pedregales*, as they are termed.

We were now in the State of Jalisco, having passed the boundary of the State of Colima a little to the southward of Tonila, and had thus arrived in a part of the Republic noted for its numerous bands of brigands. We gave orders that our party, straggling as it did over a quarter of a mile, should now close together, and unpacked the Winchester rifle and shot gun (the latter provided with buck-shot cartridges) to be ready for whatever emergency might occur.

After a ride of about five miles through country partially cultivated, there appeared to our left the stately Hacienda de San Marcos, a large and palatial building, charmingly situate on the slope of a small hill. This *hacienda* is one of the most important sugar-factories in this part of the Republic, and an enormous reach of country belongs to the estate.

The view from this place and its neighbourhood is proverbial in Colima, and although it was too late to ride up to the *hacienda*, I stopped awhile on the road to enjoy the remarkable panorama. The two volcanoes on the left, with numerous spurs projecting from their giant sides, gradually fading into the valley; a long winding range of mountains on the right, with their mantle of forests, and, mysteriously undulating along the central horizon, a broad fringe of netted vegetation hiding from view the chasm of the great *barranca*, all combined to awe us with their sublime beauty.

Another two miles, partly along a steep path, partly over a wide road which skirts the sugar-cane plantations of San Marcos, brought us to the edge of the celebrated Barranca de Beltran, which according to popular belief is the largest in this part of Mexico. The most erroneous ideas seem to prevail concerning the actual depth of this chasm, which with respect to dimensions must certainly disappoint him who has the marvels of the Yo-semite fresh in his memory. Whatever may be wanting, however, in grandeur of formation, is fully atoned for by the magnificence of the herbage and the variety of charming views which the *barranca's* course reveals with each of its many bends and curves.

I made careful aneroid measurements of difference of altitude between the plateau and the bed of the stream at the bottom, both in descending on one side and ascending on the other, and ascertained the depth to be no more than 525 feet, whilst people in Colima and Zapotlan estimate it variously at 1000, 1500, and even 2000 feet.

The walls of the *barranca* are almost perpendicular, and the construction of the zigzag road which descends one side and ascends the other must have involved enormous labour. All the larger *barrancas* possess these roads, built more than a hundred years ago by the Spaniards. They are wide, and a great portion of the original stone paving still exists, as well as the solid breastwork of masonry erected at all dangerous parts. The zigzags are composed of slopes about 200 yards long, with a grade of about one in four.

Our handy mules carefully and slowly commenced the downward path, and our small caravan soon presented a not unpicturesque appearance, as it twinkled along the densely-overshadowed road. Flowers of the most variegated tints relieved the numerous shades of green around us; splendid trees —some remarkable for the brownish-purple colour of their bark, some for their curious foliage, and others for huge thorns that studded trunk and branch —rose in profusion from the vast undergrowth, while bright, slender creepers clung affectionately to their sides; magnificent parrots, gold-winged humming-birds, and crowds of others hardly less beautiful, seemed with their voice and movement to be, as it were, the soul of this superb body. The splendour of the scene was matchless when the stream at the bottom of the *barranca* was reached, and the view extended not only up its green and precipitous sides, but also along the serpentine and sandy course of the rivulet.

We forded a narrow branch of the latter, after partaking with the mules of its delicious contents, and pursuing the opposite bank for a few yards, crossed the chief stream on an old but solid stone bridge. We now entered upon the zigzag road on the further side, and commenced the ascent. The steep incline severely taxed the powers of our poor animals. The riders all dismounted in order to walk, and with many a halt, to give breathing-time to the *mulas de cargo*, we reached the plateau just before sunset. The distance in direct line from edge to edge of the Barranca de Beltran is about a third of a mile; the length of the road down one side, across the valley, and up the other, is hardly more than a mile and a half, but it took us an hour and a half to surmount.

These *barrancas* are great difficulties in the line of communication between Colima and Zapotlan, and render transport on wheels impossible. All goods must be carried by mules, of which we met hundreds and hundreds with heavy loads on their backs, plodding slowly along. Many a poor beast was groaning beneath its burden as it toiled up the steep roads, and not a few were seen to lie, or even fall down exhausted, so perfectly unable were they to continue the journey.

The sun was just beginning to disappear behind the hills to our right when we commenced the ride over the two miles of tableland that separates the Barranca de Beltran from the wide and shallow

Barranca de Vueltas, in the valley of which is situated the large Hacienda del Platanar, where we intended to make our halt for the night. The few minutes of twilight quickly elapsed, and we were advancing in utter darkness, when we gained the edge of the *barranca*, and the path began to descend. Along an uneven stony way, between rocks and hills, and through dense vegetation, we at length saw the glimmer of lights before us. We were at the village of the plantation labourers, and had still a couple of miles before the *hacienda* building could be reached.

Marvellously strange was the appearance of this village as we rode through it in the darkness of night. The little plots of ground before the huts, contained groups of men, women, and children, chattering, eating and drinking, romping and singing, or engaged in some game that seemed to create the utmost hilarity among them, while the flickering pitch-pine on the earth shed an unearthly light over all. The scenes thus produced by these dark-skinned individuals, with their white clothing and huge hats, viewed in the uncertain light of their primitive illumination, are almost too weird to allow of adequate description. They appeared to be thoroughly happy, and so intent on their evening recreation as to take no notice whatever of our cavalcade.

It was past seven o'clock when we reached the *hacienda*, and after our forty-nine miles' ride over the wretched roads, we were not sorry to be able to dismount.

We found the interior square of the old, stone-built house full of bustle and animation. Two other travelling parties had arrived from Zapotlan only a short time before ourselves, and their men and escort were busy unpacking and unsaddling the mules and horses, and preparing for the night.

The room into which we three were shown was anything but comfortable. It was flush with the ground, without a window, nor could the door be made to close. On the stony floor we found the most primeval bedsteads of rough boards, unprovided with anything wherewith to soften the hard wood; other furniture there was none. We were so tired, however, that after partaking of supper served in the yard, and stumbling over the bodies of *mozos* and soldiers who were lying asleep in all directions, we wrapped ourselves in our blankets, and regardless of the music, both instrumental and vocal, in which some of the men indulged, had soon forgotten bad roads, hard fare and harder beds.

At four o'clock next morning our chief *mozo* knocked at the door with the announcement that the coffee was ready, and we were soon sitting down to our early breakfast in the verandah, and watching the animated sight before us in the yard. Horses and mules were being driven in from the adjacent *corral* amidst the shouts and yells of the attendants, whilst others busied themselves with kindling fires of pitch-pine, by the light of which mules were packed, horses saddled, and arms secured. There was something of martial wildness about the whole scene that reminded me vividly of a painting that I had lately seen, representing a guerrilla-band preparing for a night-attack.

After the lapse of half an hour all was ready for the start, and the escort having formed in two lines outside the *hacienda*, we rode past them with the *mozos* and the *mulas de cargo*.

The contingent from Colima had duly arrived; they were twelve men armed with carbines and revolvers of various patterns, some breechloaders.

Besides these, there were eight cavalry soldiers who had convoyed a party from Zapotlan the previous evening, and who now joined us on their way back. These men carried Remington breechloading carbines and Colt's revolvers. With our six *mozos* and ourselves, we thus amounted to the number of twenty-nine.

We rode across the bottom land of the wide *barranca* in complete darkness, but by the time we had climbed its northern side, daylight commenced to dawn. After a mile or so over the *mesa* the country began to get hilly, and we soon entered a pine forest, which, but for the smallness of the timber, seemed almost a reflection of some parts of the Sierra Nevada. The growth of pines and firs indicated a considerable elevation, and on reference I found that we were nearly 4000 feet above the level of the sea.

The track through this wood is fearfully rough, and the nature of the country most favourable to robbers, who can easily avail themselves of the numerous breaks in the ground, clumps of trees, and hillocks, to rush upon the traveller so suddenly that resistance would be an absurdity. This locality is at all times most insecure, and it was against it

F

in particular that the German Consul at Colima had warned us. Our escort here separated into three divisions—one formed a vanguard, the second remained with us and the pack-mules, whilst the third protected our rear.

This, our mounted *escolta*, proved, on a nearer examination, to be the most ruffianly half-castes I had yet seen; and their appearance corresponded so closely with the picture of a band of brigands, as description had painted it in my imagination, that the truth of my information in Colima concerning them required no further confirmation. These armed *mozos* serve as escort, if hired for the purpose, and as long as you pay them are tolerably honest; but should you venture to travel unprotected, these versatile gentlemen will resume the brigand part of their business, attack, and rob you. They are determined to live on the traveller one way or the other, and alike constitute the evil and supply the remedy. There exists in the State of Jalisco, and in many other states, an important class of these people, who, ever ready to favour disturbance, welcome heartily any revolution, when they side with the faction which pays them best.

The state authorities, who have often to thank this clique for their advent to power, do not throw many obstacles into the way of their predatory proceedings; and even if murder be committed, the perpetrators are rarely brought to justice. The population has become so hardened to news of robbery and murder, and so disused to the thought of punishment for crime, that they have grown perfectly callous. It is usual for Mexicans in the State of Jalisco, after hearing some sad story of murder on the road, to simply shrug their shoulders, and with the expression, "*Pobrecito, que desgracia!*"* at once dismiss the whole story. On expressing your indignation, you will hear them say, "What good can be done by talking? the authorities won't bother themselves about it, why should we?"

Soon after the forest had been left behind, we came to the edge of the large Barranca de Atenquique, the main features of which closely resemble those of the Barranca de Beltran. Atenquique is deeper than Beltran by at least a hundred feet, but as the former is about double as wide, its depth is less apparent; the rich vegetation, enchanting scenery,

* " Poor fellow, what a mishap!"

and dense population of splendid birds, are however the same.

Arrived on the northern *mesa* of the *barranca*, a ride of a few miles brought us within sight of a small Indian village, consisting of about half-a-dozen low huts, and being told that one of them was a "restaurant," we dismounted before a wretched structure, consisting of a square of *adobe* walls about eighteen inches high, on which rested fragile walls of matting supported by sticks, and overlapped by a roof of rice-straw. We had to stoop low to enter, and soon found ourselves seated round a rough table on rougher stools; but the meal that was brought in almost immediately was surprisingly good, considering the "coffee-room" in which it was served. We had what Americans call "scrambled eggs," fried pieces of *langaneza* (a very long, thin sausage of smoked pork, highly seasoned with garlic), *frijoles*, and *tortillas*, besides some excellent chocolate, which, I believe, is better in this part of Mexico than anywhere else in the world. Through the open door which afforded a peep into an adjacent hut, a girl was seen kneeling on the ground preparing *tortillas*, whilst another was busied in taking them out of the primitive oven and bringing them to our table, keeping us well provided with a constant supply of hot ones, and removing those that had become cold, as is usual at native repasts.

Continuing our journey for several miles, the road led over another *pedregal* formed of huge layers of ancient lava. The volcanic composition of this part of the country is very apparent, though it is difficult to understand the cause of its presence, the distance from the Volcan de Colima being too considerable to allow of the supposition that an eruption from that source could have been the origin.

About three miles before reaching Zapotlan we entered a wide road, entirely out of repair, and harrowed by the last rains into ruts, pools, and microscopic *barrancas*. The adjacent fields under cultivation were carefully fenced off from the road by rows of the *nopal* or prickly-pear cactus (*Opuntia vulgaris* and *O. tuna*), and we noticed ditches nearer the town.

The fields are extensively planted with the *maguey* or *metl* (*Agave Mexicana*), a large species of the American aloe or century plant of the United States, of which I never lost sight as long as I remained in the *tierra templada*.

The different uses of the *maguey* in Mexico are manifold. About five years after it has been planted, a long shoot that springs from its centre rises to a height of ten to fifteen feet and carries the blossom. This is cut off at about a foot from the ground, and the sap that oozes from it is collected and allowed slightly to ferment. This liquid is the native Mexican beer, and among Indians and *mestizos* greatly appreciated. It has the colour and consistency of milk-and-water, and smells and tastes like yeast. Zapotlan is famous for its *pulque*, as this beverage is called; and before our entrance into the town we passed many a hut and low *fonda* where pigskins were suspended full of the liquor, and hollowed gourds arranged on shelves as its receptacles.

Mezcal and *tequile*, two kinds of spirits, are likewise manufactured from the *maguey*. They are exceedingly strong, and the latter (*tequile*) much renowned for its purity.* Besides this, the fibre

---

* There are various kinds of *maguey*, and besides those mentioned above, three other sorts of spirituous liquors, called respectively *sotal*, *tusca quesca*, and *pinus*, are distilled from other genera of the plant.

of its thick leaves is utilised for strong rope, excellent matting, and horse-girths.

At eleven o'clock A.M., after a ride of seventeen miles, we reached Zapotlan, and our long caravan entered the monotonous, straight streets, lined with the customary low and solid houses, amidst an assemblage of the natives, who from their doors curiously surveyed our entry.

The inhabitants of Zapotlan do not enjoy the best of reputations. They are said to be more or less connected with brigandage; and whenever a revolution gives them the opportunity, the male population turn out on the roads in great numbers, to lighten travellers of money, luggage, and clothing. Even in quiet times like the present the vicinity of Zapotlan is considered most dangerous.

The priests retain a powerful hold on these people, and if their influence were properly employed, much might be done to better them. But I have heard of ecclesiastics themselves as the chieftains of robber-bands; and even the best of their order are only too ready to ignore the evil, so long as the people attend confession, burn candles before multitudinous shrines, and last, but not least, pay the money demanded for absolution and the like. In this manner even murder is condoned by the clergy. No wonder that the poor Indians and low *mestizos* remain in the most degraded condition of moral and mental darkness. Riding through the wretched streets of the outskirts, tenanted by these tribes, I noticed small placards of pink paper fastened to the wall or door of almost every house, and on examination found them to contain some printed lines invoking the protection and blessing of some saint or other on the dwelling and inhabitants in question!

We soon reached the *fonda* on the large *plaza*, a house most uncomfortable in all its arrangements. A room was apportioned to us, blest with little but two antediluvian bedsteads, and destitute alike of light and window. It was closed by massive folding-doors, and fastened by means of a lock a foot square, with a gigantic key weighing several pounds.

This inviting chamber opened on the filthy and fragrant yard. As it is considered unsafe to entrust the key of a room to a stranger when its occupant is absent, it may be imagined what a struggle there was between us as to the individual on whom the charge of that ponderous instrument was to devolve.

The rest of the day was spent in exploring the town, which is one of the oldest in Mexico. The *plaza* is much larger and brighter than that of Colima. The same stone or *adobe* benches are ranged all round, and trees render the walks pleasant to sight and sense. The streets are wider than at Colima, but the pavement is inferior, and the low one-storied houses have an older and meaner air. In fine, there is not so much "style" about Zapotlan as Colima, and the inhabitants appear less favoured by fortune.

While strolling through the streets we perceived a number of houses in which fighting-cocks were exposed for sale. Small square stalls were disposed round the walls of the rooms, in which the warriors were displayed. Cock-fighting is a favourite sport with the Zapotlanians, and enjoys with them a greater popularity than bull-fighting, as it offers a greater scope for betting.

Near the *plaza* are the ruins of what has once been a fine cathedral, destroyed, I believe, about sixty years ago, by an earthquake, and to this hour as uncared for as if the catastrophe had happened yesterday.

Although this town can boast churches sufficient to accommodate a population ten times as numerous, a new cathedral has been commenced near the remains of the old one; but the structure has not advanced much above the foundations, although years have elapsed since they were laid. The day we spent in Zapotlan happened to be Sunday, and we were much amused by a fat and ancient priest, who, himself comfortably seated in a light waggon with some friends, directed with the most pious energy the poor of his congregation, who were now pouring out of church, to proceed to a quarry some three miles off, there to collect stones and carry them to the site of the cathedral, in order to assist in the work of building. A great number, principally of the fairer sex, followed his bidding, and were seen late in the evening returning with heavy loads of stone and sand on their heads, whilst their bloated " medicine-man " was calmly driving his mules.

Zapotlan (which on maps and official documents is often called Ciudad Guzman) contains a population of about 20,000, and is situate in a most fertile country, at an elevation of 4300 feet above the level of the sea, in north latitude 19° 41′. Its climate has the reputation of being all but perfect. Possessed of all the advantages of the tropics, whilst exempt from excessive heat, and in the permanent enjoyment of a moderately warm summer, Zapotlan is one of the most delightful localities in the *tierra templada*, or temperate zone of the Mexican plateau. Of course the mid-day sun aims his rays with tolerable vigour, but the mornings and evenings are charming, and the atmosphere deliciously clear, pure, and light. I am assured that the town is most healthy, and that epidemics are wholly unknown.

Zapotlan is noted for its soap-factories, and provides all the neighbouring states with this commodity. Besides this, it produces a large supply of *pulque*, a fair quantity of *mezcal*, while the *haciendas* in the vicinity manufacture sugar, molasses, and a kind of rum called *aquardiente de caña*. The country around the town will bear almost everything except plants which require tropical heat, but is only partially tilled. The same causes as elsewhere in Mexico — insecurity of life and property, as well as lack of means for transport and communication—have hitherto prevented the development of its natural advantages. The hills and mountains surrounding the town are reported to be rich in minerals of various kinds. During my stay I was shown specimens of stone brought from the immediate vicinity, apparently containing a large percentage of cinnabar, and of this ore I was told that enormous quantities exist. At present considerable cargoes of quicksilver, extensively used in the "beneficiating *haciendas*" of the silver-mining districts, are imported at large cost from abroad, whereas if sufficient enterprise were forthcoming, there is little doubt that a large supply could be obtained here at a much smaller outlay.

At seven o'clock next morning we departed from Zapotlan on our way to Sayula, eighteen miles to the northward. The road being considered safer than that traversed the previous day, we reduced our escort to six men, which were engaged for us by a merchant of Zapotlan. With our six *mozos* we accordingly numbered fifteen in all. Immediately after leaving the town the road leads through a broad valley and along the marshy shore of a small lake. This spot simply swarmed with birds. The water was hidden by duck and teal, whilst large cranes, herons, and other waders were strutting and lounging on the banks. In the trees and bushes small *cardinales* entirely red, tiny glittering humming-birds, and many others were flying from branch to branch, whilst the mute-like *zopilotes*, quietly perched in a commanding position, were calmly expecting some morsel which might gratify their not over-fastidious palates.

About three miles out of Zapotlan the road passes over a *pedregal* of the worst description, where attacks from brigands are said to be very frequent, especially on the diligences which pass here regularly. The nature of the ground necessitates a funereal jog, and effectually debars escape.

About a fortnight before we passed, the coach which left Zapotlan at two o'clock A.M., and had consequently arrived at this spot in utter darkness, was assailed by a band of ten men. In accordance with their tactics, one of them jumped from his ambush before the door of the diligence to open it, and with cocked revolver force the travellers to descend. But the passengers, three only in number, appeared this time to be well prepared, and unlike the generality of Mexican travellers, who prefer robbery to resistance, they shot the brigand dead the instant he approached the door. The others seeing their comrade fall, and the passengers ready for defence, immediately took to their heels. The dead brigand was tied to the top of a pole, and left there as a scarecrow for others. At Zapotlan we were promised the treat of this interesting spectacle, but on reaching the spot one of our men informed us that the gentleman had been released the previous evening and buried by his friends. We were thus happily spared this disgusting sight, and only beheld the blood-stained pole and the new grave by its side.

Along all Mexican roads rude graves of this kind are numerous. The majority have a primitive cross erected over them, and often bear a rustic inscription, recording the familiar tale of attack by bandits and interment on the spot where the victim fell. The few heaps which lack a cross cover the remains of those brigands who themselves perished in their attempt upon the life and property of others.

The flourishing trade of brigandage in Mexico is for the greater part sustained without combat or bloodshed, and it is only in exceptional cases that travellers use force in trying to prevent their despoliation. It seems to be perfectly understood that your life is safe if you quietly submit to be plundered of all that you carry. If you quit the coach willingly when your masked assailant asks you, and comply with the request of "*cara en tierra*," which means to lie down with your face towards the ground, there is no further inconvenience attached to the operation than the loss of money, portmanteau, and clothes; and if it does not happen to be particularly cold, the journey to the next town in a semi-naked state, with a newspaper in lieu of your usual garments, may not prove too thrilling an adventure.

Those Mexicans who prefer travelling by diligence to riding on horseback, generally restrict their luggage to a very small handbag, take no valuables, and often no arms. They yield unconditionally when attacked, and besides their clothes are only mulcted of the few dollars which they take care to carry in their pockets so as to escape the beating invariably bestowed by the brigands on the traveller impertinent enough to be without coin. At times, when objects of value are at stake, conflict is preferred to concession; and I am assured that the majority of cases terminate in the retreat of the brigands, who, as a rule, are cowards, and ever mindful of the old Spanish proverb, "*La pintura y la pelea desde lejos las ojea.*" *

It is evident that they do not sally forth with the intention of fighting, which, in the result, would only imperil their own precious persons, a contingency to which these gentlemen seem to entertain the strongest objections, and might possibly involve them in difficulties with the authorities; their object is to rob, and they do all they can to attain that object, if only the use of arms on the part of their prey be rendered impossible.

Brigandage has greatly decreased in Mexico within the last year. The absence of civil disturbances has enabled the state governments, despite the

---

* A picture and a battle are best seen at a distance.

inefficiency of many, to supply the roads with escorts and police to a moderate extent; and although the latter very frequently make common cause with the robbers, yet on the whole the measures taken appear to have caused some amendment. Wherever I went, however, tales were plentiful about the events of only a month, a week, or a few days ago, and on arriving after the day's journey, the first question put to us invariably was, "Did you meet with any *novedad?*"—*novedad* (novelty or news) being in this case the periphrastic and vulgar term for brigandage.

After leaving the small lake, the road begins to ascend, and for some miles leads over successive hills, continually increasing in height until the summit of the pass over this spur of the Sierra Madre range is attained. The country here is wild and uninviting, the narrow road winding its way through undergrowth composed of cacti and a variety of shrubs, overtopped at times by a deformed and sickly tree. The path seems until quite recently to have been much narrower, for the shrubs and cacti felled to effect the clearing are still cumbering the ground. This improvement was carried out mainly to render the road less liable to surprises. Arrived at the highest point of the pass, at an elevation of about 5500 feet above the level of the sea, a magnificent view was revealed to us. Before us, and stretching from the foot of the mountain on which we stood, lay an extensive plain, bordered miles away to the northward by another range of emerald hills, and dotted with villages and *haciendas.* On the margin of a lake we descried the town of Sayula with numerous steeples and towers, covering a large expanse of ground. The land appeared carefully tilled, and an air of thriftiness and wealth seemed to belong to this locality such as I had not before observed in Mexico. The fields were waving with corn of various kinds (and this in the month of December), whilst acre upon acre was sprinkled with rows of graceful *magueys,* interspersed at short intervals by trees of numerous descriptions.

The remarkable clearness of the atmosphere, as well as our commanding position, caused us to believe that the end of the day's journey was very near, but to descend the heights and to traverse the plain proved a ride of many miles; and when we reached the end of the wide road lined with *nopales*, and separated by a broad ditch from the adjacent fields, which leads into Sayula, one of the ancient church bells was just proclaiming the hour of noon.

CHAPTER V.

SAYULA TO GUADALAJARA.

A family likeness—Sayula—Its climate—An extensive vista—An attempt at swindling—First experience of a *diligencia*—Departure from Sayula—Closely packed—Cavalry escort—Lago de Sayula—La Cofradia—Carbonate of soda or *tequesquite*—A cotton-tree—Cebollas—Mexican *diligencias*—*Cocheros* and their assistants—Laguna de Zacoalco—A horrible road—Mismanagement of public works—Pozos—An extensive plateau—Santa Ana Acatlan—Santa Cruz and Christmas processions—The valley of Guadalajara—Mexican waggons and carts—Travelling *Indios*—A small but dangerous *barranca*—An agreeable change—Arrival at Guadalajara—Comfortable quarters.

THERE is such a sameness about small Mexican towns, that the stranger at first sight can hardly discern any difference between them. Sayula in its general features is so much like Zapotlan, that I almost thought we had been led in a circle, and returned to our starting-point. There were the same streets, the same badly-paved roadways, and the same low *adobe*, whitewashed houses. The similarity extended to the inn accommodation; our room, although larger than the one we occupied at Zapotlan, was furnished in the same primitive

STREET IN SAYULA

manner, and the meals were composed of the same dishes.

Sayula is as old a town as Zapotlan, and Spaniards settled there immediately after the Conquest. It has a population of about 10,000, mostly engaged in agriculture, preparing *pulque*, and the manufacture of salt.

Its climate is very salubrious, being situated in about the same elevation as Zapotlan (4400 feet above sea-level). It is not visited by any epidemics, and without the annoyance of excessive heat basks in a perpetual summer.

A merchant of Sayula, to whom we brought letters, conducted us after dinner to the top of a hill outside the town, from which we enjoyed a splendid view of the neighbourhood.

From our position, the town and surrounding country was spread out before us as on a map. There were the straight streets, the flat-roofed houses with thickets of green in the *patios*, the never-missing *paseo* lined with shady trees, the cosy *alameda*, and the eternal *plaza* with a church as one of its sides. In front, at the foot of the eminence on which we were, an ancient cathedral was shown, said to have been erected by Cortez himself (*all* ancient churches in this country enjoy this reputation), and its peculiar old-Spanish architecture, its pillars, fretwork, and images, together with the mysterious arcades which communicate with the stately palace of the bishop, were certainly most quaint and remarkable. To our left stretched the waters of the Lago de Sayula, with numerous houses nestling near its shores, and hundreds of birds skimming its mirror-like surface. To our right were the verdant fields of the fertile plain, bordered at no great distance by the wooded mountains with which our morning's ride had acquainted us.

The scene breathed so much of peace and calm that the mere mention of war and revolution seemed a profanity in connection with it; and we gazed at it from a rocky seat till the sun had disappeared behind the domes and tower of the town, when we returned in darkness.

As we had arranged to complete our journey to Guadalajara in the diligence, we here paid our men and discharged the animals. After the principal of the escort had received the money for all his subordinates, some altercation ensued between them, and

STREET IN SAYULA.

two of the men repeatedly appealed to us, asseverating that they had been cheated out of their portion, whilst their villainous chief insisted that we had paid him too little. Seeing, however, that we remained impervious to all their demands, they mounted their horses and galloped away about an hour after our arrival, as they proposed a return to Zapotlan the same day. Late in the evening, a telegraphic message* arrived from our friends in Zapotlan, inquiring whether the escort's story of our refusal to pay them was true, as they had that instant arrived declaring they had not received a cent. They had evidently forgotten the power of the—here rarely used—electric wire, which speedily frustrated their designs.

We were unpleasantly surprised to find that the coach, instead of starting at six A.M. as we had been led to believe, was to arrive at half-past three A.M. from Zapotlan, and leave immediately afterwards. According to regulation our luggage had to be taken to the diligence office the previous evening, where we were charged outrageous sums for the

* A single telegraphic wire, supported by rough poles, has for some years connected the principal towns of the Republic. When not interrupted by *pronunciados* it works fairly well, but is chiefly used for Government purposes.

extra weight, only an *arroba* (twenty-five pounds) being allowed free.

At half-past three next morning, we were waiting in the draughty yard of the *despachio de las diligencias* for the coach, which soon made its appearance. There is something unearthly in the thought of experiencing a Mexican stage-coach for the first time in the utter darkness of night, and being obliged to step into the close and repulsive conveyance, without a chance of reconnoitering the interior or the *compagnons de route*.

We delayed entering, whilst the mules were unharnessed, and the eight fresh ones got ready; but after this and the packing had been completed, by the blaze of the pitch-pine burning on the ground, the decided *vamos* of the *cochero* urged us to push our way into the vehicle and find our places as best we could.

We were hardly seated when the driver cracked his whip, as if he were firing pistols, and with shouts of *Vamanos mulas ahah ha-a-a-h!* we rumbled at a sharp pace over the awful pavement of the good old town of Sayula. The moon was invisible, and a large torch, held over the side by the

driver's assistant, was the only light by which the *cochero* could steer, but both he and the mules were evidently initiated into the secrets of the road.

When my eyes had become accustomed to the darkness, I found the diligence closely packed, for besides ourselves there were six other passengers, and thus all nine seats were occupied. This, on the whole, is rather an advantage in this country; like an addition of sawdust or straw in a packing-case, it prevents the contents of the coach from the painful friction with another, which would occur, through the horrible incongruities of the roads, were there ampler room for movement.

After a couple of miles, we left the wide cactus-lined road leading out of Sayula behind us, and entered a narrower way bordered on both sides by trees and bushes. Here we were joined by three fearfully shabby cavalry soldiers, whose duty it was to escort us. They may be very useful to frighten intending robbers by their presence, as indeed a scarecrow generally is in the case of intruding birds; but in event of attack, I presume, they would have modelled their conduct on that of the same scarecrows, when the seeds are filched in spite of them.

Like their comrades at Colima, and those that had formed part of our escort from Platanar to Zapotlan, they were the most disorderly soldiers possible. Their filthy canvas uniforms were in this instance hidden by a *sarape* wrapped round their shoulders and half their faces; their *machetas* were fastened to the saddles, and passed under the leg of the rider and the girths, whilst their carabines were secured lengthways along the body of the horse.

They kept up with the coach for some time, and were then suddenly lost to view.

We soon reached the margin of the Lago de Sayula, the shores of which we followed for a considerable distance.

After a rough drive of fourteen miles, we reached the first halting-place for change of mules, a miserable village called La Cofradia, where we arrived at about six o'clock, when the first rays of the rising sun peered over the mountains. The wretched houses built of undisguised *adobe*, and a few thatched huts, were all discernible, and the *tout ensemble* was so repulsive that we did not feel inclined to leave the coach.

Starting again, we continued along the banks of the lake, over ground thickly crusted with a white alkaline salt (carbonate of soda) which is deposited by the lake when subsiding after the rainy season. This substance, which Mexicans call *tequesquite*, is a source of wealth to the population of this district, although its presence deprives the country of agricultural fertility. From the Lago de Sayula northward, the land is much inferior for producing purposes to that between the coast and Zapotlan, with the exception of that part of the plain of Sayula which lies between the hills to the south and the lake. The *tequesquite* is transported to all parts of the Republic, and especially to Zapotlan, for the manufacture of soap.

On the waters of the *lago* we observed the same variety of "*raræ aves*" noticeable before in similar localities.

At this time we were travelling on a wide road, bordered on the right by the lake, and on the left fenced off from the *ranchos* by the usual stone walls. The fields on the undulating ground composing these *ranchos* were partially cultivated, whilst on the portions left fallow two or three kinds of trees, as well as an assortment of cacti, were worthy of remark. Amongst the trees, one carrying pods filled with a substance closely resembling cotton, was most conspicuous. Mr L——, who is a cotton manufacturer at Guadalajara, has repeatedly tried to use this tree-cotton as a substitute for the ordinary material, but all his experiments have been futile owing to the shortness of staple in the tree produce, and its want of strength.

Towards nine o'clock the second stage was reached at a wretched village called Cebollas, where, however, we were pleased to find breakfast in readiness for us. The *fonda* looked miserable enough; its cracked tumble-down walls, and general squalor, did not certainly excite an undue expectation within us, but we found the table neatly laid, and the meal plentiful, well cooked, and remarkably cheap. After three-quarters of an hour's stoppage, eight fresh mules were harnessed to the coach, and the usual "*vamos señores*" of the *cochero* was the signal of departure.

The *diligencias* in use in Mexico are the Concord

coaches of the United States, and considering the labour they have to perform, are undoubtedly the best that can be found for the purpose. They are run by a company styling themselves "*Impresa de diligencias generales,*" and are employed in carrying the mails. The coaches are in two different sizes, the smaller to hold nine, the larger twelve passengers inside. The seats are arranged in three rows, at right angles with the pole, the middle bench being provided with a movable back, and running from door to door. The carriage rests on stout leather bands, which are themselves suspended from strong old-fashioned springs, and thus the jerking and jolting occasioned by the execrable roads is to a great degree alleviated. If it were not for this contrivance, to travel by diligence in Mexico would be next to impossible; even with these Concord coaches it is one of the most awful ordeals to which any one can be subjected, and people are tossed in the stage-coach like dice in a cup. The diligences are drawn by eight mules, or small horses; two are harnessed to the wheel, then four abreast, and finally two in the lead, and are driven by the *cocheros* in the most skilful manner. The driver works a powerful break with his right leg, by placing his foot into a hook at the end of a lever, by his side. An assistant performs much of the shouting, as well as the whipping and stoning of the animals. The latter operation is resorted to when the whip proves ineffectual; stones of the size of an egg, are thrown at the lazy animal, and with such precision that they never miss their aim, and always produce the desired effect. This *muchacho* of the driver is a hard-worked individual; besides the duties above mentioned, he must attend to the luggage, and when occasion requires urge on the animals by running beside them, or by his own weight balance the coach, when, owing to the uneven ground, there is danger of tilting over on one side or the other. The poor man is always on the move by the side of the diligence, now jumping upon the right step, now changing to the left, then rushing forward to whip or stone a mule, then tightening a strap or a chain, and finally mounting the box perfectly breathless, only to undergo the same torture a few minutes later. Both the *cochero* and his *muchacho* generally wear *chapareras* made of goatskin with the long hair on the outside, which gives them a savage aspect.

After leaving Cebollas, we soon came to the margin of the Laguna de Zacoalco, which for a considerable time formed our view on the left; whilst on our right, some distance off, and to which, on account of the higher ground, the waters of the lake do not extend, the land was fenced in and partially cultivated.

We drove over another tract of alkaline deposit, and as we proceeded the roads grew worse and worse. We had frequently to abandon the coach, whenever it was jammed in the mire, and find our way on foot as well as we could over deep pools of reeking mud; and when the impetuous gallop of the mules happened to pull us through these quagmires, we received our full share of the ooze as it splashed over the coach. Mexican roads baffle all description: it is utterly impossible to convey a correct idea of them, and only he who has suffered can know what they really are.

A journey under these circumstances is naturally very slow: including stoppages for changing mules and taking meals, we proceeded at the rate of about five miles an hour.

The importance of a good road from the Pacific to Guadalajara, by way of Colima, is as patent to the Mexican as it is to the visitor. But the sluggish indifference of the people, the bungling which distinguishes native operations, and the corruption that pervades the monetary administration, have hitherto effectually thwarted the desired end. More than five years since, a road was projected from Colima northwards, but owing to the combined causes of war, mismanagement, and continual want of funds, the work is still in its infancy. On the way from Colima to Tonila I observed some signs of the intended improvement, and at one point even labourers actually engaged; though another portion, completed as it was, and waiting for a juncture with the former, was rapidly falling into decay from constant neglect and the summer rains. At a *barranca* near Tonila the supports for a bridge intended to span the stream at a small height from the bottom, and solidly constructed of stone, are all but perfected, and a number of men were busily employed when I passed. The supports will perhaps be finished shortly, but according to every precedent in this country, it will probably take years and years until the bridge (apparently an iron one) is transported to the spot, and the structure finally completed. What the object can be of building the road piecemeal, instead of continuously, and allowing the rains of years to destroy one part before the others are placed in connection with it, is I presume a matter only comprehensible to Mexican minds.

At Pozos, a village composed like the others of low *adobe* houses neither plastered nor whitewashed, and inhabited almost exclusively by Indians, we again changed mules, and striking away to the northward, left the lakes behind. Our road had hitherto conducted us through broad valleys surrounded by mountains about fifteen miles apart, and now after slightly ascending for some miles we found ourselves on a more extensive plateau. Cultivation became somewhat more general, and we now and then passed extensive *hacienda* buildings. Some portions of the road were fenced off from the estates by wide ditches, with an *adobe* or mud-wall on the further side, and an additional hedge of *nopales*, a double and most powerful protection, prompted probably by fear of brigands.

At about three o'clock we reached the town of Santa Ana Acatlan, famed for its population of robbers, and notorious for miserable low houses, and excruciatingly paved streets.* A church with lofty towers, added to many less stately companions, is sufficiently large to accommodate the inhabitants of half-a-dozen Santa Anas; and it is evident that each of these edifices must have cost at least twice as much as the remainder of the town put together.

* A few weeks after I had passed this locality in safety, a terrible disaster happened there to a German family of Guadalajara, whose hospitality I had the privilege of enjoying when at the latter place. Mr B—— was returning home from Colima, accompanied by his wife, child, and a recently-arrived German physician. When within three miles of Santa Ana Acatlan the coach was stopped by eight or ten men. The passengers descended, and Mr B—— and his friend opened fire on the brigands, who, however, at the first shot were reinforced by from twenty to thirty *ladrones*, who had been hiding in the vicinity. In the ridiculously unequal fight that now ensued the doctor was immediately killed, whilst Mr B——, unsupported by any of the other passengers, fought gallantly until a robber, riding up behind, split his skull with a *macheta*. Not content with this, the fiends subjected the surviving passengers to the most brutal treatment, before they allowed the ransacked diligence to proceed. The soldiers stationed on the road had been seen shortly before the appearance of the band, but they did not arrive at the spot until the fight was nearly over, and even then decamped immediately they were fired at. It was not until several weeks afterwards that some of the band were *said* to have been caught and brought to justice, but the truth of this remains very doubtful.

Leaving Santa Ana Acatlan, the fearful road leads up a hill, from the top of which an extensive view is obtained of the surrounding country. In spite of the infamous reputation of the people, there were traces of a less scanty agriculture than in the country we had just left behind; and beyond the stone walls and fences we descried rippling fields of sugar-cane and various cereals.

As we neared the village of Santa Cruz, we met several processions of Indians dressed in all the finery of holiday accoutrement, and bearing aloft a cradle of straw, surrounded with coloured paper and tinsel, and containing a waxen image of the Infant Christ, embedded in paper shavings and gold leaf.

The crowds were headed by children with burning tapers, and the rear was composed of a motley throng that let off crackers, and shot up rockets in the broad daylight. This being the 23rd of December, these were the preparations of the *hacienda* labourers for the celebration of Christmas at one of the churches in Santa Crux.

Ever since Santa Ana Acatlan we had been gradually ascending a low ridge of mountains, and now as we passed San Augustin, the last stage before Guadalajara, the road led down from the hills, into a large plain with many villages, hamlets, and *haciendas*, and a seemingly numerous population. The nearer we approached the capital of Jalisco, the more we observed its influence on the surrounding country, and the traffic on the road swelled palpably the further we proceeded.

On account of *barrancas* and other difficulties, almost the only means of transport employed between the coast and Zapotlan are mules; we rarely met a cart or a waggon. From the latter place, however, towards Guadalajara and other inland towns, the porterage of goods is divided between *mulas de cargo* and rude heavy waggons and carts. In order to afford mutual protection, they always travel together, and we were now meeting great numbers, which often blocked the way and kept the diligence waiting until they had moved aside. These waggons and carts are in the shape of an oblong box, clumsily constructed of a framework of logs of wood, and mounted on large wheels, connected by weighty bars of rough timber for axles. The wheels are peculiar; they rarely form a true circle, the felloes being formed of several pieces of wood rounded to an arc on one side, and fastened to a solid square block on the other, which latter forms the inside of the wheel, as there are no spokes.

The waggons, which sometimes convey tremendous loads piled up to a great height, are mostly drawn by mules, from four to sixteen or more to the team.

The carts, whose two wheels are of enormous size, are, as a rule, drawn by oxen—two, four, or more, yoked by the head, somewhat in the South German and Italian fashion. The teamsters guide them cleverly, but employ the cruel method of pricking the poor brutes with a sharp spike mounted at the end of a long, slender pole.

Besides trains of pack-mules, and caravans of waggons, we frequently met families of Indians and low *mestizos* tramping on foot, or with one mule among half a dozen of them, carrying in huge frames of wickerwork a quantity of brown earthenware vessels, baskets, or *maguey* matting. The loads borne by these people along the dusty roads under a hot sun were quite enormous, and we could not help compassionating them, whilst admiring such apparent industry and endurance. An occasional party of well-armed horsemen would next pass us, or a family-carriage jogging along slowly, though far from surely, surrounded by servants and escort.

About fifteen miles before we reached the city, the road winds through the all but dry bed of a stream, forming a small *barranca*, the result of continued action of the water on the sandy soil. During the few rainy months the coach has to make a long detour, the stream being too high to allow of a passage. This small *barranca*, with numerous caves and crevices in its steep walls, is a favourite resort of brigands, and a few soldiers are always stationed there. These six or eight men and the three cavalry soldiers that accompanied us out of Sayula, were the only indications I observed of the much-vaunted escorts that the authorities are said to have now distributed all over the roads. It was certainly only owing to our good luck, and not to the care taken by the Government, that we escaped unmolested.

Our Mexican fellow-passengers became more and more anxious as we approached Guadalajara, for it is in the immediate vicinity of large towns that attacks occur most frequently, and of all the queer places in the Republic, the capital of Jalisco is the worst.

The wide road that for the last ten miles leads towards the city, was torn up into numberless miniature *barrancas* by the rains; and it required all the dexterity of the driver to steer the coach safely over the winding path.

A league outside the town, we were met by two horsemen, relatives of Mr L——, who had come to welcome him back to Guadalajara; and a little further on, several carriages were drawn up containing more of his friends. I accepted the invitation to complete the journey with them, and was heartily glad to be able to quit the stuffy coach. An abundance of Winchester rifles and revolvers were secured in every corner of the carriages, and on my expressing some surprise, I was assured that robbery and murder in the city and its neighbourhood were at present as rife as ever. The steeples and towers of the town gradually dawned upon our view, and the graceful twin-spires of the cathedral stood out proudly above the rest. The number of domes and lofty buildings created an impression far beyond my preconceived ideas.

The fast horses of my friends soon trotted over the remaining couple of miles, and having passed a few tumble-down *fondas* and *rancho* buildings by the wayside, we entered the execrably paved, straight streets of the capital of Jalisco. Low, wretched houses form the outlying quarters of the town, and the people appeared miserable and poor; but when we drove into the better districts, the two-storied mansions, and fine churches, soon convinced me that I had as yet seen nothing in Mexico to compare with the city of Guadalajara.

At seven P.M. we halted before Mr L——'s house, where the greatest kindness and warmest hospitality awaited me; and the society of his relatives, and their agreeable conversation, soon made me forget the discomforts of my first day of diligence-travel in Mexico.

CHAPTER VI.

GUADALAJARA.

The state of Jalisco—Situation of its capital—Its climate—Streets and houses—Architecture—Wretched outlying quarters—The *plaza*—The cathedral—The *palacio*—The *portales—Dulces*—Native toys—Clay images—*Cajones*—Composition of the population—Cotton factories and paper-mill—The Salto factory—Brigands and *plagiarios*—A pic-nic interrupted—Brave men—Insecurity of the city—Juan Panadero—A happy editor—Voz de Jalisco, the priest's paper—A violent pamphlet—Hospital de San Miguel de Belen—A morbid taste—The department for the lunatics—The schools — The Cimenterio de Belen—*Gavetas*—The burial-place of the poor—The Hospicio de Guadalajara—A town of charities—The *cuna*—Customs encouraging immorality—The schools—Superior embroidery—Trades for youths—The church and a doll-show—Girl's school of San Diego—The *teatro*, a Roman ruin—Fine interior—A Mexican Italian-opera troupe—Bull fights, and the bull-arena—An enthusiastic audience—The *paseo*—The *alameda*—A Guadalajaran Rotten Row—Walks in the *portales*—Evening *vueltas* on the plaza—A practical arrangement — Female seclusion — Serenades without music—A simple pulley—Middle-age habits retained—Strange contrasts.

THE State of Jalisco, which comprises the greater part of the territory which, under the Spanish regime, was called the kingdom of La Nueva Galicia, is one of the largest and most renowned in the Republic. It covers an area of 50,120 square miles, and its population is estimated to number about 900,000. Guadalajara,* its capital, is next to the city of Mexico and Puebla the most important town in the country, although in point of population it is surpassed by Leon, a city which will claim a subsequent comment. It possesses about 75,000 inhabitants, and is situated in 20° 41′ 10″ north latitude, and 103° 21′ 15″ longitude west of Greenwich, at an elevation of 5200 feet above the level of the sea. This altitude in the tropics has the advantage of a climate very little short of perfection. Guadalajara forms no exception to the rule. Its inhabitants are in the enjoyment of perpetual summer, a light clear atmosphere, and a sky as bright and blue as sapphire itself.

Despite a total absence of any system of drainage, or other sanitary measures, and the habitual filthiness of the people, it is free from epidemics of all kinds, and sickness, as a rule, is easily and quickly cured.†

---

* The word is taken from the Spanish town of the same name, the birthplace of Nuño de Guzman, the conqueror of the old kingdom of Tonala, the present Jalisco.

† An exception to this rule occurred in 1833, when a terrible visitation of Asiatic cholera carried off 3200 people in the months of August and September, the population then numbering about 40,000.

The straight streets of the town are from thirty to fifty feet in width, indifferently paved, and at night very sparsely illuminated by oil-lamps.

In the central quarters the houses are solidly built either of stone, brick or *adobe*, the latter preponderating, are all plastered and white-washed, and display, some of them, tasteful frescoes on the outside. The majority are built in the peculiar fashion of the country, following no recognised style of architecture, and are provided with an archway, closed by heavy wooden doors with enormous antique locks, and large square windows secured by a grating of iron bars. A few are more artistic in their design, and follow the Moorish or Arabesque style. They are all nearly two-storied, the windows of the upper floor being mostly furnished with narrow balconies, which in their turn are often tastefully ornamented with iron railings. The roofs are flat, and provided with the peculiar horizontal waterspouts (gurgoyles, as architects would say) emptying the rain on the pavement, and upon the very heads of the passers-by. The interior arrangements are the same as elsewhere in Mexico; every house has its square inner yard, round which the building is constructed, and according to the use that is made of the house, it is either employed as a garden with trees, shrubs, and flowers, or as a store-room for cases, bales and boxes. All the rooms open into this *patio*, and where there are storeys above the ground-floor, a gallery runs all round the interior of the quadrangle.

About half-a-dozen houses in Guadalajara are three-storied ; the most conspicuous of these is the Hotel Hidalgo, the rendezvous of the diligences, and a building of rather imposing an appearance. The accommodation, however, is said to be very indifferent.

The outlying quarters of the town are composed of very inferior buildings: one-storied, low, *adobe* houses, mostly with sloping tiled roofs, dirty and cheerless in the extreme. The inhabitants are in keeping with their domiciles, and struck me as being poorer and lower than even the wretched denizens of the small villages passed on our road.

The *plaza*, as in all Mexican towns, forms, in Guadalajara, the centre of all out-door life. It is a square of about a hundred yards each way, with broad walks round the four sides, lined with orange trees, and provided with seats. In the middle

LA CATEDRAL GUADALAJARA

there is a fountain from which paved paths radiate to the sides. As in Colima, lamp-posts of the ordinary type are profusely distributed over the *plaza*, but as the manufacture of gas is still an enterprise of the future, and the oil-lamps seldom lighted, they are evidently intended for ornament more than for use; though, as it happens, unfit for either purpose.

The cathedral entirely occupies one length of the *plaza*, an extensive and imposing edifice, with two tapering steeples, and a fine dome covered with tiles of various colours, laid down in figures resembling mosaic. The effect of its beautiful proportions is marred by the tasteless application of the colours with which the outside is painted. The interior of the cathedral is noble and chaste, and the altar boasts four life-size statues of saints of rather superior execution—one at each corner. Owing to the prevailing darkness, the accompanying photograph of the interior is unfortunately wanting in detail, but will nevertheless give a better idea of the building than any necessarily meagre description can convey.*

---

* The ground-stone of this cathedral was laid in 1571, forty-one years after the conquest of this part of the country, and the edifice completed in 1618.

On the opposite side of the *plaza*, and also occupying an entire length of the square, stands the *palacio*, as an inscription over the large window in the centre indicates, the *Casa de Gobierno del Estado*, the house of the State Government. It is a tasteful, two-storied, comparatively modern structure, but nevertheless commencing to succumb to the inroads of time.

The two other sides of the *plaza* are occupied by the *portales*, as Guadalajarans call the covered way formed by pillar-supported arches over the pavement. Under the *portales* are the best shops of the city. The spaces between the massive pillars are the resort of stall-keepers, who exhibit for sale a variety of articles, the principal being *dulces* (sweetmeats), for which Guadalajara enjoys no inconsiderable reputation. Mexicans, generally, have an amiable weakness for sweet things, and *dulces* are manufactured throughout the Republic; but none, I am told, can compare with those of this city. Under the *portales*, stall after stall exhibits scores of these preparations, as also huge cakes covered with preserves and sold in slices, as well as refreshing drinks made from the juice and seeds of various fruits.

INTERIOR OF CATHEDRAL. GUADALAJARA

Dulces are such necessaries of life, and regular articles of consumption, that the different kinds have all their distinctive names. Thus the *dulce* prepared from lemons is called *limonate,* that from pine-apples *piñate,* from chirimoyas (or chirrimollas) *chirimoyate,* and so on. All the numerous kinds of tropical and semi-tropical fruits, grown either on the plateau or in the *tierra caliente,* are preserved or candied, or otherwise prepared, to add to the number of these Mexican delicacies.

Other stalls are gay with toys, the manufacture of which is purely Mexican. Some of the pieces are most singular and original, whilst others are simple imitations of imported goods, but they are all cleverly made, and cost next to nothing.

The most curious production sold under the *portales,* however, are the clay figures, manufactured by Indians near the city. In some cases they are almost worthy to rank with works of sculpture, a fact which excites the more astonishment when it is known that they are the handiwork of a people possessing no artistic training whatever, or even ordinary education. It is an indigenous craft, handed down from generation to generation, and was practised, doubtless, long before Cortez introduced Spanish blood and customs. The images represent work-people, *arrieros*, beggars, water-carriers, charcoal-vendors, soldiers and the like, in their peculiar costumes, and are finished with the utmost accuracy and fidelity to nature. I am informed that these Indians produce life-like portraits of any one who will give them a sitting, or will work by the aid of photographs or paintings.

A large number of the stalls are provided with a locker, in which the wares are kept over night. These bear the name of *cajones* (boxes), and hence the name for all "*portales*" stalls. They are owned by Indians, or half-castes of a deep dye, who reside in the *portales*, where they also ply their traffic; at night they sleep either in front of their *cajones*, or on one of the neighbouring doorsteps.

There are fewer pure Indians in Guadalajara than in the towns so far visited by me, the great bulk of the population being *mestizos*. The foreign inhabitants, though as regards wealth important, are numerically few. There are about fifty Spaniards, as many Germans, about twenty Americans, perhaps a dozen Frenchmen, and but very few English.

The Germans rank first commercially; of the entire trade of Guadalajara, about two-thirds is in their hands, though the imported goods are mostly of English manufacture.*

Four cotton-factories, and a large paper-mill, are in operation not far from the city. The latter is owned by the richest family in the State of Jalisco, and supplies a great part of the Republic with cigarette-wrappers (of which the consumption is enormous), and with various descriptions of common paper. Of the cotton-factories, the one called "Salto" is the property of my kind hosts, the five brothers L——, who were alone at the time able to work their mill profitably. The other manufactories were at work, though on a reduced scale, with the sole view of preventing their entire suspension. The articles of produce, as at Colima, are *mantas* and coarse yarns; whilst there are a large number of minor establishments where considerable quantities of *rebozos*, *sarapes*, and *fajas* are woven.

* The chief home industry of the Guadalajarans consists in tanning leather, the manufacture of *sombreros*, and in the spinning and weaving of wool and cotton.

The "Salto" factory is about three miles from the city, where a small but deep stream leaps into a lovely cascade over rocks of lava formation, and causes the motive-power through the medium of a turbine-wheel. The buildings are surrounded by fields, gardens, and orchards of some extent. In the former a small quantity of cotton is grown, which at the time of my visit was just ripening, whilst in the latter vegetables and delicious fruits loaded ground and tree; here I gathered magnificent strawberries in abundance on Christmas-day.

Many are the stories of brigands and *plagiarios* (kidnappers) in connection with this factory. Nothing short of confirmed habit and thorough acclimatisation can induce the owners of this property to remain in a country that offers but few material advantages, whilst it involves dangers and discomforts of a serious character.

About two years ago, the eldest Mr L—— was kidnapped whilst on his way from the factory to his town residence, carried off to the mountains, and there detained for more than a week, until ransomed for 4000 dollars. The miscreants were never punished, nor even tracked by the authorities.

The reader must pardon these repeated allusions to brigandage, but, as it forms one of the chief topics of conversation throughout Mexico, its constant introduction into my journal is explained.

At the time of my arrival in Guadalajara, an event that had happened some weeks previously was still in every mind and on every tongue. I refer to an accident that befel a picnic party of about twenty ladies and gentlemen belonging to the best families of Guadalajara. They had gone in carriages and on horseback to a retired spot, three miles from the town, to enjoy an afternoon in the country. No sooner had they arrived at their destination, and scarcely had they commenced arrangements for the intended meal, when they noticed the approach of twelve men, whose designs were not to be mistaken.

As usual in this country the gentlemen of the party were well armed, but apprehending an attack they relinquished all thoughts of protecting those under their charge; and with the exception of one plucky father and his son, the whole gallant company hastily mounted their horses, and decamped as fast as they could, leaving wives, children, and sisters, to the mercy of the *ladrones*, who at once proceeded to strip them of all they possessed. The ruffians, as it turned out, were without fire-arms of any sort, and were only equipped with *machetas* and sticks; no one was wounded, but the ladies had the intense mortification of returning considerably lighter both in purse and apparel than when they set out.

Although cowardice in everyday-life is the rule, and not the exception, in Mexico, yet the behaviour of these runaways was so contemptible and ridiculous, that they became the butts of satire and opprobrium throughout the city. The papers commented upon their conduct, and the affair was made the subject of a farce at one of the small theatres. In spite of all this, however, there are many good citizens who loudly approve of the act, as the only means by which bloodshed could be averted.

During my stay at Guadalajara, similar attacks on houses and individuals were of daily occurrence, and it was considered hazardous to walk through the streets after sunset. In returning home of a night we invariably walked in the middle of the road, to avoid a surprise at the corners, and never dreamed of venturing out after dark without loaded revolvers. Several times between nine and ten o'clock in the evening, the report of heavy firing was heard only a few streets off, proceeding, as we learnt next morning, from systematic attacks by large bands on the house of some individual citizen. One of these gangs was dispersed by the garrison, and some of the robbers taken prisoners, when it was found that the Chief of the Police was not only one of their band, but actually at the head of the lawless crew.

One of the numerous and singular newspapers published twice a week in Guadalajara, a tiny sheet composed of eight pages, each measuring six inches by four, called *Juan Panadero* (John the Baker), was literally crammed with nothing else but accounts of misdeeds by brigands and comments thereon. This Liliputian journal is the most popular of all Jalisco publications, and enjoys by far the most extended circulation. It serves no party, but fearlessly exposes as many crimes and defects of administration as its limited space will allow.

Happy editor! He is never in want of news, and could, without the slightest effort, fill a daily sheet as voluminous as the *Times*, instead of his dwarf-issue.

Another newspaper, of slightly larger size, and also published twice a week, is the *Voz de Jalisco*. It is owned and edited by the priests, and its contents are in accordance with their aims and opinions. The number seen by me was almost entirely absorbed by an article fiercely attacking Protestants and Protestantism, and containing the most sophistical arguments ever advanced.

There are no daily papers in Guadalajara, but from eight to ten bi-weekly and weekly chronicles, which are, however, for the most part short-lived. Almost every week witnesses the demise of one publication, and the birth of another; so that at the end of the year one or two alone have survived the vicissitudes of existence.

A pamphlet published by a well-known priest, and directed against the American missionaries, who are beginning in small numbers to work all over the Republic, was the subject of some conversation. The utterly ludicrous arguments of the writer, his clumsy flatteries when speaking of the citizens of Guadalajara, and the vehement language in which he inveighed against the missionaries, gave rise to pity rather than to indignation, and to feelings of mirth rather than of anger. He repeatedly remarks on the high degree of civilisation to which Mexico, and the Guadalajarans especially, have attained, owing to their fidelity to the Roman Catholic Church, stigmatises all that emanates from the United States as barbarous, and pronounces the English language to be fit for dogs alone.* Surely, this man cannot himself believe

* On March 1st, 1874, the Rev. Mr Stephens, an American Protestant missionary at Ahualulco, in the district of Guadalajara, was attacked by three hundred individuals armed with daggers, sticks, and stones, who amid furious cries burst open the door of his house. Mr Stephens took refuge in the yard, but was soon reached by the fanatics, who speedily murdered him, afterwards quartering and otherwise fearfully mutilating the poor man's body. The local authorities rather aided than resisted the wretches, who finally pillaged the house and destroyed everything they could not carry off. It was after the termination of the Roman Catholic service that this barbarous act was committed, and that in consequence of a vehement sermon delivered by the priest of Ahualulco against the Protestants. He concluded his address with the words : " A tree bearing bad fruit ought to be cut at the root ; my friends, interpret these words as best you understand them," and out rushed the ignorant, bestial crowd, like so many wolves, to interpret their instructor's utterings in the only way conceivable to them.

what he writes; but he evidently understands his readers; and there is unfortunately no doubt that nine-tenths of them accept his every word as truth, and unhesitatingly adopt his view.

During the week of my stay in Guadalajara, I had ample opportunity for seeing all the "lions" of the place; for there are but few.

In company with one of the first physicians of the town, I visited the two great benevolent institutions, of which the citizens are justly proud. In the midst of such numerous abuses, and among a population as corrupt as they are bigoted and superstitious, these charities shine out as bright stars in a dark and clouded sky.

We commenced by the *Hospital de San Miguel de Belen*, a series of one-storied buildings, very plainly but substantially constructed of stone and *adobe*, all in communication with one another, and standing on an extensive piece of ground. On entering, I at once came to a circular hall, the meeting point of six long chambers, which radiate from the centre in the same manner as the corridors of modern prisons. The three chambers on the left are sick wards for men, the three on the right destined for women. One ward in each division is set apart for contagious diseases, another for ailments of a non-infectious kind, and the third for patients sent in from the prisons. These latter wards are guarded by soldiers. The men's wards are open towards the central hall, whilst those of the women are shut off by large folding-doors. I inspected one of the former, and though almost each bed was occupied, the atmosphere was perfectly pure, and the utmost cleanliness prevailed. The wards are very lofty, and the ventilation and arrangements generally admirable. The women are attended by Sisters of Charity, whilst the men have male nurses.

The rooms on a corridor near the wards are set apart for medical students, of whom there are always a large number at the hospital. One of them was most pressing in his desire to show me the dissecting-room, which contained the mutilated body of a young half-caste.

This room was full of sight-seers, who apparently devoted as much or more time to this melancholy spectacle as to viewing the rest of the building. Such is the taste of the people!

The buildings of the *Hospital de Belen* proved to contain not only an hospital, as we understand the term, but also an asylum for the insane, a school for little children, and finally (and this struck me as the strangest of all), a large burial-ground, the principal cemetery in Gaudalajara. The different departments of the institution are kept entirely distinct, and are separated by tastefully planted parterres. The portion devoted to the lunatics comprises a suite of spacious rooms, and a yard surrounded by cells. The latter are intended for the raging mad, of whom there were about half-a-dozen at the time of my visit, whilst a large number of harmless individuals were moving about without restraint. A few miserable beings clad in rags, and unspeakably ugly, were squatting about the walls, or seeking a cowering concealment in corners as we approached: these were cases of hopeless idiocy; and the poor creatures were left in their tattered state, as new clothes would be reduced to the same condition almost as soon as received. There are several rooms set apart for the insane of rich families, who pay for the superior accommodation, which accounts for the absence of white patients in the public wards.

After visiting the dispensary, kitchen, and store-rooms, all managed by Sisters of Charity, we came to the school-rooms, where children from two to six years of age obtain rudimentary instruction gratuitously. Sisters also superintend this department, but although much of the work is in their hands, they have no share in the supreme direction. A committee of citizens conduct the latter.

Before leaving the hospital we examined the burial-ground, known by the name of *Cimenterio de Belen*, which covers a space of about six acres within its walls. It is entirely different from all similar places in the United States and the greater part of Europe.[*] The square ground is bounded on three sides by broad colonnades, each of about 120 yards in length. The inner sides of these arcades contain six tiers of *gavetas*—*i.e.*, niches in the wall intended to receive the coffins. These *gavetas* are two feet square, and have eight feet horizontal depth; when filled, the open square in front is closed, and receives the stone with the inscription. A hundred

[*] Similar arrangements exist in some parts of Spain and Southern Italy.

dollars is the price of the freehold of a *gaveta*, but they may be rented for twenty-five dollars for a period of five years. If, at the end of the term, however, the lease is not renewed, the coffin is removed, and the *gaveta* is at the disposal of the next applicant. To judge from the number of empty niches distributed over the walls, it would appear that five or ten years have a most soothing influence on the hearts and memories of the pious people of Guadalajara.

There are a number of graves and vaults in the open space, where interments, according to our own custom, have been made; and in the centre of the cemetery stands a well-designed, but now timeworn chapel-like edifice, underneath which lies a vault containing the remains of countless ecclesiastical dignitaries.

Very little care seems to be bestowed on the gardens of the cemetery; there are no memorial garlands on the graves, no trees planted, except several rows of orange trees, leading up to the chapel, and which, when I saw them, were heavy with the golden fruit.

Next to this part of the cemetery, and separated

from it by a substantial wall, is the burial-place of the poor. It is a dismal, desolate place. There are no *gavetas* here, nor, as far as I could see, individual graves; the moneyless dead seem to command even less respect here than the moneyless living, and have apparently to share a common tomb.

Our next visit was to the *Hospicio*. This is a grand institution, not only in regard to size and building, but chiefly as concerns its truly benevolent purposes, and the objects it so efficiently realises.

What with us is divided among a large number of charities is here united in one vast organisation; and whilst, on the one hand, its aim is to rear and educate for the battle of life those who through circumstances lack the assistance of parents and friends, it forms on the other an asylum for those who, in their old age, find themselves deprived of the means of sustenance.*

---

* According to the "*Constituciones*" of this institution, drawn up in 1802, and approved by the King of Spain by decree of September 5th, 1803, the following are entitled to admittance in the *Hospicio*:—1st. Children of both sexes "exposed" in the same (foundlings). 2nd. The aged of both sexes, who owing to advanced years are unable to work for their sustenance. 3rd. The blind, the deaf and dumb, the crippled and infirm, and incurables of all ages. 4th. Boys and girls of tender age, who are either orphans or have been deserted by their parents, and sons of fathers who, on account of poverty, are unable to keep and educate

The *Hospicio* is situate on the eastern side of the small stream which runs through the town, and divides it into two unequal parts, and is approached by a wide street lined with orange trees. Walking up this street, the façade of the building forming its termination affords an imposing view, with its pillared portico and graceful dome. Right and left from the entrance run out high, substantial walls, enclosing the entire establishment, which covers an area of upwards of eight acres.

The institution includes solidly-constructed buildings, mostly one-storied, and closely resembling those in the *Hospital de Belen*. Each block is constructed round the sides of a *patio*. There are

---

them. 5th. Daughters and young sons of married men belonging to the second and third classes, no matter whether the girls are suffering or in good, robust health. 6th. Boys and girls not exceeding ten years of age, whose fathers wish to place them in the establishment for purposes of correction, and who are willing to pay for their maintenance and clothing. As appears from the same document the following are the subjects to be taught to boys: Reading, writing, arithmetic, the principles of geometry, and drawing. To girls, reading, sewing, embroidering, washing, ironing, spinning, making stockings, ribbons, *fajas* (see page 58) and buttons; cooking, and other occupations fitted to their sex. Youths are to be instructed in the combing and spinning of cotton and wool, in the manufacture of stockings and other hosiery, caps, gloves, ribbons, *fajas*, and buttons, and other work suited to their age and respective circumstances; and to all generally is to be given instruction in the articles of the faith.

STREET IN GUADALAJARA LEADING TO THE HOSPICIO

no less than twenty-four such blocks, and consequently as many interior squares, with bananas, orange, lemon and coffee trees. The different departments are all mutually connected, and over the entrance to each its name is inscribed in large letters. The entire establishment is under the management of Sisters of Charity, assisted by some members of the priesthood. As far as outward appearances can testify, their duties are performed to perfection.

One of the Sisters conducted us over the whole institution, to see which employed an entire afternoon.

That which at home would be termed the "Foundling Hospital" is one of the most interesting. It is a large and lofty hall lined with cradles, in which poor innocents are commencing an existence—doomed perhaps to be the less smooth and happy from the peculiar circumstances of their birth. Here we saw white infants nursed by dark Indian women with a cheerfulness and loving care quite pleasant to behold, equalling, if not surpassing, the attention that the little unfortunates could have received from their white mothers.

Noticing that some of the cradles were much superior to others, and furnished in a rich and luxurious manner, I inquired the cause, and was informed of a curious fact in connection with this department.

The great majority of infants deposited at the Hospicio are born of mothers belonging to the better classes; and a few days after the reception of a foundling, money, clothing, and other necessaries are not unfrequently sent to be devoted to the child. In most cases the names of one or even of both the parents are disclosed, and regular payment is made until the child leaves the home. This can hardly be considered real charity, and the continuance of the practice will doubtless operate against the interests of morality.

What we should term an Orphan Asylum is represented in the Hospicio by a number of large, airy saloons, used partly as dormitories, partly as schoolrooms. Up to the age of three the children remain in the "*Cuna*" (the department above mentioned, the word signifying cradle), when they are promoted to their first school. We found the schoolroom alive with little learners, who politely rose as we entered, and treated us to a half-song, half-chant, amid regularly performed motions of hands and arms. In this school they remain till the age of six, when the sexes are separated, and what has hitherto been classed under the collective term of *infantes*, is now divided into schools for *niños* and schools for *niñas*, which are two departments complete and distinct in themselves. After the age of twelve the boys enter another section directed by masters (mostly priests), instead of the Sisters of Charity, who up to that point are entrusted with the entire government, whilst the girls enter a superior class, still under the guidance of Sisters. In these grades both boys and girls receive instruction in music, which, favoured by the natural talent of Mexicans for this art, attains a degree of great excellence; in drawing, painting, and in the study of foreign languages. We visited a number of rooms belonging both to *niños* and *niñas*, the walls of which were hung with capital specimens of drawings, paintings, and geographical maps.

Progressing further, we found the girls who had outgrown the schools, employed in sewing, knitting, and embroidering, or assisting in the culinary department, according to their different tastes and abilities. The embroidery worked in the Hospicio is celebrated throughout Mexico, and I for one was much struck with its delicacy. The brightest silks are by this accomplishment developed into landscapes and portraits, and I invested in a Mexican eagle of many hues wrought on both sides, and a marvel of the art.*

The boys after leaving school are received into workshops of various descriptions. I saw them apprenticed as bakers, tailors, bootmakers, carpenters, locksmiths, printers, weavers, and other trades. Almost every requisite for the Hospicio is made by the adults of both sexes in the establishment itself.

The young men, at the age of about twenty-one, generally quit the institution, and easily find employment in their various trades and professions, as pupils of the Hospicio are engaged in preference to any other applicants. The girls are

* See frontispiece.

sought after as governesses and superior servants, or remain in their early home until their marriage.

It must not be inferred from this, that the institution occupies itself with foundlings and orphans alone. On the contrary, the great bulk of its inmates is composed of children recruited from all classes of society, who for the greater part reside with their parents, and frequent the Hospicio daily for tuition. The poor are provided with clothes besides gratuitous instruction, whilst those who have the means pay for all they receive. There is also a High School in the establishment, where the rising generation may profit by the erudition and talent of the city.

We next proceeded to the quarters of the aged men and women—the infirmary, the dispensary, the kitchen, store-rooms and other departments; and, before leaving, visited the church within the precincts of the institution. It is an elegant building, with fine dome, shapely pillars, and walls profusely ornamented with paintings. This being Christmas-time, an extraordinary doll-show was, as it were, the reredos of the altar, representing the birth of Christ in the manger, with cows, and asses, and the seven wise men.

So far it resembled similar arrangements in Italian and Spanish churches at this period of the year, but the shepherds and shepherdesses who surrounded the chief figures were unmistakably of Tyrolese nationality—the men with breeches and alpenstock, and the women with short petticoats and pointed hats. Some German trader had no doubt received a cheap cargo of these Alpine figures, and the ignorance of the purchasers added to the already puerile performance another ludicrous feature.

The *Hospicio* contains upwards of a thousand inmates, including the Sisters of Charity, masters and attendants. Of this number seven hundred are children, and about two hundred aged men and women. The establishment possesses a certain income of its own, but the city of Guadalajara has to contribute yearly to its funds.

On another day we visited the girls' school of San Diego, which, as far as I could see, appeared to be excellently conducted. Until about seven years ago the building which it occupies was a convent; it is a substantial two-storied edifice, enclosing a fine square. The school is entirely under lay management, and rejoices in perfect immunity from the priests. The system of tuition is based on the same plan as that of the upper forms in the Hospicio, and the arrangements generally appear very similar to those of the latter, but I found the girls brighter and more cheerful, and one seemed to breathe a freer atmosphere. The embroidery worked at San Diego equals, if it does not surpass, that at the Hospicio.

I had no opportunity of visiting more schools, but was told that a fair number of them for both sexes have been established during the last few years; that they are well conducted, and receive due attention from the authorities.

Guadalajara possesses two places of public entertainment: the theatre and the bull-arena. The former, when first indicated to me, appeared like an old Roman ruin, and I could hardly believe that this pile of apparently antique walls, columns, and loose, straggling stones, could show a capacious, symmetrical, and tolerably decorated playhouse as its interior. But such is the case. Here is another instance of that neglect so ordinary in Mexico: an imposing structure, well planned, commenced in grand style, but after a time left unfinished to crumble to ruin. The building covers a large area, and if perfected would doubtless have been magnificent; at present there seems to be no hope of its final completion.

The inside is almost as large as that of Covent Garden Theatre, and is six storeys high. Five of the tiers are devoted to boxes, and the sixth forms the gallery. On account of the climate, the furniture in the theatres is not encumbered with superfluous and stuffy draperies, as with us, which at first sight lends them a cold and almost comfortless aspect; but the briefest experience will attest the advantages derived from the use of the most simple accessories. Thus the box-tiers are built exclusively of white-washed masonry, thin iron railings about two feet high serving as partitions, the breastwork in front being of the same fabric but a foot higher. There is no division on the ground-floor for pit and stalls, but the space is filled with rough chairs, and all seats rank alike. The house is lighted by oil-lamps fixed in all its parts; they are, however, wholly insufficient for the brilliance so essential to theatrical effect.

"Il Barbiere" was the opera I heard in this house, performed in Italian. Besides the *impressario*,

however, who was also the baritone, there was not one other Italian amongst the company. The rest came from South and Central America, and "Rosina" was impersonated by a Mexican, and a native, I believe, of Guadalajara. Opera performances take place twice a week, and are well attended; the large house was almost full when I was there, though it can accommodate over three thousand people. The singing was fair, and the whole entertainment much better than I was led to anticipate.

Bull-fights are prohibited in most states of the Mexican Republic, but in Jalisco they continue to flourish. Whatever may justly be urged against the cruelty of the practice, and its demoralising effects on the population, it is, certainly, when considered from a physiological point of view, one of the most extraordinary sights imaginable.

A performance had been announced for Christmas-day, but as, contrary to all old-established rules of the dry season, it then poured with rain, it had to be deferred, and I witnessed one of the regular Sunday-afternoon entertainments.

The bull-arena is close by the *Hospicio*, and the entrance to it is in the same broad street that fronts the latter. It is a solid stone building, similar in shape and arrangement to the ancient Roman amphitheatres, and much resembling the Spanish arenas of the present day. It consists of a circus about 150 feet in diameter, open towards the sky, and enclosed by seven tiers of sittings, of which the uppermost alone is roofed over. The latter is broader than the rest, and provided on the shady side of the ring with chairs, for the accommodation of those who wish to pay for that luxury. The great majority of the audience, however, are seated on small cushions placed on the stone benches, whilst the common people crowd into the sunny portion of the arena, where seats or standing-room cost a mere trifle. The flat narrow roof of the top tier is generally occupied by a detachment of soldiers, under the command of an officer, to act in case of disturbance.

In the morning the performers paraded the town on foot and on horseback, attired in gaudy costumes, and accompanied by drummers and trumpeters, who succeeded between them in evoking a hideous din. At two o'clock in the afternoon, the band took its post in the street, outside the *Plazo de Progreso* (as the place in which the

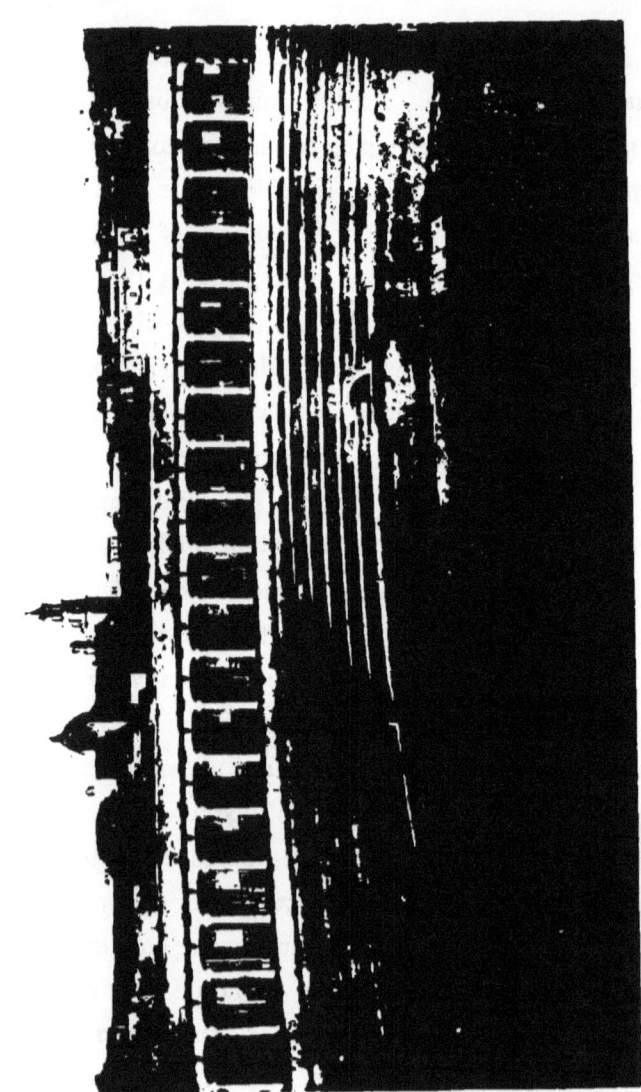

BULL-ARENA. GUADALAJARA.

arena stands is appropriately called), and played their choicest pieces, until, at four o'clock, the commencement of the fight was announced. The musicians then proceeded to their allotted space within the circle, and throughout the performance prolonged their inspiriting strains.

Bull-fights have been described a thousand times, and the feats of *matadores, banderilleros,* and *picadores,* are almost as familiar to the general reader as the *tours de force* of acrobats on the tight-rope or the trapeze. It is, therefore, unnecessary to repeat the details of a performance, the main features of which are the same in all latitudes; but I cannot refrain from a record of the enthusiasm and vigour with which the entertainment was watched by the applauding audience, who followed every movement of man and beast with an extraordinary eagerness.

This savage Spanish custom could have cast its seed into no more fertile soil than that of Mexico; and it has so acclimatised itself, that the pure-blooded Indian now enters into the practice with the same keen interest as the true descendant of old Spain, or the half-bred *mestizo*. *Corridas de Toros* (bull-races, as they are politely termed) have attended the Spaniards in all their wanderings, and have become the chief national sport of their colonies, whatever may have been the aboriginal element. But it is doubtful whether there is any place where the custom is more ardently sustained and the popular spirit more thoroughly enlisted in its favour than in Guadalajara.

Bull-fighting appears especially suited to the Mexican character: there is enough of bloodshed to gratify their cruel tendencies; enough of seeming danger to stimulate a morbid craving for excitement, and an abundance of opportunity for the disgusting display of swagger and mock-heroism. The risk incurred by the combatants is in reality exceedingly small, and the whole performance an exhibition of execrable cowardice.

The "play-bill," printed on red paper, announced in conspicuous type that *cuatro arrogantes toros* would be "fought to death," but the poor brutes looked anything but arrogant when they entered the ring, with an iron spike driven into their loins to goad them to fury. The young and ill-fed bulls were startled rather than infuriated by the unwonted appearance of the audience, and it required the combined efforts of music, shouts, red cloths, and various instruments of torture, to nerve them to self-defence. The wretched animals, however, are hopelessly confronted by swarms of men, armed not only with deadly weapons, but with a variety of appliances calculated to divert the animal's attention, when in the act of charging any individual opponent. The latter have likewise the advantage of sheltering screens, if too closely pressed, whilst his horns, the only weapon of the bull, have been previously shortened by several inches, in order to reduce the danger of his adversaries to a minimum. They are thus teased, worried, and tortured, and when at length their various discomforts have sufficiently gratified the spectators, a sword-thrust in the region of the heart brings them to the ground, and a stab between the head and the spine ends their agonies.

The spectators side with the bull, and cheer him wildly if he shows pluck and succeeds in unseating a rider, or upsetting or wounding one of the horses. The latter, as a rule, are the only victims on the side of the attacking party. If a horse should fall, and the assailants think discretion the better part of valour, the bull will sometimes pierce the body with his horns, and nothing excites the enthusiasm of the audience in a greater degree, than to see a horse removed from the arena, with his protruding entrails draggling on the ground.

A timid bull is vociferously hissed, and the frantic occupants of the lower tiers endeavour to rouse him, by throwing at him whatever missile is within their grasp from the cushions on which they sit to their own *sombreros* and *sarapes*. If this also prove unsuccessful, shouts of "*fuera*" are raised until the bull is lazoed, dragged from the ring, and another of more mettle substituted.

The audiences of bull-fights are composed of all the various elements of the population. Neither rank, race, sex, or age, interferes with its attractions; and whites, *mestizos* and *Indios*, men, women, and children, are all numerously represented.

The women take the same interest in the spectacle as the men, and if they are less demonstrative than the latter, their fiery eyes and flushed cheeks betray an eagerness and passion equally keen.

FOUNTAIN IN THE ALAMEDA, GUADALAJARA

WALK IN THE ALAMEDA, GUADALAJARA

In the evenings of Sundays and feast-days, the beauty and fashion of Guadalajara assemble in the *paseo*. This is a wide road lined on both sides by fine old trees, whose overhanging branches meet half-way. It runs nearly parallel with the small river, and along almost the entire length of the western part of the city—a distance of about a mile and a quarter. At its northern termination is situated the *alameda* or public garden, prettily arranged and covering about five acres, surrounded by a high wall with quaint old iron gates, and a wide ditch on the outside. It is laid out in broad walks, centred on a circular space, where a fountain trickles into a marble basin. Trees, shrubs, and flowers are worthy of the city and its climate.

The *paseo* is the Rotten Row of Guadalajara. The ladies appear in carriages, tricked out in their best, whilst the men in all the glory of the *charro* prance about on their small horses with their huge saddles. The carriages that congregate here form the oddest mixture of vehicles; they are of all denominations, sizes, and patterns; some profusely painted and embellished, others plain; some imported from the

United States, others from France and England, but nearly all shakey and shabby.

Their inmates are either arrayed in plain and becoming black, or in less sober colours, their bare heads veiled with the *mantilla*, and may be seen exchanging smiles and greetings with the *cavalleros*, who are in the habit of forming line at the corner of the *paseo* and the *alameda* (on the left hand side in the accompanying photograph), allowing the carriages to pass before them—*tout comme chez nous* in Hyde Park.

During the day, when the sun is too powerful to allow of walks being taken in the open, the *portales* are the fashionable promenade. There young ladies accompanied by their mothers, or attended by an old servant, indulge in the interesting occupation of shopping, or strolling up and down the shady walk; young men, who contrive to absent themselves from their occupations, will be waiting to catch a glimpse of a charming *señorita;* officers of the Jalisco guard, or the gensdarmes, may be admired as they strut jauntily in their high top-boots and clattering spurs, whilst knots of beggars line the doorsteps, and the

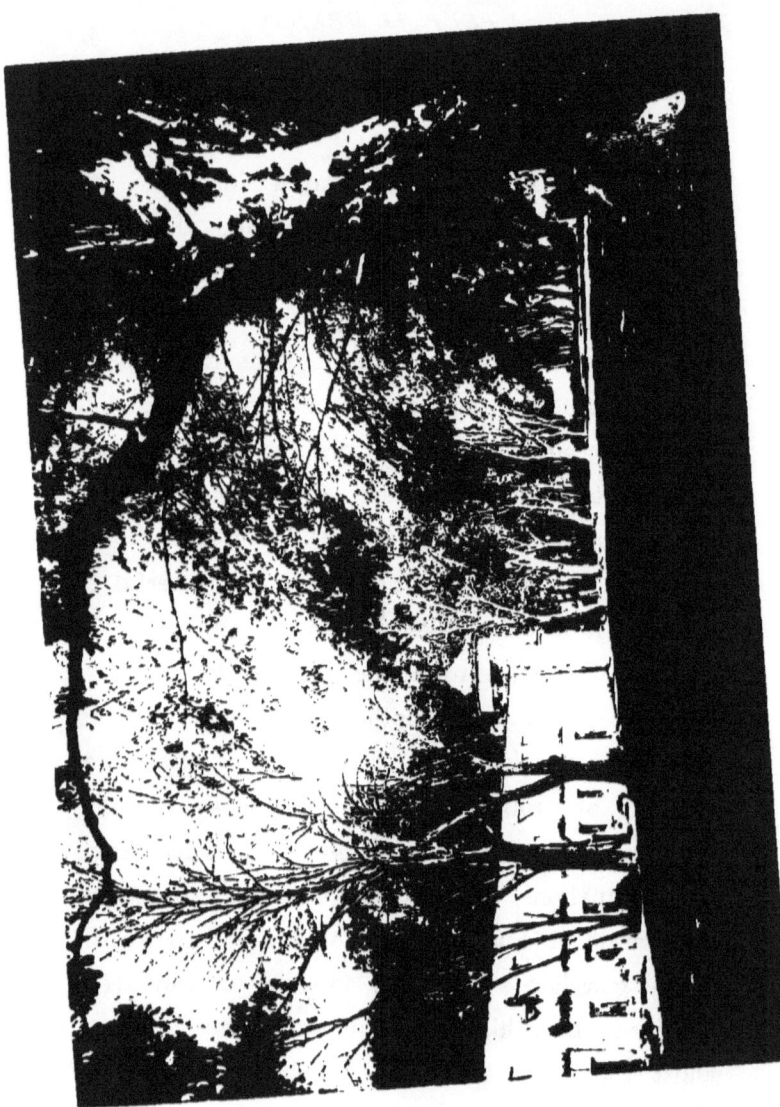

stall-owners and their friends assist in effectually crowding the thoroughfare.

After dinner in the evenings, the *plaza* is the favourite place of assemblage. Every other day military bands perform there between the hours of seven and nine, and all the town turn out to enjoy the music and to perambulate the square. This is managed in a most regular and systematic manner, which, under similar circumstances, might elsewhere be imitated with advantage. The ladies keep strictly to one side of the avenue, and the gentlemen to the other, whilst they move round in opposite directions, thus continually confronting one another. This tacit arrangement is, I am told, never violated, and forms the main attraction of the *vuelta* after dinner.

It is only on these and similar occasions that the youth of Guadalajara have an opportunity of meeting. Social intercourse of the better classes, is placed on a perfectly different footing from our own; and if French, Italian, and Spanish seclusion with regard to young girls is a matter of surprise to us, the customs observed in Mexico are still more so. Unless their respective families are very intimate, no young man is admitted into the houses of people who have grown-up daughters, and such a phenomenon as wooing and winning, as we understand it, is perfectly unheard of. Dinner-parties and balls are almost unknown among thorough Mexicans, and even in the capital, more European in many of its customs than the rest of the Republic, where a large number of foreign residents may be said to be acting as educators, social gatherings of any kind are quite exceptional.

Such being the case, young people look upon the *portales*, the *plaza*, the theatre, the bull-ring, and the *paseo* as the only places of legitimate meeting; and if, by the eloquent language of the eyes, and the subsequent instrumentality of mutual friends, a couple have decided to unite for life, the lovers' path is still strewn with thorns, and their meeting most jealously prohibited. Even if the parents approve of their children's wishes the suitor is not admitted to his *fiancée's* house; and until the wedding-day their companionship is restricted to midnight conversations whispered from the balcony of the lady's room into the street below. Such scenes

VIEW TAKEN FROM AN AZOTEA, GUADALAJARA

were by no means scarce in Guadalajara, and every night I saw many a fair maiden draped with the *mantilla*, softly signalling to her lover beneath, who, with *poncho* thrown over his shoulder, reminded me not a little of operatic serenades, the absence of the guitar forming the only difference. If the old adage —"necessity is the mother of invention"—required any additional illustration to establish its truth, it might be found in the handy appliance, invented by the fair sex for the purpose of exchanging correspondence, and consisting in nothing more romantic than a pulley of string reaching from the balcony to the ground. These, to us, ridiculous practices, are here the acknowledged form of courtship, and although reserved for the quiet of night, and apparently cultivated in a clandestine manner, are well known to and approved of by the parents.

All provincial towns of Mexico, and especially those of the State of Jalisco, reproduce in a hundred ways all the life, manners, and customs of the fifteenth and sixteenth centuries; and whilst in the Old World they now exist in books and tradition only, a walk through the streets of a Mexican town, or a peep into its houses, or a visit to its churches, supply an unquestionable proof that in this part of the New World they still endure and flourish.

Coming from the United States, as I did, the thorough contrast between the two portions of the North American Continent afforded matter for perpetual comment. In the States, activity, energy and enterprise, on every side; in Mexico, lassitude, indifference and stagnation: there, customs and society on a level with the highest European civilisation; here, habits and usages, handed down unchanged from the barbarism of the Middle Ages: there, prosperous towns rapidly increasing in size and population; here, cities and edifices almost untouched since the first Spanish colonists built them, now dilapidated and crumbling to ruin: there, new inventions, modern machinery and railways; here, the clumsy remnants of mediæval appliances—no steam engine,* no locomotive, but roads whose fiendish unevenness can be only appreciated by those who have experienced them: there, a hardy race constantly recruited from the best material of the Old World, to whose power and energy the aborigines have

* There is not a single steam-engine of any kind in the entire State of Jalisco.

been forced to succumb; here, the degenerate descendants of a people, originally too weak to avoid admixture with the indigenous tribes, and now but an isolated half-caste breed, endowed with all the conceit, but none of the chivalry of the conquerors, nor any of the virtues of the natives; there, the enlightened ideas of reformed religion, tolerance, philosophy and education; here, the dark, superstitious, idolatrous creed, which a corrupt and crafty priesthood has for generations ingrafted on the hearts of a feeble and yielding people—in a word, the fanatical intolerance and ignorance, fostered and encouraged by all the arts and perseverance of Roman Catholicism.

CHAPTER VII.

FROM GUADALAJARA TO GUANAJUATO.

Departure from Guadalajara—San Pedro—A poor district—Beggars—The valley of the Lerma—Lago de Chapala—Puente de Tololotlan—Zapotlanejo—A joke—Puente de Calderon—Tepatitlan—Sterile country—La Venta de Pegueros—A forced halt—San Juan de los Lagos—Its saint and its fair—*Organo* fences—Lagos—A clean *diputado*—*Arboles del Peru* or Peruvian Pepper trees—Enter the State of Guanajuato—Leon—Silao—Rugged country—Marfil—Arrival at Guanajuato.

AT five o'clock in the morning of the last day of the year 1873, I quitted Guadalajara on my way eastward across the Republic.

A vehicle similar to that which had brought me here was now about to take me further; and both *cochero* and cattle were, to judge from externals, the twins of their predecessors. The passengers' luggage, according to regulations, had been weighed on the previous evening, and, as far as I was concerned, tremendously charged for, so that no time was wasted in setting off at the hour appointed.

My ticket had been taken as if for one

Señor Mendoza, since it was feared that the name of a foreigner might stimulate the ever-watchful *plagiarios* to a stroke of business in the way of kidnapping, and I rejoiced in that distinguished cognomen until my diligence troubles had ended.

There were seven passengers inside the coach besides myself; consequently only a single vacant seat remained, for which, as it happened to be between an Austrian gentleman and myself, we agreed to pay, so as mutually to enjoy a little more space.

Away we rattled through the dark streets of Guadalajara, and over the indescribable pavement, the *cochero* cracking his whip, and encouraging his eight mules with shouts and exclamations.

Among the passengers there were four sons of one of the richest men not only of Jalisco but of all Mexico, and in order to protect them the coach was accompanied by an escort of ten cavalry soldiers, wrapped in their ragged *sarapes*. They were, however, so forlorn in their appearance that I reposed more confidence in our own arms, should occasion call for defence, than in the doubtful services which these men seemed capable of rendering.

After leaving the city, the gardens and *haci-*

endas of the suburbs, we traversed a flat country, here and there varied by slight undulations, and bordered on all sides by distant hills and mountains. Cacti, dwarf trees, and stubbly grass appeared to form the only vegetation. Five miles out of Guadalajara we reached the miserable town of San Pedro, composed mostly of rough *adobe* houses with thatched roofs, and during the ten miles following we passed through several wretched villages inhabited principally by Indians. There appeared to be little cultivation in this district, but herds of cattle were frequent. It is difficult to imagine on what the people of this locality rely for their subsistence; the country seems so poor that it is a matter of surprise that the inhabitants do not remove to some more favoured spot. Yet in spite of all this apparent poverty a really downcast face is rarely discovered: the people are not used to luxuries, and *frijoles* and *tortillas* are everywhere amazingly cheap!

Whenever the coach halted in a town or village the passengers were regularly besieged by an army of beggars, chiefly old women, and a crowd of cripples defying imagination. A more hideous and utterly disgusting sight is incredible, and each fresh parade of their infirmities, each grip of the listener's coat, excited a corresponding shudder. It is, I am told, inclination rather than necessity that prompts these unfortunate wretches thus to beleaguer diligence travellers.

For the next fifteen miles the country was unaltered in its features, and after crossing a small stream we entered upon a strip of rich land. Here the soil seemed favourable, partly stocked with crops of maize and other cereals, partly prepared for the reception of new seed. Fine tall trees of various growths, and an occasional plot of rich pasturage, gave the locality a most pleasing appearance, and contrasted agreeably with the tame scenery through which we had just travelled. Brakes and bushes densely overarched the road, with outstretched branches; and whenever the *cochero*, to avoid some obstacle, steered near its edge, the coach would brush by them, causing a rattle as of volley-firing, and rendering a look-out a most hazardous proceeding.

This change in the nature of the land was due

to the vicinity of a large river, known in Guadalajara as the *Rio Grande*, which we were now fast approaching. This river, one of the largest, and perhaps the most important in Mexico, rises from the Lago de Lerma, a small lake about twenty-five miles south-west of the city of Mexico, and flows for 600 miles in a north-westerly direction towards the Pacific, which it reaches about twenty miles north of San Blas.

After the first 325 miles of its course, the river falls into the *Lago de Chapala*, a large sheet of water covering about 520 square miles, and situate thirty-three miles south-south-east from Guadalajara. The river, which from its source to its influx into the lake is called *Rio de Lerma*, enters it at its north-eastern side, and emerges from it barely fifteen miles to the northward. The lake would thus appear to form a huge backwater of the river, and acts as a never-failing reservoir, supplying the stream with an abundance of water during all seasons. From the Lago de Chapala to the sea, a distance of 270 miles, the river is known by the name of Rio de Santiago, with the exception of the district of Guadalajara, where it is simply called *Rio Grande.**

The valley of this stream, along the greater part of its course, is composed of bottom lands of the greatest fertility, and adapted for crops of the most varied description. At times the valley is thirty miles wide; at others, where the river winds its course through hills and mountains, and *barrancas*, it is necessarily narrow, but on an average it possesses a width of about fifteen miles, which, added to a length of about 600, forms a very considerable and the most productive area in the *tierra templada*. The wheat and barley† grown here are of very superior quality, and said to be the best in the Republic.

The land in this splendid valley, although divided into *ranchos*, and in the most favourable spots, graced with a fair number of hacienda-buildings, is comparatively little cultivated. If, however, means of transport were at hand to convey the surplus grain either west to the Pacific, or east to the

---

* The native name of the river is *Esquitlan*.

† Barley is not only grown in Mexico for purposes of brewing, but chiefly for fodder for horses and mules, being much preferred to oats, which latter are scarcely, if ever, cultivated.

Gulf, it could be made to yield perhaps ten times as much as it does at present, and would be able to compete with similar produce from Chili, California, and other parts of the United States.

About an hour after we entered the valley we reached the river, a fine stream with a slow current, and at this spot about 150 yards wide. It is spanned by an old but very substantial bridge, the work of the Spaniards more than a century and a half ago, and called *Puente Nacional de Tololotlan* after the name of the small town at its eastern end.* This bridge heralds a series of narrow valleys and *barrancas* through which the river flows after leaving this point for a distance of about 120 miles. Some of these *barrancas* are described as most beautiful and picturesque, but I was, unfortunately, unable to visit them, as well as the celebrated waterfall of *Juanacatlan* in the vicinity of the village

---

* The *Puente de Tololotlan* was commenced in 1700, and finished in 1717. It is, including the approaches, about two hundred yards long, twenty-six feet wide, and supported by twenty-seven pillars forming twenty-six arches. The bridge possesses a few statues, inscriptions and other ornamentations, now all in a state of utter dilapidation, and on the Tololotlan side it is provided with a gate, which formerly closed the passage at night.

bearing the same name, and ten miles above the Bridge of Tololotlan.

The *Rio Grande*, at that point 180 yards wide, thunders over a precipice sixty-five feet deep, in a most magnificent waterfall.

A short drive from the river brought us to a *hacienda*, where we breakfasted, and after another four miles we arrived at Zapotlanejo, a tumble-down place of about 6000 inhabitants. The same elements that compose all smaller Mexican towns—low *adobe* houses in straight, narrow streets, diabolical pavements, and a large, costly cathedral worth a dozen times the value of all its surroundings, were likewise to be found here. Zapotlanejo is situated on the edge of the valley of the *Rio Grande*, on a small tributary of the latter, and the country in its immediate neighbourhood appeared arable and fertile.

From here the road slightly ascended, and we soon found ourselves again in the vast undulating land of the Mexican plateau, much less rich than the valley we had now left behind, and at times even arid.

About three-quarters of an hour after turning our backs on Zapotlanejo, the diligence suddenly stopped, and looking out we could perceive two men on horseback speaking to the *cochero*, and presently approaching the door of the coach. Finding three revolvers pointed at them, however, they immediately became very civil, and smilingly informing us that they simply intended to perpetrate a joke, hurriedly wheeled round, and galloped away at full speed. If it had not been for our pistols we should probably have been relieved of some luggage.

Another hour brought us to a narrow ravine with a small stream running at its base, spanned by a strong stone bridge called *Puente de Calderon*,[*] after which the road wound over the same monotonous country for twenty miles, when we arrived at Tepatitlan, a town of about 8000 inhabitants, and in appearance the exact counterpart of its other and similarly sized brethren.

A clown clad in red and yellow, with painted face, and large artificial nose, was parading the streets on horseback, accompanied by a trumpeter and followed by a crowd of children. Stopping

---

[*] This bridge, constructed in 1807, is celebrated in the annals of the great revolution, by the battle fought there on January 17th, 1811, between the Spanish General Calleja and the Mexican patriot Hidalgo.

at every corner, he proceeded to proclaim in a loud tone the unparalleled fighting qualities of two bulls, which were to be "Done to the death" on the morrow. He finished his harangue with a little joke, immensely appreciated by his youthful audience, who could not contain themselves for laughter.

The clown was just commencing a repetition of his story in front of the *fonda*, where the coach had halted to change mules, when the *vamanos* of the driver invited us to proceed. Off we went in jumps and jerks, over the murderous stones of the Tepatitlan streets, and ascending a low hill continued our journey over a road which, as usual, was merely a perforated bog, with its intermediate spaces strewn with rocks. How it came to pass that we did not upset has remained a mystery to this day, for the coach was swaying to and fro like a small boat in a cross sea.

The twenty-one miles from Tepatitlan to *La Venta de Pegueros* led over a tract of country more stern and barren than any part of Mexico I had as yet seen. It forms a vast plain, hemmed in the far distance by mountains just peering over the horizon, now hilly, and now rising up abruptly to an inconsiderable height. The soil is composed of a yellowish-brown sand, at times thickly strewn with boulders and stones, and seemingly fit for no other produce but a few crippled cacti. Luckily some rain that had fallen a few days previously had hardened the ground, otherwise the dust we should have had to encounter, and of which we had some sad experience subsequently, would have been terrific.

At last, after thirteen hours' continuous shaking, I was truly thankful to see the coach stop before the large *hacienda*-house at La Venta. We had started at 5 A.M., and arrived at 8.30 P.M., having travelled a distance of seventy-three miles.

The house at which the *diligencias* stop, where the stage company have their office, and a few rooms are set apart for the accommodation of travellers, is the chief building of the *hacienda*, La Venta de Pegueros being really nothing but the village formed by the houses belonging to this extensive estate, and the huts of its workpeople. Besides this large quadrangular building with the usual *patio* inside, the place is hardly anything but a collection of low *adobe* houses.

New-Year's day, 1874, found me up at half-past

two A.M., and an hour later inside the diligence, and under weigh.

In lieu of a passenger who remained at La Venta, a very fat half-caste lady was seated in the coach, who was engaged from morning till night in incessantly smoking cigarettes. This habit, so universal amongst the weaker sex of all stations in Mexico, was developed to perfection in the specimen which faced me, to my lasting advantage, throughout the day.

We had barely quitted La Venta, when the coach stuck in a mud-pool, and all the passengers, but the corpulent *señora*, had to descend to lighten the vehicle. In the many violent attempts to extricate the diligence, some of the harness, at all times in a deplorable state of rottenness, was broken, causing altogether a delay of over an hour, during which time we had to wait in this veritable slough of despond, unable to stir to the right or the left.

Our route, at first over a gentle incline, conducted us for about twelve miles across a flat country of a more fertile nature than that traversed the previous day, till at a small town called *Jalostotitlan* we crossed a tributary of the *Rio Verde*, a river which rises in the State of Zacatacas and flows south into Lake Chapala. From here, for the next two or three miles, we toiled up hill after hill, over loose rocks and *pedregales* of awful formation, until we arrived at a plateau about 7500 feet above the level of the sea, and fully 1000 feet higher than the surrounding country. After eight miles of comparatively plain sailing the road suddenly commenced to descend, and looking ahead I found the country composed of glens and small *barrancas*, all parallel to one another, and at right angles to our route. Each range of hills, forming these gulleys, was lower than the preceding one: their sides were hidden by trees and shrubs, growing denser and taller as the altitude diminished; and the rivulets in the valleys gleamed like silvery serpents as the bright sun shone on their spiral course. We now wound in and out through this labyrinth of obstacles, down steep inclines, up hills and across streamlets, until we reached a tolerably well-paved zig-zag road, that led down the last and steepest hills. One by one the lofty towers and steeples of *San Juan de los Lagos* came in view: the lower we came, the more their number increased, and at length passing over two solid stone bridges that span the two arms of the *Rio de Lagos* (a tributary of the *Rio Verde*), at 11 o'clock we entered the town.

San Juan numbers about 8000 inhabitants, and is rather a cheerful little place. Its houses (the usual low, whitewashed ones) are here and there tattoed with a few wavering lines of red and green, and its small *plaza* is remarkably well kept, and deliciously inviting. An enormous cathedral, with a magnificent façade, and a long flight of broad stairs as its approach, as well as twin-towers of exquisite taste and considerable height, stands proudly out from the other buildings like a man-of-war in the midst of a crowd of row-boats. The interior is majestic and imposing, and, as far as architecture is concerned, a masterpiece of the art; but when the spectator reflects that thousands and thousands must have been wrung from the wretched population to construct this edifice, that the people have had to undergo privations, to toil and to suffer, before this priestly stronghold could be called into existence, the philanthropist would, I presume, rather behold superior dwellings, greater comfort, and less ignorance amongst the laity, than all this clerical splendour. It was on New-Year's day that I visited this church; its steps and interior were thronged with worshippers, mostly Indians, who with a burning candle in hand would drop on their knees at the door, and thus crawl up to the image or picture of the saint for whom the taper was destined, depositing, each of them, their ill-spared mite in the ever-present offertory.

San Juan de los Lagos is celebrated for the fair which is held there annually at the commencement of December, and which is the most frequented institution of the kind in all Mexico. This fair owes its origin to a most sacred shrine, containing an image of the Virgin known by the name of *Nuestra Señora de San Juan de los Lagos.* As early as 1623 this shrine attracted a multitude of pilgrims, chiefly in the first days of December, the eighth of that month being the feast-day of the Virgin. The pilgrims naturally brought a large number of traders to San Juan, and to legalise the annual congregation of so large a body of merchants, King Charles the Fourth of Spain, in 1797, granted a concession for a yearly fair, which was afterwards confirmed by the Government of the State of Jalisco.

After two hours' halt we proceeded on our journey, and, ascending anew, in a few miles arrived on a plateau about 7000 feet above sea-level, and thus 1000 feet above the altitude of San Juan. For the next twenty miles we travelled over this table-land, mostly undulating, and sprinkled all the way with a large number of *haciendas*, and villages of various sizes. The country appears the reverse of sterile, but is only partially utilised; maize, wheat, barley, and beans are the principal products.

In all the villages I noticed neatly and peculiarly constructed fences of the *organo* cactus. Instead of the stone or wooden fences, hitherto prevalent, the long straight arms of the *organos* are here lopped off from their parent, and driven into the ground so close to one another as to leave no perceptible space between them. These pieces quickly take root and grow to a height of more than twenty feet, and as they are from two to six inches in diameter, it may be imagined that they form a strong and suitable protection. Near the villages and *haciendas*, and sometimes along the roads, various trees were worthy of remark, amongst which *mezquites* and tamarinds predominated.

As we approached *Lagos,* numerous species of cacti became abundant, especially *nopales,* which extended over acre upon acre, and seemed almost to have been purposely planted.

The situation of Lagos is much like that of San Juan, in a deep valley traversed by the Rio de Lagos, and at least 800 feet below the plateau which we had just traversed. The town was perfectly concealed from the view until the circuitous descent was commenced, when it gradually emerged.

It was five o'clock when we entered the town and halted before the *fonda,* distinguished for the usual execrable accommodation, where I had to share a small room without a window with two other passengers. One of these was a *Diputado* (Member of Congress), a man of superior intelligence, and to whom I am indebted for much valuable information. My gratitude, however, did not prejudice me so much in his favour, as to prevent me from noticing the alarming fact, that not once since our departure from Guadalajara until we started from Lagos, a space of two days and two nights, did this amiable legislator think it necessary to apply soap and water, either to hands or face, and that he cherished an additional predilection for sleeping clothed in all his habiliments, excepting only his boots.

Lagos is a gay and pleasing town, with a pattern *plaza*, a shady *paseo* along the *Rio*, and a charming *alameda* with fine orange and lemon trees, and numberless white rose bushes, which were all in full blossom when I walked through. The town has an elevation of 6300 feet above sea-level, and over 15,000 inhabitants, mostly engaged in agriculture.

There is a very extensive flour-mill near the *alameda* which we visited. The wheat employed is all grown in the immediate vicinity of the town, and the motive-power is supplied by water, tapped from the Rio de Lagos, and led over an enormous waterwheel said to be sixty feet in diameter. The cathedral at Lagos is rather smaller than that at San Juan, and less costly in its structure and ornaments. It is nevertheless sufficiently large for a town ten times the size of Lagos, especially as there are at least eight other churches to keep it company. The population of this entire district have the reputation of being as bigoted and fanatical as they are poor and ignorant.

Lagos is the junction of the diligence route to Durango and the north generally, with that from Guadalajara to the capital. When we started the morning after our arrival, a coach proceeded northward at the same time as our own started for the east, carrying with it the *Diputado* just mentioned, who intended paying a visit to his constituency. The *diligencias* from this place eastward are more roomy than those from Guadalajara to Lagos, accommodating twelve passengers inside instead of nine, although the increase in size is in no way proportionate to the augmented number of sitters.

At five o'clock A.M. we were off. Crossing the Rio de Lagos on a good stone bridge, we proceeded on a somewhat less barbarous road lined on both sides with splendid specimens of the *Arbol del Peru* (*Schinus Molle*), which here so much resembled weeping willows, that I at first mistook them for the latter.

The road for some distance followed the course of the river, and then turning off in an easterly direction, wound its way through a network of small lakes, which appeared right and left, and whose existence may have given its name to the town. The country was highly cultivated, and maize, wheat, barley, beans, filled the fields within three to four miles from the town. Later on less care appeared to be bestowed on the land; *haciendas* became scarcer, and the *ranchos* were only under partial cultivation, although the soil seemed to repay the husbandman.

A journey of twenty miles brought us to the border of Jalisco, and we now entered the State of Guanajuato, reputed to be one of the best governed in the Republic.

Two miles further took us to the top of a low range of hills, outposts of the *Sierra de Comanja*, whose rugged ridges bordered the north-eastern horizon, and then we descended into the splendid plain for which the city of Leon is celebrated. For the next eight miles we drove through this fertile and well-tilled plateau, over roads comparatively smooth, and past the signs of industry and habitation.

At ten o'clock we caught our first glimpse of

the dingy streets of the narrow suburbs, and reaching the town proper soon halted before a spacious building, the *hotel* (as it is here termed to distinguish it from the usual *fondas*) of the *diligencias*.

I had unfortunately not intended to make a stay at this remarkable place, but from what I could see of it in the brief interval between the arrival and the departure of the coach, it impressed me with the idea of being one of the most thriving towns in Mexico. It is laid out in the customary manner: straight streets, meeting at right angles, and paved with round pebbles. Its houses are larger, and of architecture superior to those of Guadalajara. They all appeared old, some ruinous, others repaired, and owe their origin, no doubt, to the energy of the old Spaniards. The present occupants confine themselves to painting the outsides and warding off utter decay from their ancestral inheritance, but not a new building or any modern improvement is to be seen. In spite of their thus living on the enterprise of bygone generations, the inhabitants of Leon show more activity than most citizens of other places, who in the majority of cases will not raise a hand to prevent the annihilation of these old and splendid buildings. Three and four-storied houses are common in Leon, some of which, from their grand proportions, doubtless formed palaces in times gone by, when the city was a centre of the old Spanish colonists. A cathedral, rather insignificant for the size of the town, and a crowd of minor churches, distributed over the place, are, as everywhere else, also to be found here, and a well-tended and spacious *plaza*, enclosed by an ornamental iron railing with the ordinary accompaniments of seats, fountain, and trees, is not missing. Facing the *plaza* stands the imposing *palacio*, and its other sides are graced with *portales*, crowded with the usual frequenters of these shady walks. *Dulce* and *agua fresca* vendors, hawkers of *sarapes* and *rebozos*, confectionary stall-keepers, fruit-sellers, and a motley multitude of vagabonds and beggars, crowded the environs of the hotel, and variegated the curious scene.

Leon, or *Leon de los Aldamas*, in regard to population ranks second only to the city of Mexico, being estimated as numbering about 100,000 inhabitants, including some outlying villages belonging to the municipality. It is situate in the same altitude as Lagos, about 6300 feet above the level of the sea, and is thus blest with the most agreeable climate of the *tierra templada*. In spite of its size, it is not the seat of the State Government, that privilege belonging to the city of Guanajuato, owing no doubt to its more central position. To this absence of official life is to be attributed the plebeian character of its population, which is principally composed of artisans and tradesmen. Leon is the supplier of many manufactures, superior in their way to any other in the Republic. Thus it is renowned for the best Mexican saddles, and saddlery in general, the most superior spurs, and other metal-work; also for its *sarapes*, and woollen and cotton fabrics.

Leaving Leon we continued our route in a south-easterly direction towards Silao, distant twenty-eight miles. The country as a whole is flat, and at times only slightly undulating. It appears fertile, while its loneliness is at times mitigated by *haciendas*, villages, and small towns.

The roads excel those of the State of Jalisco, and are frequently bordered by prickly-pear cacti, or neat *organo*-fences.

We reached Silao at three o'clock, and after a few minutes' delay to change mules resumed our journey. As we drove through, I found it to be an old and rather dirty place of the customary type, with nothing to arrest attention.

About four miles away from Silao (the direction of the road being east by north) the aspect of the country gradually changed, and we entered a mountainous district, of partially rocky formation, split into gorges and numerous ravines. We were making straight for the *Sierra de Comanja*, in a valley of which the city of Guanajuato, our destination, lies. Up laboured the mules, over rocks and stones, to the summit of an eminence, immediately afterwards descending into a deep gully, only to recommence ascending still deeper inclines as we proceeded. This repeated itself over a distance of six miles, when we entered a narrow valley, and drove along the dry portions of the bed of a stream called *Cañada de Marfil*. Crossing and recrossing the turbid waters of the sinuous rivulet, we travelled over its sandy bed for about a mile, and arrived at one of the suburbs, *Marfil*, built on both sides of the banks, which here towered at least fifty feet above the stream. Huge stone walls coated the precipitous sides of the ravine, from the top of which the back portions of the squalid habitations stared in all their hideous filth. The muddy nature of the river was caused by the mining processes for which the water is used higher up, and in these suburbs lived the miners, of whom the greater part of the city's population is composed. Further up, a part of the dry river-bed was used for the manufacture of *adobe*, for which the soil seems peculiarly fitted, and when we had arrived within a mile of the town, we already perceived large numbers of workmen engaged in constructing a wide road along the valley, by dividing its bed and damming up a portion of the stream. I noticed a number of convicts employed in this work, chained in couples, and guarded by soldiers. Still nearer the city we entered the completed part of this exceptional road, and finally, at five o'clock, halted before the *Hotel de las Diligencias*.

CHAPTER VIII.

GUANAJUATO.

From bad to good—Site of Guanajuato—Jardin de la Union—New theatre—Superior administration—Foreign residents—Fine country houses—Loza—The presas—El Cantador—A Sunday afternoon there—Riders—Mineral wealth—La Valenciana mine—A pestilential road—A valuable village—A monster shaft—Mining operations—Other mines—Yield of precious metals—Conductas—The Castillo de Granaditas—Trajes del pais—Silver figures—Situation of Guanajuato.

APPEARANCES frequently prove treacherous, and so it was with this pretentious hotel. A four-storied massive building, with a *porte-cochère* opening into the inner yard, and galleries running along every floor of the building, much in the style of old-fashioned English inns, led us to expect great things. We were, however, woefully disappointed. A room on the third floor, ten feet square, with its only window opening into the narrow yard, was all the accommodation my Austrian travelling companion and myself could obtain, in spite of remonstrances and polite entreaties. The stifling atmosphere of this stable was awful, and the *table-d'hôte* too dreadful for description. Our delight may consequently be imagined when next day, on presentation of our introductory letters, Messrs M. and Company, the leading firm in the city, most hospitably asked us to take up our quarters in their large and luxurious house in the *plaza*. And now commenced a time of real enjoyment, an episode of more instructive interest than I experienced anywhere else in the Republic.

Guanajuato is a wonderful place, and unlike any other city I saw in Mexico. It reminded me vividly of the towns of old Spain, both as regards its architecture and the quaint animation in its crooked streets.

The city marks the spot where three narrow mountain gorges meet and unite. It is built on the steep slopes of these three glens, the chief portion of the town surrounding the confluence of the streams. Its streets are necessarily curved and narrow; those running parallel with the streams are tolerably level, whilst those which are built at right angles to them are naturally hilly, as

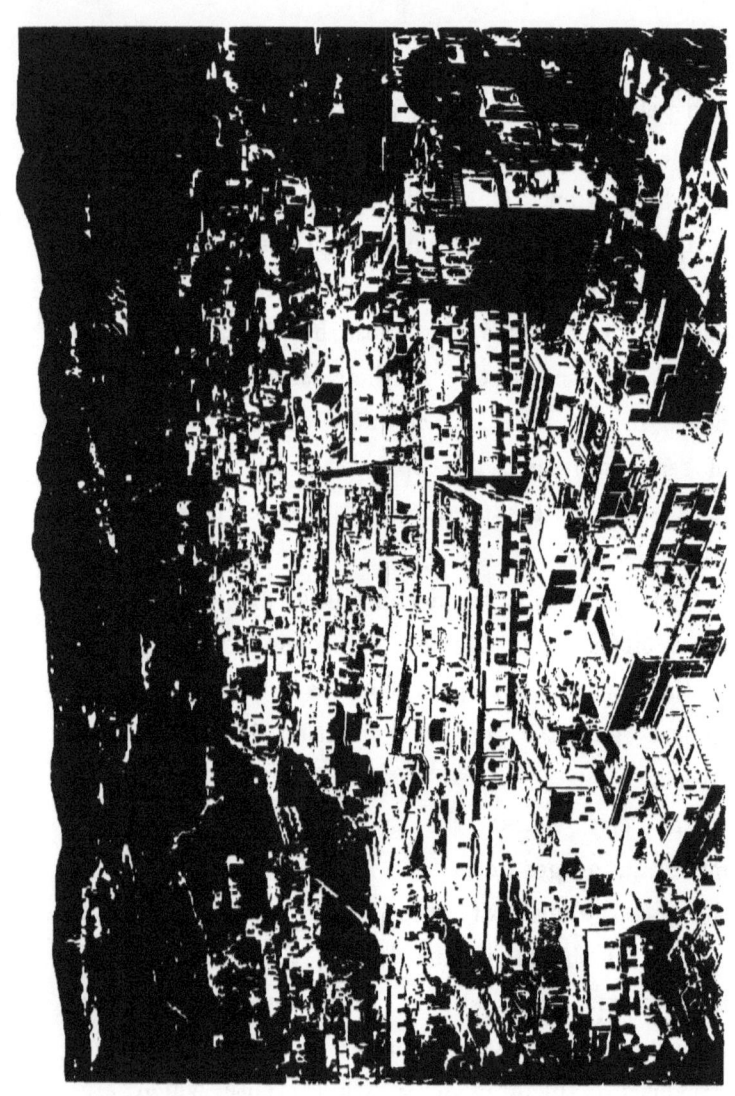

GUANAJUATO NORTH-WEST PART

they are but the steeps of the gulches. All parts of the town are thus amphitheatrically constructed, and extensive views of the different quarters are easily obtained, either by looking up from below, or taking a commanding position in one of the uppermost thoroughfares.

The town itself is due to the remarkable mineral wealth of the mountains in its immediate vicinity, and was erected by the Spaniards very shortly after the conquest. There being a scarcity of good building sites, the houses on comparatively level ground were constructed to a height of four and five stories, whilst those placed on the sloping parts were kept within the limits of from two to three floors. Thus the lower and better quarters of Guanajuato closely resemble the streets of Spanish towns, whilst the steep alleys up the hills are not unlike the *vicoli* that run right and left into the *Via di Toledo* at Naples. To eyes grown weary by the unceasing repetition of straight streets lined with low and monotonous houses, this thorough change was a most delightful surprise. But this was not all. From morning till night the streets were astir with an ever-moving, ever-shifting crowd:

miners in their white loose costume coming for the purchase of provisions, Indians from the neighbourhood carrying their produce to market, *arrieros* driving trains of pack-mules, *carboneros* with heavy burdens of charcoal strapped on their backs, itinerant hawkers of *agua fresca*, *dulces* and confectionery, were constantly mingling with the usual traffic. At no time during the day, and not even during the greater part of the night, were the streets empty, and nowhere in Mexico did I observe sights more suggestive in colouring and character for the author or the artist, not even in the animated capital itself.

My host's house was in the *plaza* here called *Jardin de la Union*, and from the balcony I was never tired of watching the tide of life below.

This *plaza* is smaller than any other I had as yet seen, owing to the scarcity of level ground, and its shape is triangular. But the citizens had made the most of the limited space, and a more elegantly-arranged park of equal dimensions cannot be conceived. The shrubs and flowers are choice, the fountain musical, while the pink-painted benches are more graceful than the seats of other *plazas.* Here, too, are tall lamp-posts which (on the "lucus a non lucendo" principle) are destitute of oil appliances; and as gas does not exist, evidently intended for ornament only. This loss of illumination, however, was fully remedied by the glittering crowd of loiterers who assembled to breathe the evening air, and hear the military band.

Two sides of the *plaza* are taken up by large private houses, tastefully and luxuriously constructed, whilst along the third side is an ancient church, with a most noteworthy façade, sculptured in the overloaded and florid style of the Renaissance. Next to the church a new theatre is in course of erection; necessarily small, it promises to be a model of its kind, if the few arches and pillars at present standing may be taken as a criterion, and unlike its sister building at Guadalajara, will be completed within a year, to judge from the manner in which the work was progressing when I saw it.

It must be evident to the most cursory observer that more public spirit and better administration exist here than in any of the towns or states hitherto mentioned. To this the new road, the activity displayed in the constitution of the theatre, the numbers of houses in course of erection to replace the old ones, the neatness of public walks and squares, the cleanliness and martial bearing of the military, and many other characteristics, bore eloquent witness. All this is due, in great measure, to the excellent governor of the State, General Antillon, who for many years has been at the head of affairs, and who, unlike the majority of state officials, does not owe his position to *guerilla* or brigand exploits. The General is descended from an old Castillian family, and by his wise administration, and rigorous execution of the laws, has not only succeeded better than any other governor in thinning the herds of brigands, but also in establishing a less corrupt system of finance. The roads in the State of Guanajuato are thus almost the safest in all Mexico; and the public exchequer directed into its proper channels, has effected improvements and introduced a general atmosphere of wealth, all the more gratifying because absent in other parts of the Republic.

There is a larger contingent of foreigners in Guanajuato than in the more westward towns. In point of numbers the Germans greatly preponderate, and monopolise the commerce of the town. The

CHIEF STREET IN GUANAJUATO, WITH CATHEDRAL

largest mercantile firms are owned by Teutons, and they also are the representatives of various trades. An English Mining Company, as well as the English direction of the Mint,* have attracted a fair number of Englishmen to the city; there is also a goodly array of Frenchmen, mostly devoted to the honourable and useful occupations of hairdressing and *confiserie*, whilst of North Americans there are but few.

One afternoon our kind hosts drove us up the banks of the chief *cañada* towards the great reservoirs which supply the city with water. After lurching along the exceedingly rough pavement of several winding streets, we entered upon a wide road, which continued the entire distance of the drive (over two miles), along the margin of the gulch. This road, which is one of the favourite drives of the people of Guanajuato, was constructed by the same company which instituted the reservoirs, and is lined the entire distance with stone-benches of the usual type, and plentifully supplied with shady

---

* By act of the Mexican Congress the English company were paid an indemnity on the 1st March 1874, and the Government undertook the working of the Mint.

trees. A short distance outside the town there were country houses of a singular kind. They were so far in advance of anything I had seen in the country, that I could scarcely trust my eyes. Following no single style, every individual owner seemed to have employed a different architect to design the plan of his residence, and almost every idea appears to have been artistically conceived and admirably executed. How far foreign or native skill is to be credited with these buildings I know not, but the result, to my mind, is most thoroughly successful and highly attractive. Some of the villas are constructed in the fashion so frequent in Southern Italy—a plain, airy building, with many windows, and a verandah on the ground floor, the outside walls gaily daubed with pink and green, and overgrown with vines and creepers; others are more pretentious, and erected entirely of stone. They are approached by pillared porticoes, finely sculptured and bright with statues arranged in numerous niches. All these houses stand in delightful gardens, distinguished by the variety and perfection which belong to this splendid climate.

The stone principally used for these buildings, as

well as for many in the town, is a peculiar sandstone called *loza*, which is found in a mountain called La Buffa, situated on the right side of the road on which we were driving, and towering above all neighbouring ridges with the bold, perpendicular rock which crowns its summit. This sandstone is of the finest grain, and its customary colour—a delicate pale green—is interlined with thin bands of brown, pale blue, and darker shades of green. The theatre above mentioned is being built of this stone, which imparts a peculiar beauty to the columns which it forms.

About two miles away from the town the reservoirs, called *presas*, were reached. They are constructed by two huge dams of masonry placed across the entire *cañada*, thus forming two extensive basins. The lower of these dams serves the purposes of a bridge, and is wide enough for carriages, whilst the upper only admits of pedestrians. These dams are of pleasing design, and unlike similar arrangements at home, conduce to the enhancement of the landscape. They are, like the road, provided with benches, and are much used by Guanajuatoans as pleasant resting-places in the evening.

The lower part of the dams contain the flood-gates, which are closed towards the end of the rainy season, to retain the waters of the stream for use during the dry months. The upper *presa* is like a small natural lake. Enclosed on all sides, but that of the dam, by precipitous and rocky hills, the placid waters of the gulch in their enforced captivity look most romantic, reflecting rocks and foliage with the distinctness of a mirror.

The water obtained from these reservoirs is considered very wholesome, though its appearance is prejudicial. It contains a strong admixture of sand and mud, which natives do not seem to mind, but which foreigners easily remove by a filter. The people are either too lazy or too ill-informed to employ the same means. When travelling we had everywhere to drink the grayish-blue liquid, which, in the face of a hundred protestations as to its sanitary qualities, was only drinkable through sheer necessity. This grayish-blue colour is by far more repulsive than the pale brown of the water in the creeks of the North American prairies.

The *Alameda* in Guanajuato is a fine public

garden, and on afternoons, especially of Sundays and Saints'-days, the rendezvous of all the beauty and fashion of the city. This small park, here called *El Cantador*, beautifies a densely populated part of the town, and is entirely surrounded by mediocre houses. It forms a square of about 150 yards each way, is enclosed by a low stone wall and laid out in broad walks, capitally disposed and kept. In addition to the foliage so often before described, rise the tall mimosas, and vases and kiosks vary the horticultural charms.

On the Sunday afternoon of my visit the *Cantador* was literally crowded. Carriage succeeded carriage, and after driving round the outside road they would stop at one of the gates, where their proprietors descended to enter the garden.

A large number of equestrians were engaged either in riding round, or taking their stand in a line near the principal gate, and would watch the *señoritas* enter and leave the park.

There was a much more of European colouring about this scene than I had found further west. The carriages were superior, betraying their recent importation either from the "States," or Europe; and although at times huge knobs of decorative brass, and blotches of showy painting, would betray a lingering taste for barbarous pomp, they were, on the whole, as good a collection as is the average in interior North American towns.

Here for the first time in Mexico I saw the big American horses, all the larger because contrasting with their small native cousins. It is considered the height of fashion to be able to harness a pair of these animals to the carriage, and the "belles" which it contains are regarded with no little envy by their sisters who have to submit to the less elegant stride of little Mexican steeds, or a pair of plebeian mules. The riders form a mixture of Mexican *cavalleros* in *charro*, and horsemen, both foreign and native, in breeches and boots. Without being able to assimilate the qualities of the European, the Mexican delights to ape him in dress. The *charro* is thus fast disappearing, and the nearer the capital, where European influence is most powerful, the scarcer is the national costume.

The foreigners on their horses and English

saddles, in riding trousers and boots, appeared natural enough, but not so the darker-skinned Mexicans, who, when on English saddles and mounted on American horses, are the most incongruous spectacles. Used from their youth to the Mexican saddle, on which a firm grip is all but unnecessary, and where a tolerably secure seat is inevitable, the bare, flat English substitute affords them no hold whatever, and their legs dangling to and fro in the most alarming manner, emphatically evidenced the agonies of these "fish out of water." If they only knew what pitiable figures they present when thus trying to mimic foreign habits, they would remain constant to their own spirited ponies and easy saddles, and be content with looking picturesque and feeling comfortable.

Guanajuato owes its existence and its fame to the silver mines. To enumerate the names of all would take several pages, for there are considerably over a hundred, of various sizes and richness. Immediately after the conquest the Spaniards became acquainted with the wealth of this region. The first houses of the city were built in 1554, and in 1560 the great vein of silver called *Veta madre* was discovered. It was not, however, until 1760 that this lode was properly worked, and it was then found that the mine called *La Valenciana* could yield by far the greatest wealth of all. It has been said—with what claim to truth I do not know—that for a number of years more silver was obtained from this mine than had ever been procured from any other in the world. Of late years, and until about twelve months ago, various circumstances had caused operations in the mine to cease, although it was well known that its stock of ore was by no means exhausted. A few years of idleness had filled the subterranean passages with water, the amount of which can only be calculated when it is known that these shafts and tunnels extend for miles.

The matter appeared hopeless until a combination of the most powerful native and foreign merchants, the German Consul at their head, leased the property of Don Miguel Rul, the heir of the Perez Galvez family, its hereditary owners, and commenced work anew. Although the difficulty of removing the water will still occupy a considerable time, this new company is already successful, and its hopes for the future are by no means feeble.

To spare the valuable horses of our hosts, we hired an old carriage with a pair of mules to drive up to the mine, which is situate to the northward of the city. After a drive through the narrow town, we emerged on the banks of one of the three streams (the one that flows from the north), which directed our course for a short distance. This part of the city is occupied by the dregs of its inhabitants, and the dirt and degradation of their dwellings and surroundings is truly awful. The stream here is converted into a public sewer, and the odour with which the atmosphere was impregnated obliged us to substantially protect the approach to our smelling organs. Crossing the gulch over a high bridge we commenced a fearfully steep road, which led through one of the suburbs. Tired of the superfluous beating and stoning of the poor mules, we accomplished the distance on foot, and seating ourselves again at the top, drove along an almost level road, which skirts one of the heights at the back of the town. From here we obtained an extensive view of the city lying immediately beneath us, and its singular situation appeared as if drawn on a map. Distributed all over the mountains that surround the town, we descried numbers of mining works resembling large ant-heaps in the distance, whilst droves of mules were carrying heavy sacks of ore towards the refining works. A short drive brought us to the Valenciana property, which does not consist of a single shaft and a few buildings, like the majority of the North American mines, but covers an area of considerable extent, and where there is a large village with an old church, and a number of enclosures—all possessing separate shafts and buildings of their own. The low houses of the village are mostly built of stones, in which lurk veins of silver that would prove very valuable in England, but which would not here repay abstraction. If in future a reduction of the export tax on silver, and cheaper "beneficiating" arrangements should supervene, this village will certainly be demolished to obtain the wealth of its building material. We entered the enclosure that contains the chief shaft, or *tiro principal* as it is called. Here not a little activity was displayed, in hauling up not ore, but large buckets of water, so as to clear the works for future operations. As this great shaft is thirty feet in diameter, and over 2000 feet in depth, communicating with numberless tunnels of enormous length, it may be imagined that the task of emptying it is the reverse of easy. The process is an arrangement of half-a-dozen large leathern buckets* which are lowered in succession into the pit, and reach the top in the same order, discharging their contents over the side.

The motive power is supplied by a small and very simple steam-engine, constructed in Manchester, after the drawings of the young Mexican engineer who is in charge of the work, and who prefers this method to pumping. For the last ten months operations have been in full force day and night, and it is thought that two years more will be required until the subterranean passages are sufficiently emptied for the miners to extract the ore. An unforeseen difficulty was experienced in using the water that was drawn up for the boilers of the engine. This, as indeed

* The untanned leather is stretched over a framework of strong wire.

all water on the property, contains such a percentage of different salts that its use was found detrimental, and thus all the requisite water has, during the dry season, to be fetched in barrels on mules' backs from a great distance, at a considerable cost. After inspecting the various appliances and workshops in this enclosure, we proceeded some way through the straggling village, and arrived at another part of the mine, where numbers of operatives were employed on the ore brought from the depths of a similar shaft. This *tiro* had for some time past been pumped perfectly dry, and it was hence that all the profits of the mine were at present derived. Blindfolded mules, harnessed to the end of a long pole and circling round, were winding up quantities of stone—mostly quartz—in which the rich metal is found. In a large open space men and boys were squatting before heaps of this stone, busied in all the various stages of reducing the large blocks into small fragments, and sorting the ore according to its richness. Hard by, in a huge shed, mules were turning a rude crushing-machine, in which the small pieces of stone were refined to the consistency of sand, and in another part again the smelters were outbidding each other in the purchase of the ore, which is sold by a kind of auction. The scene was one of great industry and animation, and several hundreds of workpeople were employed in this enclosure alone.

On our way homeward the various *haciendas de beneficio* (works where the silver is extracted from the ore), were pointed out to us, scattered over the bases of the hills containing the mines. The bullion, when separated from the stone, is exceedingly rich in silver, as only the very best ore is "beneficiated," and the mode of dividing the dross from the metal is through amalgamation with mercury. A great amount of the latter is thus constantly consumed, and the profits consequently much dependent on the price of quicksilver, which at the time of my visit was exceedingly high. There is also some gold to be found in nearly all the bullions, which is generally extracted by the Mint.

Besides the Valenciana a great many other mines are prosperous at present; amongst their number *La Luz*, *La Joya*, *Rayas*, *Mellado* and *La Sirena* were specially mentioned. The English Mining

Company not have been very fortunate. Their possessions, the *San Cayetano*, *Buenos Ayres*, and *Ovejera* mines are scarcely paying their expenses; but their chief mine, the *Jesus y Maria*, is latterly reported to have much improved. It is to be hoped that they too may share the *bonanza* which so large a number of the others are enjoying.

There is a mine called *Los Cedros*, the ore of which is almost all embedded in limestone. The fragments are stamped by the black imprints of a fern, such as is often found in similar formations. This fern, in its outlines, much resembles a miniature cedar, and it is uncertain whether the mine took its name from the fossils, or from the circumstance that cedars formerly grew on the hill. There are, however, not a few Guanajuatoans who firmly believe that the imprints on the stones have been caused by the previous presence of the trees, of which, they say, the fossil ferns are the reduced images.

The total value of precious metals yearly exported from Guanajuato was named to me as amounting to about six millions of dollars. Of this sum five millions is converted into silver *pesos*

(Mexican dollars) by the Mint, half-a-million coined into gold by the same establishment, and the remaining half-million exported in bars and ore. On minted silver the Mexican Government now exact an export duty of five per cent.; it used to be considerably more.

Owing to the insecurity of the roads, the transport of precious metal is attended with some ceremony and much precaution. The Government themselves undertake its conveyance for a certain charge or tax, and three times a year (until lately it was four times) they organise so-called *conductas*,—a convoy protected by from three to five hundred soldiers, according to the state of the country. In the dry season the coin is conveyed in waggons, and during the rains on mules, on account of the soft state of the ground. They travel in short, easy stages, taking over a week to go from Guanajuato to the capital, a distance which the diligence performs in three days.

Such a *conducta* was just preparing to start for the city of Mexico when I happened to be in Guanajuato; all the merchants talked of nothing else, and remained working till late in their offices to complete the necessary arrangements. Only once in the history of this institution has it happened that a *conducta* was robbed. In this instance, it is said that the Government themselves were in such urgent need of funds that they went through the farce of an attack on the convoy so as to secure the treasure. They, however, only considered it as a forced loan, for some time afterwards all the owners were fully reimbursed.

One of the most conspicuous buildings of the city is the *Alhóndiga de Granaditas*, a square, massive edifice, with a few small windows securely protected by close iron lattice-work. In spite of its ponderous character, it is pleasing in design, and possesses a finely-executed doorway. *Alhóndiga* means granary, and that was the primary purpose of the building. Later on, however, in the wars of independence, it was employed as a fort, for which use it might seem almost to have been destined; and many a fierce struggle is recorded between the Spaniards and the Nationalists, in the commencement of the present century, for the possession of this building. For Mexicans it has a great historical significance as the spot where their great patriot Hidalgo met his death in 1811. After his defeat by General Calleja, he and the three other insurrectionary chiefs, Gimenez, Aldama, and Allende, took refuge in the *Alhóndiga*, but were captured and killed; their heads were fixed on the four corners of the flat roof, where they remained for ten years, till in 1821, after the final destruction of Spanish rule, they were removed. The iron hooks on which the heads were suspended exist to this day, and form the chief objects of interest in the *Castillo de Granaditas*, as it is now generally called.

The plastic skill of the Indians in and near Guanajuato is exemplified by their traditionary accomplishment of moulding rags into figures illustrative of the different costumes of the country —*trajes del páis*—exactly in the same manner as the clay figures of the Indians near Guadalajara. In spite of the less pliable nature of the rags, these images are fully equal to those of clay, and on account of their less fragile nature much preferable for packing purposes.

Images and figures of a much superior kind, however, are cast in Guanajuato from the soft silver-amalgam of the *haciendas de beneficio*. When the silver ore has been crushed to powder, and the mercury applied to it, the outcome is an amalgam, which is a soft, pliable paste, in Spanish mining phraseology named *limadora*, from which statuettes of all kinds are easily shaped. Exposed to heat the mercury soon evaporates, leaving the image in very porous, but perfectly pure silver. The figures, as a rule, are coloured to resemble nature, by a clever process of enamel, and represent every phase of society from an *arriero* or a *cárbonero* to a complete representation of a bull fight.

The State of Guanajuato is the most densely populated department of the Mexican Republic. On an area of 12,170 square miles, it numbers 874,000 inhabitants, thus possessing about 72 to the square mile, whilst the adjoining State of Querétaro, which ranks next in this respect, has only 52, and Jalisco only 14 to the square mile. The city of Guanajuato, situate in north latitude 21° 0′ 50″ and 100° 54′ 27″ west longitude of Greenwich, at an elevation of 7200 feet above the level of the sea, numbers 63,500 inhabitants, including the population of the outlying villages of the mines.

CHAPTER IX.

FROM GUANAJUATO TO THE CAPITAL.

Departure from Guanajuato—Irapuato—Improvement in the country—Salamanca—Celaya—Artificial irrigation—The plaza—Baños—Apaseo—Indian village—Enter the state of Querétaro—Arrival at the State capital—Superior hotel—Aspect of the town—Its manufactures—Situation and population—A hard day—Questa China—An oasis in the desert—San Juan del Rio—Enter the State of Mexico—The watershed—Arrival at Tula—Our clerical fellow-passenger—Venta del Refugio—A sermon—Traffic on the road—Huehuetoca—A finely balanced coach—Cuautitlan—Wide and shady roads—Tlalnepantla—The valley of Mexico—Irrigation—Modern Aztecs—Approach the capital—Arrival in the city of Mexico.

ON leaving Guanajuato, at three A.M. on January 6th, the diligence quitted the city on the same road along the bed of the *Cañada* by which we had entered it, this being the only highway connecting the town with the road-system of the country. By the banks of the muddy stream, in the village *Marfil*, we were joined by half-a-dozen horsemen, who had been waiting the approach of the coach before their dingy low houses. They were the escort of the diligence, and in this instance not soldiers, but a private guard specially picked for the service. Arrived at the junction of the various roads with the *Cañada*, the *cochero* chose that leading in a southerly direction towards Irapuato. After descending from the heights to the plateau, and leaving the hills behind, the country seemed promising as far as about ten miles from Guanajuato, when the usual irregular and partial cultivation supervened, and the familiar stone fences and low *rancho* buildings formed the only features of the landscape. The twenty-six miles, mostly down hill, to Irapuato were accomplished in four hours, and at seven o'clock we halted in the *plaza* of the latter town, a snug place of about 10,000 inhabitants. The exterior of the houses in the vicinity of the *Despachio de las diligencias* I found painted with tasteful and rather artistic patterns. Otherwise I could distinguish nothing of the town excepting the interior of a humble *cáfé*, where we procured some capital chocolate and *pan dulce* whilst the team was being changed.

Irapuato is about 6000 feet above sea-level, and it is here that the two routes from Guadalajara to the city of Mexico converge. The way which we travelled runs, with a few slight deviations, east-north-east from Guadalajara to Guanajuato, and thence south to Irapuato, whilst the other route leaves Guadalajara in a south-easterly direction until the *Lago de Chapala* is reached, traverses that lake in a small steamer started by an American resident at Guadalajara, and from La Barca, at the eastern extremity of the Lago, runs north-east to Irapuato.

Leaving the town we entered upon an elevated road, and crossed two rivers on stone bridges before we had proceeded two miles. About three miles below the bridges they unite, and ten miles further south fall into the *Rio de Lerma*. The more we approached Salamanca, our next halting-place, and eleven miles distant from Irapuato, the richer became the soil and the more numerous *haciendas*, *ranchos*, and tilled fields. The influence of the *Rio* on the country was apparent in more than one way. In many places the land was already ripe for the sickle, whilst in others maize, wheat, and barley showed various stages of growth. The numerous villages looked clean and thrifty;

the small plots of land belonging to each house or hut were neatly hedged with *organos*, and the roads shaded by *mesquites* (*Prosopsis glandulosa*), *arboles del Peru*, and other trees.

At half-past nine A.M. we reached Salamanca, a clean, straight-streeted town of the ordinary type. It contains about 8000 inhabitants, mostly engaged in the old-fashioned style of manufacturing *mantas, sarapes,* and *rebozos*. Indeed, this is said to be one of the first towns in Mexico which produced sufficient *manta*-cloth to supply other places after satisfying its own demand. The large convent *de los Agustines*, with a fine church attached, forms one of the most conspicuous buildings in the town. Appropriated, like all former possessions of the church, by the State, it has now been converted into a prison for both sexes, instead of, as formerly, for one.

After partaking of *almuerzo*, and a walk round the pretty garden at the back of the *fonda*, we continued our journey.

Salamanca is situated about five miles to the northward of a sharp bend of the Rio de Lerma, which flowing north to that point, from there turns to due west. At that bend it receives the waters of an important tributary, the Rio de la Laja, the course of which we followed for the rest of the day.

The first few miles led us across a splendid plain, but as we proceeded eastward the soil seemed less fitted for agriculture, and after about eighteen miles became perfectly barren. Shortly afterwards we traversed a plain white with a thick deposit of *tequesquite*, which continued until we had approached within two miles of our next halting-place, *Celaya*, where we arrived at one o'clock.

Celaya is distant about twenty-five miles from Salamanca, and situated 6200 feet above the level of the sea, in a tolerably fertile but naturally dry portion of the country. In order to render the neighbourhood productive, artificial irrigation has been resorted to, and all around the town the land is intersected by narrow canals and ditches, much like similar arrangements in Holland. These wide channels extend for a mile outside the town, and irrigate smaller ditches, in the adjoining fields. The latter appeared to be used as kitchen gardens, and were rich with every sort of vegetable, whilst here and there luscious fruit glistened amid lofty branches. Men, women, and children were busy in these fields, in either gathering, planting, or watering, and there was altogether a charming air of homeliness about the whole scene.

Celaya is a gay and cheery town, with remarkably trim houses, all clean, and tastefully coloured on the outside. It was founded in 1570, under the name of *Concepcion de Celaya*, and the original narrow and not very straight streets still remain intact, lending it a rather quaint and venerable appearance. The town swarms with places of worship. Besides a large cathedral, there are three other churches of enormous size, and more than half-a-dozen smaller ones—more than sufficient for the entire State of Guanajuato. Its population numbers about 25,000, engaged in the manufacture of harness and saddles and other articles of leather. Soap is made in large quantities, and many hands are employed in a woollen manufactory possessing a small steam-engine.

Celaya has the prettiest *plazá* of all the provincial towns through which I passed. The walks are quite artistically arranged in beds of eccentric shape and grouping. Indeed the arrangements of this square would have done credit to any gardener at home. In the centre of the rich plantations, there is a monument erected in remembrance of the Independence of the Republic, formed by a column of white stone, rising from a fountain.

Opposite the *fonda* where we stopped there is a bathing establishment, which is supplied with warm water from an Artesian well. The baths are practical as well as practicable. There are a series of private compartments, and a large public basin sufficiently deep for swimming purposes. The white-washed walls are gay with fresco paintings, more amusing than artistic, and represent two European gentlemen attired in the newest fashion in active conversation with a Mexican *cavallero* robbed in *charro*. This magnificent specimen of native art is executed in life-size, and covers the entire wall.

Refreshed by a dip in the *baño* we resumed our journey, and after passing the gardens and green fields outside the town we crossed the Rio de la Laja on a compact stone bridge flanked by obelisks and columns. Our route led us on an elevated and partially paved road across stubbly land. Scarcity of water prevents a more extensive improvement of the soil, which is here only used for stock-farming. Horses, oxen, and pigs are bred in large numbers in this district, whence the States of Guanajuato and Querétaro draw their chief supplies. Whenever we came near a *hacienda* or a village, artificial irrigation was observable, and trees and crops were seen in the neighbouring gardens and fields. As we approached *Apaseo*, a small town ten miles from Celaya, a great portion of the country was planted with the *maguey*, which in the immediate vicinity of that town is replaced by well-watered fields of vegetables, interspersed with orange, lemon, and other fruit trees. After leaving Apaseo we continued over a loamy plain dotted with numerous *haciendas* and small villages, surrounded by well-irrigated fields, clumps of trees and little enclosures separated by *organo* fences. Fourteen miles further brought us to the border of the State of Querétaro, near which we changed mules for the last time before reaching the State capital in a village of Indian huts. The inhabitants of this *pueblo* were a race of natives perfectly different to any I had previously met. They appeared to be inferior in physique and intelligence to the Indios of the Pacific slope, and their huts were, unlike those of the latter, constructed in a most slovenly and fragile manner.

Our first acquaintance with the State of Querétaro was marked by the toils of a steep and formidable *pedregal*, and the allurements of a terrible road fenced in by walls of broken lava, and *nopales*. The roads throughout the States of Guanajuato were much superior to any over which I passed in the rest of Mexico. In Querétaro, however, everything has the reputation of resembling the institutions of Jalisco; thus bad roads and probable attacks from brigands were awaiting us. This fearful road, which was fortunately only three miles long, was literally lined with rude modern crosses, indicating the graves of the victims of *ladrones* with which this particular locality is said to abound.

An hour more and we arrived at the top of the hill, from which we descried the city of Querétaro, most picturesquely situate on the summit of another hill rising from the splendid valley that intervened, and commanded by a semicircle of heights in the background. There were still seven miles to the city, which took us an hour and a half to accomplish, although at first sight we imagined the distance to be much less. The road through the rich dell is lined with fine trees —*arboles del Peru* and *mezquites*—beyond which extends refreshing strips of cultivation. At last, at six o'clock, we entered the straight streets of Querétaro and halted at the *Hotel de las Diligencias*, having travelled over 90 miles since the morning.

The hotel was an agreeable surprise, and by far the best I had as yet visited in Mexico. It is a fine building, well proportioned, and three storeys high, with a large *patio*, and easy, wide flights of stairs leading to the upper galleries. The rooms are well-appointed and remarkably clean; this, coupled with good attendance and superior *cuisine*, reminded me almost of European or North American comforts.

Querétaro, since the fall of Maximilian's empire, and the death of that unfortunate prince on the *Cerro de las Campanas*, a hill in the immediate vicinity of the city, has acquired a memorial fame, and the circumstances connected with that event, as well as the general features of the town, have been repeatedly and minutely described. Apart, however, from the melancholy end of the emperor, the *Cerro de las Campanas* does not deserve the most cursory inspection; and when the fact of Maximilian's imprisonment in the convent of *Los Capuchinos* is disassociated from the building, it is not more interesting to gaze upon than any ordinary edifice of the same kind.

The narrow streets of the city look gloomy; the comparatively lofty houses, with their quaintly-barred windows, stone balconies, and clumsy wooden doors in the *portes-cochères*, possess an ancient and sombre appearance; which, added to the melancholy and monotonous tolling of the unharmonious bells of twenty-five churches, imparts to Querétaro more of mediæval seclusion and strangeness than I had yet noticed. Some of the footpaths are paved with a pink kind of sandstone called *loza*, like its light-green relative at Guanajuato; but the pink species is not so pretty, and cannot so well resist the onslaught of the weather, changing its colour to an ugly ash-gray after a short exposure. There are considerable quantities of this stone in the quarries near the city.

The town is supplied with water by an aqueduct, which brings it from the surrounding heights, and which forms a conspicuous object in the landscape of the country.

The inhabitants are largely engaged in the manufacture of soap and cigars, the latter from tobacco grown in the neighbourhood; they also brew a considerable quantity of *pulque* for home consumption. But its chief claim to the appellation of manufacturing town is owing to the cotton factories belonging to the Rubbio family. The one called *Hercules* is by far the most important of the two, and has the reputation of being the largest in the entire Republic. The motive power is supplied partly by water, partly by two steam-engines of English make. The chief articles produced are *mantas* and yarns.

The State of Querétaro covers an area of 504 square miles, and contains a population of 180,000. The metropolis is situate at an elevation of 6600 feet above sea-level, and numbers 55,000 inhabitants. In importance it ranks fourth in the Republic, only yielding to Mexico, Puebla, and Guadalajara.

At 3.30 A.M. on January 7th, I was again seated in the diligence, continuing my route to the capital. That day's journey was described as the longest and hardest of the entire route between Guadalajara and Mexico, and my informants, unfortunately, were not in error. The distance to Tula, our destination that day, is 42 *leguas*—109 miles—leading over the most horrible roads of any I had yet traversed, banked half a foot high by yellowish-brown dust, which in dense clouds enveloped the coach the whole way. I have undergone many fatigues, have tramped many a mile over steep and rugged mountains in a broiling sun, and camped many a night on the snow-covered prairies, with only an ineffectual wall of canvas between me and the piercing north wind, but I can recall no hardships comparable with these sixteen hours of almost continual jolting and jostling, in an atmosphere composed of three parts of dust to one of air.

As I had frequently done before, I now exchanged my seat in the interior for one behind the *cochero* on the roof of the diligence to secure a wider view. This certainly offered me a purer atmosphere, but the motion was naturally less equable, and forced me to grasp the rails with both hands to retain my equilibrium. As I never relinquished my gun during the whole time of my stage-coach travels, it may be imagined that I was far removed from the temptations of listlessness or indolence.

Immediately after leaving the city we toiled up a steep hill of rocky formation through a wild and arid country, productive of nothing but *nopales*. The stony soil, however, seemed to suit the prickly pear cactus, for on both sides of the wide road dense forests of it stretched away as far as eye could see. This hill is called *La questa China*, and is infested with brigands. This had been emphatically mentioned by everybody of whom we had sought information, with a sympathetic smile and shrug, as much as to say, "If you get through elsewhere you will be sure to catch it *there*," but our good fortune continued, and we passed in safety. In spite of the bad reputation of this locality, and the impotence of the authorities to stamp out the robbers that ply their trade there, only four tattered cavalry soldiers escorted the diligence.

After reaching the summit of the hill our route continued over a plateau, on wretched roads across the most forbidding and sterile country imaginable. With the exception of a miserable *pueblo* of huts, called *La Palma*, there is no town or village, or even hacienda, the entire way between Querétaro to *San Juan del Rio*, a distance of thirty-five miles. We changed mules at poor-looking *ranchos*, consisting merely of palsied and solitary houses, and mostly surrounded by *maguey* fields. The latter, and *nopales*, seem to be the only plants that can feed on the soil. This whole vast plain appears to be of very ancient lava formation, and its thin layer of earth only coats it at intervals. Pieces of lava and grim boulders strew the gloomy waste, which is at times patched with ragged stubble, besides the wild-growing prickly pear cacti, but otherwise utterly nude and dismal.

At nine o'clock our eyes were gladdened by the view of a green and fertile valley lying in the direction of our route, as an oasis in a desert,

This defile is formed by one of the head-streams of the large *Rio de Montezuma*. It is a pretty little river with gently sloping green banks. On the stream and cradled among trees and luxuriant herbage is situate *San Juan del Rio*, whose steeples and houses gradually rose as we approached. Splendid *huertas* outside the town were a mass of fruit-trees and magnificent flowers, and the wide road which we followed was sweet with umbrageous *mezquites* and *arboles del Peru.*

Crossing the river over a good stone bridge, we drove up the main street, and halted before a rather modest *fonda.* This main street is a very wide, tolerably well-paved road, overarched on both sides by rows of beautiful trees, under the shade of which the people were comfortably installed in numerous benches. The houses are gaily painted, perhaps to excess in many instances, but rendering the town peculiarly pleasing. Here for the first time I noticed substantial wooden gratings before the windows instead of the usual iron bars, which gave the houses a doubly piquant appearance.

Continuing our journey we soon left the fragrant gardens, and the fresh green fields of San Juan behind us, and again plunged into the same barren plain. After four miles we crossed the frontier and entered the State of Mexico, and at eleven o'clock we halted at a *hacienda* to partake of luncheon. Whilst we were seated the *diligencia* from Tula, with the passengers bound west, arrived. They, like ourselves, were parched and cloaked with dust, and in the same state of uncleanliness. For more than three hours after resuming our route, the country underwent no change, until at about three o'clock in the afternoon the mountains, which had all day bounded the plain, commenced to dawn on our view and approach one another. The road gradually ascended, and we entered the mountain range called *Sierra Arroyada*, which in this part forms the watershed between the Atlantic and the Pacific. The scenery became varied and picturesque; right and left the country was composed of numerous hills, with dimpled dales between them, carpeted by soft, short velvety grass, and studded with groves of tall trees and matted brushwood. Cotton trees, with full pods, from which the fleecy substance was already bursting, were abundant, as were tamarind, and Peruvian pepper-trees, grouped in knolls or growing isolated, and giving to the country the appearance of a park. After crossing several small streams and fair vales, both deliciously and delicately fresh, the road commenced to ascend more rapidly, and by degrees the vegetation became thinner, and presently ceased.

The country assumed a bleak aspect, and everything indicated that we had reached a considerably higher altitude. At a forlorn-looking *rancho*, where we changed mules, we had arrived at the summit of the pass, 8300 feet above the level of the sea. Thence we gently descended, and a little further followed the margin of a deep, sandy barranca, without a particle of vegetation to warm its cold and yellow sides. As we proceeded the declivities grew exceedingly rocky, and the road led over a succession of loose stones and boulders, that forced the *cochero* to walk his mules at a snail's pace. There appeared no end to this wretched stand-still torment. All the occupants of the diligence, half-suffocated with dust, and sore all over with knocks and bruises, were silent and sulky, and our arrival at the last hill before Tula had no other effect than to add symptoms of anxiety to the many of fatigue hitherto manifested; for this precipitous hill was the hunting-ground of a much-feared gang of *ladrones*. It was perfectly dark when we descended this height on a steep road that skirts one side of it, whilst a yawning *barranca* spread its chasm beneath the other.

Twenty minutes more landed us safely before the *fonda* at Tula, without our having met the dreaded brigands, who that very morning, as the inn-people informed us, had plundered a private party travelling in a carriage of their goods and chattels, mules and all, leaving the bare vehicle on the road and dispatching its occupants back to Tula in a perfectly nude condition. And this took place within 300 yards of the *fonda!*

It was eight o'clock before we sat down to dinner that evening, and as we had to start again early next morning, it was impossible to see much of the little town. As far as the hotel was concerned, however, we found the accommodation afforded almost as good as at Querétaro, and much superior to what we had hitherto been inured. Our approach to the capital was thus announced by the presence of additional comforts and luxuries.

The next day's stage was comparatively short. The distance from Tula to the city of Mexico is 20 *leguas*, or about 52 miles, less than half the previous day's journey, and accordingly ought to have been completed in half the time, viz., eight hours. But instead of giving the travellers the benefit of the shorter distance, the Stage Company cleverly profit by it themselves, much preferring the interest of their own pockets to the comfort of the passengers. This is performed by providing fewer changes of mules, thus reducing the speed; and whilst we had hitherto advanced at the rate of seven miles an hour, including stoppages, we to-day only made a little over five.

Starting at half-past-six A.M., the sun had risen sufficiently high to allow of an inspection of Tula, as we drove through its streets; but there was nothing to distinguish it from the generality of Mexican towns of equal size. A certain air of freshness, however, was connected with the place, owing probably to a profuse distribution of bright trees, that contrasted pleasantly with the gloom and dulness of similar towns. Tula boasts a very fine cathedral famed for the purity of its Gothic architecture, as the *curé*, who here joined the diligence, informed us. A few of the inhabitants had assembled in the doorway of the hotel to bid farewell to this priest, who was about leaving his parish for some time; and it was amusing to see the eagerness of the people (mostly women), to shake hands with their "pastor and master." In return for their few and quickly delivered speeches, he would simply pronounce the word "*felicidad*" in a reserved, dignified manner, and appeared rather annoyed at his flock's importunity. One enthusiastic admirer of the *curé* was in attendance on horseback, and "escorted" the coach for more than two miles along the road.

Tula is situate in a narrow valley, at an elevation of 7100 feet above the sea-level, and immediately after leaving the town we commenced ascending anew on our way to still increased altitude. For ten miles we drove slowly up hill, over a terribly dusty but not particularly rough road, leading through thinly cultivated fields planted with the usual cereals, and at half-past-eight o'clock arrived at *Venta del Refugio.**

Whilst the team was being changed we visited a most charming little waterfall, formed by the impetuous rush over some gaunt rocks of the waters of a small tributary of the *Rio de Tula*, which winds its craggy course a few yards from the Venta, and adds a grateful moisture to the luxuriant growth of ferns and trees.

Refreshed by our little excursion we resumed our journey, and were soon interested in a vehement sermon which the *curé*, who had improved the interval by becoming more familiar with us, began to fulminate against the present Republican Government, the measures they had adopted to impair the influence of the priesthood, and the iniquitous spoliation, as he called it, of the church

---

* *Venta* (a word which forms part of the name of a great many small places in Mexico), was originally used to designate halting-places in the open country. They were gradually established, in the early years of the colonisation of Mexico, on all the principal roads, and at distances from one another equal to a day's journey on horseback. In the course of time, and owing to the increase of population, a large number of these *Ventas* were transformed into towns and villages, or received additional *rancho*-buildings, while others retain their original shape to this day. A *Venta* pure and simple, consists of the *posada* or *meson*, the hostelry, containing sleeping accommodation and stables, the *fonda*, where food and drink may be obtained, and often a general store called the *tienda*.

property. As I listened attentively to his eloquent harangue, remained silent when I differed from his views, and now and then ventured a word of assent when he by chance brought forward an argument with which I agreed, he so misunderstood my conduct as to believe me a staunch supporter of his views, and we became bosom friends. In return for the kindly sentiments for his party with which he credited me, he politely indulged in a eulogy of European and especially of English institutions, and endeavoured to impress two young Mexican fellow-passengers, who were returning to College after a holiday, with the superiority of the Old World civilisation. The two students, however, were true *Mexicanos*, who, like all the rest, are convinced that Mexico is the first country in the world. They incredulously refused to accept such a secondary rank for their native land, and having received an ultra-republican education, treated the *curé's* discourse with something very like contempt. Between the two parties in the coach the divine now became much excited, and adding violent gestures to still more violent words, threatened to shout himself hoarse, and us deaf. Exertion and dust, especially the latter, soon commenced to produce their effects; the *padre* gradually diminished in vigour, and finally, subsiding into a corner, wrapped his head in his cloak, and regardless of the severe jolting of the coach dozed peacefully to sleep.

We had meanwhile passed the summit of the mountain range which we had been ascending all the morning, and were travelling on a gently descending road round the hills and over the glades of the *sierra*. At one time, the way led along the margin of a long, narrow, but very deep *barranca;* at others, through sloping woodlands. The road thickly piled with dust, and anything but smooth, became more and more animated as we approached the capital. It was often so crowded that the diligence had to wait several minutes until it could pass, and the clouds of dust generated by the traffic were too awful to be described. Long trains of huge waggons, upon which the goods were stacked to an enormous height, drawn by from eight to sixteen mules, and ox-carts (of a superior description to those seen further west, and with civilised wheels) were literally blocking the way, whilst an enormous number of pack-mules, in defiance of a few useless *arrieros*, would spread all over the road, and often knock their protruding loads against one another or the coach. Meeting an unwieldy train of *mulas de cargo* when on horseback is quite a perilous affair. The beasts are devoid of the slightest idea of distance, and in spite of your exertions to get out of their way, will often stubbornly face you and bring their loads in collision with your legs and your animal. Many accidents—some very severe—are constantly occurring in this way; the best means to avoid them being to wheel round when the train approaches, and move in the same direction as the mules until a fitting opportunity arises for escape.

The waggons proceeding towards the city were mostly freighted with large bales of cotton, whilst those tending in the opposite direction principally contained manufactured goods. The mules chiefly transported barrels and building stone.

Seven miles from the *Venta del Refugio* there suddenly appeared a rift in the hills, which until then had supplied, as it were, an emerald setting to the landscape, and the road led through a gap called the *Puerto de Montero* into a straight causeway, which in another four miles brought us to *Huehuetoca* at half-past ten. The small town is situate in a splendid valley girdled by mountains on all sides, excepting towards the south, where the view is bounded by the waters of the *Laguna de Zumpango*. To our right rose the peak of the *Cerro de Sincogue*, whilst on the left many a jagged crest towered above the range, the two most conspicuous being the *Cerro Blanco* and *Cerro Colorado*. The slopes of the hills and the valley are fruitful, and a perfect patchwork of *haciendas*. Fields of maze and other cereals succeed large *maguey* plantations and a number of orchards hedged off by substantial walls.

After partaking of luncheon and admiring the musical talent of some mocking-birds caged in the *patio* of the fonda, I took my seat next to the *cochero* not to miss any feature of the celebrated valley of Mexico we were now nearing. The broad causeway was bordered on both sides by wide ditches which communicated with large canals, of which we crossed several on stone bridges before we reached our destination. The road, lined by tall poplar trees, soon assumed a very European and specifically French appearance. The surface of these *chaussées* was by no means even, the left wheels of the coach sometimes running several feet above the level of the right. My conversation with the driver elicited the fact that by shifting of luggage or some other trifling accident the equilibrium of the diligence is easily disturbed, and that "spills" are not at all rare occurrences. This intelligence brought to mind the account of an upset recited to me by the driver of a Californian concord coach, when a few months previously I was travelling from Knight's Ferry to Chinese Camp in Tuolumne County. Pointing out a somewhat nasty piece of road, he exclaimed:

"At that spot Bill's coach was upset the other day."

I understood that Bill was his colleague, and proceeded to inquire how the accident had happened.

"It wasn't Bill's fault, it was all owing to that confounded nigger sitting by his side."

I ventured to ask what the darky had done.

"He was chewing a tremendously big quid, sir; those awful niggers always do."

I hinted my inability to comprehend how the quid could have interfered with the safety of the vehicle.

"Well, sir," he replied, "he selected that very place to turn the tobacco from the right side of his mouth to the left, and over went the coach."

A mile from Huehuctoca we crossed the small *Rio de Cuautitlan* on a stone bridge called *Puente de Guadalupe;* two miles further the *rancho Los Pájaros*, and after another mile the small *pueblo Coyotepec* were passed on our right, while continued crops of corn and plantations of *maguey* attested the skill of the agriculturist and the husbandman. Eight miles more, on the straight road, brought us to Cuautitlan, a pleasing little town. From here, that we might avoid a hill over which the main road leads, we turned off to the left, and after a mile arrived at Tultitlan, where our team of mules was exchanged for one of small gray horses. Rejoining the *camino real*, after a short distance we continued over the wide road, for two miles, with the narrow channels at its side, and the slim poplars, *mezquites,* and *arboles del Peru* overhead, when an ascent commenced, and we soon found ourselves toiling over a neglected causeway. Quitting the highest point, we began the steep descent at a rapid pace, and passing the *rancho San Pedro Barrientos* soon arrived at the dirty little town of *Tlálnepántlá*, after leaving which we at last entered the long-expected valley of Mexico.

From Tlalnepantla the road turns off to the left, and as soon as the houses were past, the two giant volcanoes, the chief features of this famed region, with their huge peaks of snow, sparkled in the distance. The sky was marvellously keen and clear—a real, intensely blue Mexican sky—and the atmosphere, when free from dust, deliciously light and invigorating. Objects far away, and beyond the range of vision in any ordinary climate, here appeared quite near, and the hoary heads of the venerable *Popocateptl* and *Ixtaccihuátl* stood out as sharply against the sapphire sky as if only two instead of fifty miles intervened between us and them. On the whole, however, the first sight of the valley of Mexico disappointed me. My position was not sufficiently commanding to obtain an extensive *coup d'œil*; and finding myself on low ground, surrounded by

Q

fields and trees, at no time distinguished much of the landscape.

The road continued consistent to the end of our journey—a wide, straight causeway, in bad repair and fearfully dusty, with its wearisome border of dykes and poplars. The ditches communicated with a number of canals, large and small, which frequently intersect the road and over which are solid bridges. The harvest around owes its richness to this plentiful irrigation. The plain bristles on all sides with cones and hill-tops, under whose shelter repose drowsy villages and *haciendas* belted with green glades, and each overshadowed by its huge white church.

The nearer our approach to the city the greater the animation on the road, and the busier traffic of waggons, carriages, riders, and pack-mules. Indians carrying heavy burdens, and in costumes different from those hitherto seen, added a new feature to the scene. In a frame of wood called *huecalito* by the natives, strapped on the back by a leather thong passed across the forehead or chest, men and women were carrying heavy loads of charcoal, wood, vegetables, and pottery, as well as coops of poultry for market. The lineaments as well as the dress of these Indians were by no means identical with those previously met with. They are the descendants of the old Aztecs, and it is a most curious fact that though their ancestors were in advance of all the aboriginal tribes, and though they dwelt close to the very centre of all Mexican civilisation, they have remained truer to their native instincts than any of the other Indian races. They are said to have altered but very little since the conquest, and their customs and culture, if at all affected, are believed to have deteriorated rather than improved since Cortez first set foot upon their soil. Their clothing is of the simplest description, consisting merely of a large *sarape* in which the entire body is swathed, and a pair of short white drawers. The women wear a short petticoat, and a square cloth on their heads, closely resembling the head-gear of the Roman peasant girl.

I am informed that these people manufacture themselves nearly all materials they require, and that by the same primitive process which was in vogue before the Spanish settlement. In the

Valley of Mexico intermarriages between Europeans and Indians are less general than almost anywhere else in the Republic, and the *mestizos* who people the capital in great numbers have mostly migrated from other portions of the country.

Two miles from Tlalnepantla we reached the small village San Bartolo, at the foot of the fine *Cerro Tenaya*, and turning to the right we entered a causeway six miles long, which runs in an uninterrupted line up to the city gates.

The road improved as we proceeded through clusters of villages, *haciendas, fondas,* and *pulquerias*. There was plenty to occupy eye and mind: before the houses, especially the inns, Indians, *arrieros* and others, lolled in lazy groups, their animals or vehicles waiting on the road, whilst their various contents tempted me to ask a thousand and one questions. To our left, two miles away, a chain of mountains bounded the view, at the very foot of the *Cerro Guerrero*, (the last of the range) glittered the village and cathedral of Guadalupe. In the far distance to our right, and founded on a sheer and towering rock, rose the historic stronghold of *Chapultepec*, and before us the towers and domes of Mexico came gradually in view. At a quarter to four o'clock we entered the purlieus of the city—low, straggling, and distinguished alike for size and squalor. Further on we passed through the *Garita de Vallejo*, one of the city gates, and driving over a level railway (the Mexico and Vera Cruz line), where we just escaped the passing train, entered the suburbs of the City of Mexico. Through dingy streets, and wretched dens, tenanted by the lowest classes, we quickly reached a thoroughfare of nobler appearance. The houses were larger in size and of better architecture, the streets were cleaner, the inhabitants looked more civilised, and the further we advanced the more imposing became the scene. Turning to the left, and rattling through two or three more streets, we finally reached the *patio* of the stage-coach office, and with it the end of our diligence travel, "*sin novedad.*"

CHAPTER X.

IN THE CAPITAL.

Hotel Iturbide—Arrived in the *tierra fria*—*Plaza mayor*—The Cathedral—The *Sagrario*—The *Palacio del Gobierno*—*Portales de Mercaderes*—*Casa de Cabildo*—*Lonja*—*Portales de las flores*—View from Cathedral tower—The *Alameda*—Statue of Charles IV.—The *Paseo de Bucareli*—The Tacubaya tramway—Tacubaya—*Plagiarios*—The *plagio* of Señor Cervantes—The Tlalpam Railway—Chapultepec—*Ahuehuetes*—Spanish moss—Puente de Alvarado—Aqueduct of San Cosme—Fuente de Tlaxpana—Tree of the *noche triste*—Tacuba—The *teocalli*—Trivoli de San Cosme—Guadalupe—A stone frigate—*Paseo de la Viga*—The canal—*Indios*—Guatemozin's bust—*Garita de la Viga*—Floating gardens—The Roldan market—Santo Anita—Ixtacalco—A strange burial-ground—The calendar stone—Aztec war-god—Sacrificial stone—The Museum—The Academy of San Carlos—Cimenterio de San Fernando—The *Cinco de Mayo*—Theatres—Situation of the city of Mexico—Its buildings and streets—Climate—The people—Foreigners.

THE *Despachio de las Diligencias* adjoins the large *Hotel Iturbide,* and their *patios* are connected with each other. Declaring my intention of repairing to the latter, half-a-dozen porters seized my luggage, and forming quite a procession took me to a splendid room on the first floor, comfortably furnished, and opening into a long balcony commanding the busy *Calle de San Francisco* beneath. The hotel used to be the palace of the Emperor Iturbide, but inhabited by him only for a very short period. It is an immense and magnificent building, of which any European city might be proud. A large archway leads to the enormous *patio*, at least fifty yards square, round the side of which rises the elegant though gigantic pile. Balconies are attached to every window both towards the quadrangle and the street, and the rooms are spacious and lofty. My apartments faced the shady side of the street, and I felt quite chilly, and was thus forcibly reminded that I was now in the *tierra fria*, at an altitude of 7600 feet above the level of the sea. The mornings and evenings were so pitilessly cold that I had to take refuge in an overcoat, and it was only in the middle of the day that the temperature was at all compatible with the probabilities of the latitude.

The hotel proprietor does not furnish any of the meals; they are supplied by a French restaurant established in an inner *patio* of the building. The tables are arranged in a large saloon, and also in small arbours which brighten the rustic grounds of an adjacent garden. After the rough and primitive *fondas* of the interior, this sudden change was most delightful, and by offering the comforts of New York, London, or Paris, seemed to annihilate the distance from them.

It is not my intention to repeat in this chapter what has often been described by much abler pens. I shall only touch upon a few of the many objects of interest it has been my good fortune to view under peculiarly advantageous auspices; not that I can hope to reveal any absolute novelty to the reader of the many special books on the subject, but simply to acquit this "*Peep*" from the imputation of entirely ignoring the capital of the country.

Quitting the *Hotel Iturbide* the visitor emerges on the *Calle de San Francisco*, and turning to the right, the straight street called at its further end the *Calle de Plateros* will bring him to the *Plaza mayor*, the grand square of the city. It is a large space of oblong shape, measuring 270 yards in length and 200 in width. Its northern side is entirely taken up by the magnificent Cathedral, and the adjoining *Sagrario*, the chief parish

THE CATHEDRAL, CITY OF MEXICO

church, which is often supposed to belong to the *Catedral*, but is in reality a distinct edifice constructed in a totally different style. The Cathedral occupies the site of the old Aztec pyramid and its temple (*teocalli*). It is very majestic, crested by a fine dome and two lofty and artistically worked twin-towers, of which the accompanying photograph will convey a much better idea than any description of mine. The façade of the *Sagrario* is very singular; it exhibits numerous reliefs of the most "*bizarre*" sculpture that can be imagined—appears too florid, and is as a whole certainly more elaborate than artistic, although some of the detail is admirably conceived.

Along the eastern side extends the charming *Palacio del Gobierno*, and although only two stories high, does not fail to strike the beholder. It flanks the entire side of the *plaza*, and its interior affords accommodation for not only all the Government offices and the Hall of Congress, but also for the President's apartments, small barracks, and a guard-house. The reception rooms are spacious, elegantly but simply furnished, and enriched with several valuable *objets de vertu*, acquired, I am informed, by the late Emperor Maximilian. The *palacio* was built in 1693, on the spot where Cortez had constructed a palace for himself, and which up to 1692, when it was burnt, served as residence for the Viceroys.

Opposite the *palacio*, *i.e.*, on the western side of the *plaza*, a row of houses supported by a colonnade lines the road; and the street, similar to that of Guadalajara, is called *Los Portales de Mercaderes*. Under the *Portales* some of the very best shops in Mexico are to be found. Tailors, hatters, milliners, jewellers, and one or two restaurants, are the chief occupants, whilst silver spurs, native filigree work, and a variety of knick-knacks, are offered for sale in the booths and *cajones*. This thoroughfare is all day long literally packed with people, who in their different costumes are a wonderful and curious crowd.

On the south side of the *plaza mayor* stands the *Casa de Cabildo*, the seat of the *Ayuntamiento* or municipal body, containing also within its walls the hall and rooms of the *Lonja*, or Merchant's Association. On the same side as this building

PORTALES MERCADERES, MEXICO

PLAZA MAYOR. MEXICO.

extend the *Portales de las Flores*—arcades similar to the other *portales*. The spacious area of the *plaza* was an open waste until about seven years ago, when the central part was transformed into a splendid public garden, after the designs, it is said, of the Empress Carlotta.

In the middle of the square a circular raised platform, surrounded by iron railings, and approached by steps, displays a pretty bed of flowers, round which the musicians group themselves when playing in the evening. This circular platform is encompassed by tastefully arranged walks and flower-beds, whilst fine trees supply spreading shade, and comfortable benches the opportunity for rest. Although this garden is of considerable size (120 yards square), still a very large portion of the *plaza* on the east and west sides remains empty, affording space for ranks of hackney coaches of an inferior description, and mostly drawn by mules.

One morning I ascended the west tower of the Cathedral, and, arrived at the top, was able to survey the famous valley in all its loveliness. From my position I could see the wide reach of plain wholly girdled by mountains, the sunny lakes, the solitary cones, the prim canals, and straight causeways, while hamlet, harvest and pasture, each added fresh tints and touches to the exquisite picture. Eastward glimmered the wide expanse of Lake Texcoco as far as the encircling ridges of the background; southward rippled the calm waters of the *Lagos de Chalco* and *Xochimilco*, parted by their tiny barrier of land. In the west Chapultepec's shaggy crag rose from the ground; whilst to the north the white walls of Guadalupe Cathedral reflected the glaring rays of the sun. In the far distance, towards the south-east, the cowled head of Popocatepetl and Ixtaccihuatl's outstretched shoulder, the "burning mountain" and the "white woman," scornfully lifting their snowy summits above all their compeers, were projected in sharp relief from the intense blue of the sky. My learned cicerone traced the roads by which Cortez and his army had entered Montezuma's city, the way he fled when defeated on the *noche triste*, as well as the buildings and localities connected with the romantic records of the conquest; and forgetting the present in the contemplation of the past, all the familiar names and deeds of Prescott's graphic history assumed life and reality as I gazed upon the classic ground.

Leaving the *plaza* by the same *Calle de Plateros*, and continuing through the entire lengths of the *Calla de San Francisco*, we arrived at the *Alameda*, a most magnificent specimen of the Mexican public garden. It is a parallelogram of 530 yards length, and 220 yards width, and divided into four similar squares by broad walks. Each of the smaller parallelograms is itself traversed by diagonal paths, which converge in circular plots, each cool and sparkling with the spray of its own fountain. Nothing can exceed the overpowering beauty of this park. Ash-trees, elms, and aspens vie with a hundred shrubs and flowers for the supremacy in foliage, and scent the air with delightful fragrance; nor must we omit the sequestered nooks and crannies so well known and appreciated by the Mexicans.

Pursuing our walk in the *Calle de San Francisco*, past the *Alameda* for a quarter of a mile, through one straight street which is named afresh at each succeeding *manzana* (block of buildings), we reach a small open space that forms the setting to an equestrian statue of Charles IV. of Spain, which until the declaration of independence in 1821 stood in the *plaza*. The republicans removed the monument, and for twenty years it was concealed from view, but in 1852 it was reinstated in this place, to front the wooden and now abandoned Bull-arena.

Turning to the left we can look along the noble avenue of the *Paseo de Bucareli* extending in one unbroken line to the *Garita de Belen*, a distance of three-quarters of a mile. Twice at intervals of four hundred yards, the *paseo* widens into fountained crescents, and at its end plays the *fuente de la Liberdad*, so named after the statue emblematic of liberty rising from its basin. It is thus a vista of majestic trees and feathery jets of water. The road, which is about fifty yards wide, reminded me not a little of the *Champs Elysées*, and in the evenings it is thronged with all the rank, beauty, and fashion of Mexico. My visit happened to coincide with the session of Congress, when the assemblage in the *paseo* is most brilliant. The luxury lavished on carriages and horses astonished me, I must confess, and was scarcely to be distinguished from similar scenes in Hyde Park and the *Bois de Boulogne*. I am informed that Mexicans will stint themselves at home to shine in public. The better Mexican families are, as a rule, not rich, but their vanity and pride are generally in inverse proportion to their means; and rather than let the outer world suspect their indigence, they will revel in *frijoles* and *tortillas* all the year round, and inhabit barely-furnished rooms, allowing the liveried coachman, the well-appointed equipage, and the American horses to absorb their diminished income. I was irresistibly led to ask myself, on hearing of these characteristics, if this was an epidemic wholly peculiar to the citizens of Mexico. As no description of social gathering is enjoined by the canons of Mexican fashion, and as visiting generally is restricted to the most intimate friends, the caprices of vanity can be indulged without an opportunity for the unwelcome cat to leap out of this tinselled bag.

Among my many excursions to the environs of the city I paid a visit to Tacubaya and

Chapultepec. In order to become acquainted with the customary means of locomotion, we selected the tramway-cars in preference to any saddle-horses or other carriage. The *ferro-carril de Tacubaya*, which has been in operation several years, is a street railway with large cars, on the American pattern, and drawn by horses. It commences in the *Empedradillo*, the street which runs from the *plaza mayor* along the west side of the cathedral, and turning to the left follows a parallel street of the Calle San Francisco, past the north side of the Alameda, the Bull-arena with King Charles's statue, and leaving the *paseo* to the left, finally quits the city, on a fine road canopied with spreading trees.

The Tacubaya railway is four miles in length, although the actual distance from Mexico is only three. The little town is splendidly built on rising ground, and its site is much finer than that of the capital. It is said that shortly after the conquest a mandate arrived in Mexico from the King of Spain to transfer the seat of government from the old Aztec city to the spot where Tacubaya now stands. The order, however, was thwarted by the violent opposition to the Viceroy offered by the generals and nobles, whose landed interest would have severely suffered by the change proposed.

Tacubaya numbers many beautiful villas and mansions, mostly standing in their own grounds or parks, planted in a princely manner. All the skill of modern gardening is here displayed to perfection; all European improvements and appliances have been pressed into the service of the proprietors; in short, everything that art can supply has been secured, and thus a faint idea may be formed of the result in a climate where nature yields so readily to the hand of man. I had the pleasure of inspecting one of these estates. Its many acres abound in long avenues of tall trees, lawns as smooth as billiard-tables, ponds and little streams stocked with water-fowl, mazes and shrubberies, bowers, kiosks, fountains, and beds replete with a choice and cosmopolitan flora.

The mansion was a miniature palace and the whole establishment the perfection of perfection. Without being actually envious, I could not quite overcome the possibility of being so when my round was completed, and I thought for a while that life in Mexico might be made tolerable in the possession of such an Eden. My surprise may be imagined when I learnt that the owner had not resided there for years, and that the gentlemen who were fortunate enough to call these oases their own dared not permanently occupy them for fear of being kidnapped on their way between Tacubaya and the capital. No case of *plagio* had, however, now occurred for a long time, and it was hoped that the proprietors might consider it sufficiently safe to return; on the other hand, it was maintained that the recent absence of these crimes was owing to the want of opportunity for their perpetration, as no one was willing to hazard the slightest risk. The fact, however, that hardly any precaution can exterminate these crafty *plagiarios* is illustrated by an incident that occurred about eighteen months before my visit. Señor Cervantes, a Mexican gentleman, in the act of entering his own house in one of the most frequented thoroughfares of the capital, was one evening seized by several men, who, huddling his head in a cloth, quickly hustled him into a vehicle at hand for the purpose. Driving off at full speed, the miscreants, after endless detours, halted before one of the wretched houses near the *Puente del Molino,* where they deposited their victim in a hole under the floor already prepared for his reception. When Señor Cervantes was found missing, all the detective machinery of the Government was brought into requisition to trace him, but no clue to his whereabouts was discovered, especially as the *plagiarios,* intimidated by the vigorous measures taken, failed to make any overtures as to the ransom required. A fortnight wore away in fruitless search, when a relative of the missing gentleman accidentally discovered the house where he was concealed. Informing the authorities, a rapid and sudden raid was made upon the place, Señor Cervantes, more dead than alive, rescued, and four of the criminals taken prisoners. After a summary trial, they were shot before their own house, and I myself saw the riddled walls which testified to the tragedy.

A walk through a few of the slovenly Tacubaya streets brought us to the railway station of the Tlalpam line, whence a train soon conveyed us to Chapultepec, a distance of only a mile and a half.

This line of railway connects Mexico with Tlalpam, fifteen miles to the south-south-west, and its first section from the capital to San Angel was opened in 1866; it was completed in 1869. The work was executed by English engineers, although the rolling stock is of North American manufacture. It was quite a novel sensation to be seated in a railway car and progressing at "locomotive" speed in this country. The change from *diligencias* and murderous roads to spacious carriages and smooth tracks was as agreeable as it was surprising, and I could scarcely believe my own senses when, looking out of window, I could convince myself that we were flying past *maguey* fields and hedges of *nopales* in a veritable railway train.

The station at Chapultepec is opposite the palace, and proceeding a short distance we came to the entrance, approached by a wide road. Threading the file of soldiers ranked in front of the guardhouse, we entered the celebrated grounds, the beauty of which widely surpasses their fame. Chapultepec is one of the sights of the world, re-

ENTRANCE TO CHAPULTEPEC

markable as much for its chequered historical associations as for its rare natural splendour.

It is in fact, and not in name alone, a royal spot, the residence, during revolutionary and eventful centuries, of the leaders of the country. The fanatical and ignorant priests in the train of the conquerors demolished the ancient palace, and carried their Vandalism so far as to destroy two mammoth statues of Aztec kings hewn into the rock, but fortunately they did not oppose their barbarism to the ancient forest of cypresses where the Aztec monarchs rioted in the luxuries and magnificence of their voluptuous courts.

The castle of Chapultepec is a long and narrow building, spreading along the summit of the porphyritic rock, and necessarily following in form the outlines of its foundation. It stands on the exact site of the royal Aztec palace, and received its present shape from the Viceroy Don Bernardo de Galvez in 1785.

It is reported that during the time of its construction, opinions were divided as to whether it was intended for a fortress or a palace; but however much its architecture points to the former purpose, it was certainly the country residence of Galvez' successor, though he himself did not survive its completion.

Since then the castle's fortunes have changed with those of the country, and it has passed from the possession of Viceroys to that of Emperors and Presidents. Some years previous to the brief reign of Maximilian it was used as a military school, until the Hapsburg Prince ordered its thorough repair; and besides decorating the interior with fresco paintings and models of classical statuary,* caused a wide carriage-road to be graded up the hill. Since the ill-fated Emperor's death, Presidents Juarez and Lerdo de Tejada have added another link to its long chain of fitful inheritance.

But by far the most interesting and beautiful part of Chapultepec is the forest of *ahuehuetes* or *ahoehoetls*, by which it is embowered. The two names are the native designation for the Deciduous Cypress (*Taxodium distichum*), the former being the Spanish corruption of the latter, which is the true

---

* The manner in which the Mexicans regard these statues is a matter of great amusement to the foreign residents. Their otherwise certainly not over-fastidious sense of morality has been so much shocked by the nudity of these figures that they have resorted to the almost incredible expedient of covering them with clothes much resembling *sarapes*.

CASTLE OF CHAPULTEPEC, NEAR MEXICO.

Aztec word. These cypresses are mighty trees of extraordinary age, which can count their years by centuries. The witnesses of Montezuma's daring and his ancestors' adventures, they were regarded already by his contemporaries as objects of wonder and reverence, and are at present perhaps the most curious memorials in the world of trees. California boasts the most gigantic growths, and maintains that the Calaveras and Mariposa groves contain specimens of *Sequoia gigantea* which, with trunks of 90 feet in circumference, and 300 feet in height, surpass any rival that Australia could furnish. In comparison with the *ahuehuetes*, the palm in size and height must be conceded to their rivals, for the gnarled trunk of the largest and oldest cypress at Chapultepec, commonly called "Montezuma's tree," measures but 48 feet in circumference, and its height, when contrasted with the straight towering *sequoia*, is inconsiderable; but in all other respects the twisted stem of the *ahuehuete*, with its majestic pavilion of leafy branches and its garlands of Spanish moss hanging down in delicate ribbons from every twig, is by far the most impressive and beautiful of the two. Connect with it finally its glorious traditions, and the Californian usurper is fairly beaten from the field.

The Spanish moss (*Tillandsia usneoides*)—*barba Española*—is one of the strangest parasites imaginable. It is a tangle of pale-green tendrils, in thickness like ordinary string, and while one end is closely wound round the branch of the tree, the remainder droops in long straight festoons. Its popular name, *heno* (hay), conveys the best possible description of the effect it produces on the view, for at first sight an unaccustomed eye might think that enormous quantities of hay had been emptied on to the forest from above, and that it had remained undisturbed on the trees. If it were not for this parasite, much of the grandeur of this *bosque* would vanish: it is the *heno* that lends to it that peculiar and indefinable quaintness, which, added to its many other graces, renders it thoroughly unique. The same moss is known in most of the Southern United States, but I doubt whether it can be found in such masses; it certainly does not exist under the spell of similar surroundings.

The foliage of the *ahuehuetes*, with its downy thatch of *heno*, veils the walks as with a baldachin, on which the fierce rays of the sun beat in vain. The fragrance of the wild shrubs and herbs fills the air with delicious freshness, and the sweet songs of birds betoken that man is not the only living being that can be grateful for the wonders and the peace of this earthly paradise.

As I walked through the forest, the baths, and the approaches to the palace, my kind companion would point out to me the spots which tradition associates with the doings of Montezuma, and but a little further perhaps a favourite seat of the unhappy Empress Carlotta : strange similarity of fate ! Three centuries and a half is the chasm which separates the Aztec monarch from the Hapsburg Emperor; both were gladdened by the tranquil charms of Chapultepec, and contributed to its adornment and perfection; both, according to their own light, laboured for the good of the people, and both perished by the act of those whom they desired to benefit. Surely, the rocks and trees of Chapultepec unfold a tale of more romantic history, and have outlived greater vicissitudes of fortune, than any other spot in modern times.

Returning to Mexico by the Tlalpam railway, I awoke to a ludicrous sense of the present as I heard the hum of the crowds that thronged the trains which reminded me of the neighbourhood of London on Easter or Whit-Mondays. It was a Sunday afternoon, and great numbers had gone short distances into the valley to spend the day. Arrived within the precincts of the city, the locomotive was replaced by horses, and the railway cars were thus drawn right into the centre of the town, till they halted near the *plaza*.

Another most interesting excursion was to Popotla and Tacuba. Chartering a hackney carriage near the *Portales Mercaderes*, we drove through the western part of the city, along a broad road in good repair and terraced with luxurious villas and mansions, standing in large gardens. This is the most aristocratic quarter of Mexico, and the houses certainly appeared almost equal to those in corresponding parts of the large European capitals.

This road also is most fickle in its nomenclature. One of its designations, *Puente de Alvarado*, marks the locality where, if the story be true, the Spanish hero of that name cleared the wide trench, which then existed, by one tremendous bound of his horse during the hasty flight of the Spaniards on the memorable *noche triste*. Along the centre of this wide road runs the large aqueduct of San Cosme, a line of clumsy low brick arches, with no attempt of any kind to render the structure ornamental. It supplies the city with very good water from Santa-Fé called *agua delgada*—light water—to distinguish it from the *agua gorda*—thick water—supplied by the aqueduct of Belen from Chapultepec, and which is highly impregnated with various salts. Near the city gate—the Garita de San Cosme—which we soon passed, a fountain is built into the arches of the aqueduct, called *Fuente de Tlaxpana*. Situate as it is at a bend of the road, where the arches turn off to the left, it was soon obscure in the distance as we continued in our former direction. The fountain itself is constructed in the mixed and florid style, which for want of any other appellation is by Mexicans termed *churrigueresco.*

A mile and a half's drive brought us to Popotla, a small and miserable village, and in front of the celebrated *Arbol de la noche triste,* the "Tree of the Sad Night." It is believed that on the night of the rout of Cortez by the Aztecs, it was here that he stopped in his flight, and with one of his followers hid himself behind the tangled shelter of a huge *ahuehuete* until the pursuing foe had returned to the city. The venerable cypress fronts a church which was built soon after the conquest to commemorate the disastrous flight, and which like the tree is named *Iglesia de la noche triste.* The grand trunk of the historical *ahuehuete* was until a few years ago in a flourishing condition, and doubtless still nourished some of the very branches that screened the defeated Spanish warrior; but by the fiendish act of some fanatical priests it was set on fire, and there remains now but the hollowed trunk, torn, wrinkled, and black, with only a few live twigs, as if to prove that no petty malice of man can utterly sap the energies of the time-honoured monarch of the forest.

TREE OF THE „NOCHE TRISTE„ AT POPOTLA, NEAR MEXICO.

The stories related about the incendiaries are very numerous and differ materially, but I have been assured, on authority which is entitled to consideration, that it was set on fire by a party of low ruffians hired for the purpose by the *curé* of the neighbouring church, owing to a dispute which had arisen between him and the municipality regarding the ownership of the ground on which the cypress stands. The actual perpetrators of this act of Vandalism were brought to justice and severely punished, but nothing could be proved against the instigating priest, and he escaped scot free. Since then the tree has been protected by a stone wall, surmounted by an iron railing, which was inaugurated by President Lerdo in person to publish his opinion of the cleric's sacrilege.

A short drive brought us to the village of Tacuba, near which is situate the remains of an Aztec *teocalli*, popularly called pyramid, although the ancient structure in no way resembled any of the Egyptian giants. A mound overgrown with grass, and utterly shapeless, is all that survives of the former temple, and appears so much like an ordinary hillock that it would be passed unnoticed by all but the initiated. The narrow-gauge tramway, owned by the Toluca Railway Company—which at present only run their small mule-drawn cars a few miles out of the city—closely skirts the barrow, a small portion of which has been cut off to make room for the "Station." We wandered over and all around the vast *teocalli;* its broken surface bristles with pieces of pottery—red painted with black lines—whilst on its sides traces of *adobe* layers can be seen, which seem originally to have framed the staple of the entire structure. From the loftiest part of these remains we could survey the long line of road on which the defeated Spaniards fled from the city beneath the twilight of that fateful *noche triste*. It was, in fact, the same path which we had just traversed, and we now occupied the very point where tradition asserts that Cortez took up his position on the following day to review the attenuated remnants of his flagging and dispirited legions.

A magnificent *ahuehuete* not far from the *teocalli*, and armed with a perfect panoply of branches, is by some modern historians believed to be the real tree of the *noche triste*, as distinguished from the charred stump of Popotla; but the existence of the ancient church at the latter place renders it the more probable locality.

As we drove back we gazed for the last time on the eventful spot; pursuing our old way we soon entered the city, and proceeded to visit the *Tivoli de San Cosme*, a large pleasure garden and restaurant, the best and most fashionable in Mexico. The grounds are extremely attractive; fine trees alternate with rare shrubs and choice flower beds; ponds and brooks, fountains, bowers, and kiosks only require the presence of languishing swains and shepherdesses to make the scene thoroughly Watteauesque, while the presence of melodious and aquatic birds, added to a selection of quadrupeds, seem to bridge over a century, and almost convert it into a zoological establishment. The "*cuisine*" here has the reputation of being most *recherchée*, and it is the favourite haunt of the President for official or diplomatic dinners, as well as the much frequented resort of the Mexican "upper ten."

On another day we drove to Guadalupe Hidalago, which is hallowed by the greatest of all the Mexican shrines, that of *Santa Maria de Guadalupe*. It lies about three miles from the city; the town, though well-built, is insignificant apart from its churches, and nothing can exceed the dulness of its streets on all but feast-days. On those sacred festivals, however, I am informed, and especially on the 12th of December, the Virgin's great day, Guadalupe swarms and buzzes with human beings like a bechive, but I had not the advantage of visiting it on one of these special occasions. I have no intention of inflicting upon the reader the well-known legend of the miraculous appearance of the *Indio*-Virgin to Juan Diego, of the not less miraculous portrait of herself which she presented to the Archbishop, nor of the many and fabulous wonders which she has worked since her *début* in Mexico; nor do I wish to encumber these pages with the measure of her "most holy neck," although as I purchased on the spot a ribbon embodying the exact circumference, the statistics on the subject are close at hand. I only wish to mention the four objects most conspicuous at Guadalupe: the cathedral erected at the foot of the *Cerrito de los Gachupines*, the chapel gracing its summit, and commemorating the very spot where

CHURCH OF GUADALUPE, NEAR CITY OF MEXICO

the vision was first seen, another chapel on the brink of a sulphur spring said to have burst from the rock at the Virgin's bidding, and lastly, an immense full-rigged ship anchored half-way up the hill, and constructed of stone and *adobe*. This latter was the votive offering of a gentleman who owed his life to the Virgin's aid during shipwreck, and is a real "stone frigate," perhaps the only one in existence beyond that found in "Jack's" vocabulary. I refrain from describing both the cathedral and the chapels: this duty has been frequently—perhaps too frequently—performed by others; and, after all, accounts of such edifices are much alike in all but consistent accuracy to fact; suffice it to say, that the large church blazes with "glittering" gew-gaws, whether "gold" or not, after the repeated visitations of the Republicans, it is impossible to decide. The sacred portrait of the Virgin, the same that she herself sent to the Bishop, is to be inspected on special days, but I did not have the satisfaction of beholding it.

One of the most interesting excursions undertaken by me in the neighbourhood of Mexico was a ride in the most charming company along the old Paseo and the chief canal. Leaving the city by the *Puente del Molino* we entered the *Paseo de la Viga*, the chief promenade before the *Paseo de Bucareli* became fashionable. It is a slatternly road with a rim of old trees, and now used as a "garden of the people." Parallel with it runs the ancient canal cut by the Aztecs long before the conquest, and which, by intersecting a corner of the city, connects Lake Tescoco with Lakes Xochimilco and Chalco. This part of the surroundings of Mexico is perhaps that which has changed least since the days of Montezuma, and at a short distance from the town the visitor finds himself bewildered by the utter change, and transported into the midst of sights and sounds which have nothing in common with the half-European life of the capital, but which, in their epic simplicity and strangeness, resuscitate with the breath of reality the "dry bones" of pre-Spanish history.

The canal was alive with multifarious craft very similar to our fishing-punts, as well as with tiny canoes, all propelled by poles or paddles plied by standing Indios. The frail pinnaces often weighted with two or three sitters, seemed fated to capsize every minute, but would again dart along, skilfully handled, at an enormous pace; the heavy punts, on the other hand, often provided with awnings, and freighted with vegetables or grass, laboured slowly along under the guidance of one or two sturdy figures. There was nothing of Spain in all this, nothing to recall European habits of any kind; and surely the belief that the Indios of to-day, as seen on this canal, closely resemble those of three centuries ago, is not fanciful or untenable.

In the *paseo* stands a recently-erected monument to Guatemozin, the last of the Aztec sovereigns. It is a colossal bust, supported by a square pedestal, which on the side facing the city bears an inscription in Spanish, and on the opposite one the translation of it in old Mexican. Arrived at the end of the *paseo*, we crossed the canal on a stone bridge, the arch of which is barred by a gate called *Garita de la Viga*. Here is the city boundary, and the toll-house of the tax (or *octroi*, as the French would say) on all articles of consumption.

This collection of the customs naturally impedes the traffic, and the canal was here literally chocked with punts and canoes laden with all kinds of vegetables, either heaped on the bare floor of the boats, or piled in baskets and sacks. *Indios* with the baggy white drawers rolled up to the knee, *sarapes* round their shoulders, and straw *sombreros* on their heads, were awaiting their turn for paying the dues amid a lively interchange of conversation; and whenever one of their comrades appeared on the scene, they would salute each other in the most formal manner by doffing their *sombreros* and lowering them almost to the ground. This is a ceremony contracted from the Spaniards, and is adhered to by the *Indios* with a ridiculous observance of rigid etiquette.

We followed the canal along the opposite margin, and soon came in view of the *chinampas*, the Mexican floating gardens, whence the vegetable supplies of the city are derived. These gardens are the embankment of almost the entire canal, and are owned and cultivated by the Indian population. "Floating" was certainly a misnomer on the occasion of my visit, for the oblong patches of soft soil, which, about thirty yards in length and five in width, rise a foot or two out of the water, have in process of time taken root in the ooze below, and although anything but real *terra firma*, the present *chinampas* have ceased to be moveable, and cannot, like those of ancient days, be towed from one part of the swamp to another. We rode on a narrow path running between the canal on one side, and a ditch on the other. This ditch is fed from the canal, and feeds in its turn the numerous cuts which intersect it at right angles, and extend along the sides of the fruitful patches.

These *chinampas* are spread far and wide on both sides of this canal, and in various other places near Mexico, where the locality is favourable. The space on which they are situate is so evenly divided between water and land, that without a knowledge of their history it would be difficult to say whether the gardens had been hung on the water, or the canals and ditches burrowed out of the land. We remarked large numbers of Indians at work on these plantations, which were simply packed with vegetables, small shrubs, and brilliant flowers. The produce is easily brought to town by the punts moored alongside of the gardens, especially as the canal threads many of the streets in the easternmost quarter with an almost Venetian regularity. In one of them called the *Calle del puente de Roldan*, near the point where the canal turns off towards the *Garita de San Lazaro*, the boats come to a standstill, for here is the real port of the canal, and the most interesting of all the curious markets of Mexico. In the mornings the buyers congregate on the quay that borders the water, and a most lively and noisy scene ensues between vendors and purchasers; clamorous bargaining alternates with chaff and compliment, and all the bustle and stir attendant on unloading the boats and transferring the produce, vegetables, flowers, and poultry to pack-mules or waggons.

Apart from the view, this quarter is one of the most melancholy in all Mexico. The buildings are cracked and discoloured; the canal is turbid with garbage, and the atmosphere horribly redolent.

But this is a digression from the towing-path outside the city, along which we were riding. Following its course, we soon sighted the gay village of Santa Anita, entirely peopled by Indians. Their low, solid houses reflect their flaunting colours taperingly in the canal, and are shaded by a cool verandah in front, propped by stout pillars of masonry. Numerous *pulquerias* were to be seen among the habitations, and on the walls under the verandahs rude pictures smeared with doubtful inscriptions furnished more cause for pity than contempt, and suggested similar productions amongst the ruins of Pompeii.

The current of the canal, which we continued to follow, runs powerfully towards the city, and is occasioned by the elevation of Lakes Xochimilco and Chalco above the level of that of Tescoco, the waters of which the canal unites. The flow is said to be equal to three miles an hour.

A quarter of an hour's ride brought us to another Indian village, similar to the last, and named *Ixtacalco*, rendered romantic and mediæval in aspect by a large church built at the time of the conquest, and now partly in ruins. With evident risk to our limbs we ascended the roof by frail wooden steps and holes in the walls; but were rewarded for our exertions by a splendid view from the top. Villages, *haciendas*, *chinampas*, and canals were spread out before us, as if drawn on a map, to our right lay the fair city, and above the surrounding buttresses of the mountains the venerable volcano, his "White Wife," and the scowling Ajusco seemed to bid defiance to man and his civilisation. Attached to this church is a burial-ground, which horrifies the visitor by its utterly neglected condition, and the human bones which lie scattered broadcast. In one corner a heap of rubbish indicated the spot where tiers of *gavetas* were once arranged, nothing now remaining but fragments of coffins and skeletons. In the centre of the ground is a cross on a pedestal of rough stones and heterogeneous masonry, wholly cloaked by its accretions of skulls and bones. We were much amused by the manner in which three or four ragged *Indios* dogged our footsteps, as if afraid that we might appropriate any of the hallowed relics of their ancestors.

Remounting our horses, we crossed the canal over a tottering wooden bridge, and followed a disused road pleasingly varied by canals and ditches, which we had to ford, until we reached the causeway

TOLTEC CALENDAR STONE, CITY OF MEXICO.

called *Calzada de San Antonio Abad,* by which we returned to the city.

For the archæologist Mexico affords a fertile field. Toltec and Aztec remains are exhibited in various parts of the town, the most conspicuous being the Calendar stone imbedded in the wall of the west tower of the Cathedral. The principal collection of relics, however, exists in the Museum, which is a mine of the most curious objects ransacked from all parts of the country.

The circular Calendar, which is of Toltec origin, and thus of great antiquity, is sculptured on a monolith of basalt so rough and seemingly porous that at first sight it looks like lava. The stone is twelve feet six inches in diameter, and is let into the masonry of the church at a height of five feet and nine inches above the pavement. From this Calendar stone the system of ancient Toltec astronomy has been preserved to us. It proves the great degree of civilisation to which the Toltecs had attained, a civilisation doubtless much superior to that of their successors, the Aztecs.

Their year coincided almost exactly with that of the Julian Calendar, which till 1752 was the standard of time in England, and is to this day dominant in Russia.*

In the museum the most interesting objects are the war-god and the sacrificial stone, which, together with other ponderous antiques, are deposited in the *patio* of the building.

The war-god exults in the Azetic name of *Huitzilopochtli*, and is as ugly as it is curious. It would be almost futile to convey a correct idea of it by description alone; let it be enough to say that it is carved from a single block of basalt about nine feet in height, and six feet across at its widest part. The idol does not represent any human figure or even any approach to one; it is sculptured on all sides, and shows in the centre, both in front and on the back, a death's head encircled by human hands placed in all manner of positions. The rest of it is a fantastic combination of snakes, feathers, and other appendages for which names are not forthcoming.

---

* In 1793 the Mexican astronomer Antonio de Leon y Gama wrote a most learned and minute description of this stone, as well as of the Aztec war-god, which was republished in Mexico in 1832, and edited by C. M. de Bustamas. The book is named *Descripcion historica y cronologica de las dos piedras*, etc.

It is said that this most hideous of idols was reared aloft triumphantly on two high poles at the summit of the *teocalli* (present site of the cathedral) in the Aztec time, and smiled benignly on the altar where the human offerings were sacrificed.

It is believed that the cylindrical stone, at present termed the "Sacrificial Stone," was this very altar, on the polluted surface of which so many thousands of victims were barbarously slaughtered.

This stone, which stands near the war-god, is three feet high, and nine feet in diameter, is also of basalt, and is chased round its sides with rude figures in bas-relief. In the centre of its top is bored a shallow hole, said to have been the spot where the victim's head reposed, and thence runs a narrow groove to the edge and down the side, by which, so tradition affirms, the blood was drained off!

The *patio* of the museum includes many other antique stones, mostly idols, and in the galleries of the interior is an extensive collection of smaller objects, unearthed either in the valley of Mexico or at Mitla, Palenque, and other parts of the Republic. It has been the custom to compare these Toltec, Aztec, and Yucatan antiquities with those of the Egyptians, and the theory once started has been repeated with marvellous consistency by the majority of writers, although nearly all authorities on the subject refute the conjecture. For my own part, I cannot comprehend how any similarity between the two could ever have been discovered. In the European Museums, in that at Boolac, at Thebes, and other places of ancient renown in Egypt, I have seen nothing that bears the slightest resemblance to these Mexican relics, excepting, of course, the usual similitude *in form* where the animal or vegetable creation is imitated.

There are stored a large number of more modern relics in the Museum, connected with the conquerors and viceroys, the war of independence, and the late intervention, but like all such curiosities only worthy of notice because of their historical significance.

The contents of the Academy of San Carlos embrace saloons of pictures, carefully divided according to their various origins and schools; but, with the exception of a very few, they possess little claim to merit. The Mexicans themselves have undoubted talent for art, and will in time certainly send forth painters of note ; native efforts already far transcend the second-rate copies of the celebrated European masters, which crowd the walls of the gallery, and which are popularly believed to be genuine. If that were really the case, the Academia de San Carlos would possess one of the richest art-collections in the world.

The principal burial-ground in the capital (now fallen into disuse) is the *Cimenterio de San Fernando*, a visit to which proved of the highest interest. It is but small, and contains galleries of *gavetas* round three sides of the square. The central space is a conglomeration of graves and monuments, some of which are of noble and appropriate designs. Here repose the ashes of Mejia and Miramon, the two generals who were shot simultaneously with the Emperor Maximilian on the Cerro de las Campanas, and in two conspicuous *gavetas* lie the bodies of the republican generals Arteaga and Salazar, whose execution by virtue of Maximilian's so-called black decree was hereafter made the chief argument in support of his own sentence. A fine block of sculptured marble marks the resting-place of the late President Juarez, and near him is buried General Zaragoza, the hero of the battle near Puebla on the fifth of May 1862. The bare facts connected with the exploits of this general in no way justify the veneration in which his name is held; at all events, the deed which is his sole passport to immortality would in any other country have received the most scanty recognition. In Mexico *faute de mieux*, the *Cinco de Mayo* is the festival *par excellence;* it is the most popular national holiday, and its anniversary is celebrated with the wildest manifestations of rejoicing and triumph. And why? Because the French General Laureçnai, with 5000 men, in his endeavour to storm the Fort of Gaudalupe, (commanding an eminence and strongly fortified), was on that day repulsed by the 12,000 Mexicans which formed its garrison, and temporarily obliged to retreat.

This cheap victory, which only delayed but did not prevent the subsequent capture of Puebla, is the cause of General Zaragoza's renown and of his sepulture in the Cimentario de San Fernando among the nation's most honoured dead.

There is no town in Mexico, however insignificant, that does not own a street or a *plaza* named after this great day—the *Cinco de Mayo*.

Among several theatres, the *teatro Nacional* and the *teatro Iturbide* are the two principal playhouses. The latter, during my sojourn, was given up to Congress for their sittings, owing to the repairs which their hall in the *Palacio* was undergoing. The *Nacional* is a spacious and imposing house with wide approaches and elegant internal arrangements. It resembles a European theatre in many ways, and is much superior to those found in the provincial towns.

A French *opéra bouffe* troupe were performing the modern works of their repertoire, and I witnessed several amusing representations during my stay.

The capital of Montezuma, the ancient *Tenochtitlan*, was built (somewhat similar to Venice), on ground reclaimed from the shallow waters of Lake Toxcoco. Since the conquest the lake has gradually retreated, until the modern city of Mexico, although constant to its ancient site, not only stands on *terra firma*, but is five miles distant from the nearest part of the present *lago*. Of the old Aztec town not a stone remains; the noble city of the past was utterly razed by the conquerors, and the Mexico of to-day, rich as it is with the handiwork of three centuries ago, is essentially a new town. The streets are straight and rectangular; the buildings are lofty and massive, and although all different in the details of execution, are yet pervaded by a harmonious unity of conception, which imparts a sense of perfection and grandeur rarely met with in our own cities. The thoroughfares average fifty feet in width, are tolerably well paved, and fairly illuminated by gas-lamps. The central quarters of the city are by far the best; they present, as it were, a nucleus of palaces with an enveloping shell of hovels; for the outlying districts are squalid and miserable, both as regards tenements and tenants. The fondness for colours, so generally noticeable, prevails consistently in the capital, and most of the buildings flare with painted coatings of yellow, pink, pale green, or a blended mixture of all three. This custom, strange as it may appear, impressed me as pleasing; but it must not be forgotten that the sparkling rays of an unclouded sun, and the lavish distribution of contrasting foliage, are no mean contributors to the enchancement of the general effect.

The uniformity of the streets is frequently violated by large and elaborate churches and chapels, of which there are no less than seventy-eight, and about sixty tree-planted squares are, as it were, the oases of the town. Few cities of the same size can rival Mexico as regards magnificence of aspect; there is certainly not one that can boast of an equal situation, both as concerns its rare natural beauty and singularly salubrious climate. The vast oval-shaped valley * in which it stands rises 7600 feet above the level of the sea, an altitude which transforms the usual temperature of its latitude (19° 25′ 45″ N.) into one as unvarying as it is moderate and pleasant. The mean reading of the thermometer is 70° Fahrenheit, and there exist no great extremes, winter and summer being much alike. It is only in December and January that the mornings are at times somewhat chilly, and the

* The greatest diameter of this oval is about forty-five, the lesser about thirty miles.

T

houses standing in the shade perhaps not perfectly agreeable; but where the sun has free access no perceptible difference is experienced. The atmosphere is naturally light and of a rare transparency; and the sky, which is seldom streaked with a single cloud, is ever brilliant with the keenest, fullest blue.

The thoroughfares are always lively. At no time from early morning till late at night does the ever-surging hum of voices and ever-moving tramp of feet abandon them, and the multifarious costumes of the mixed populace invest the streets with a strange atmosphere of outlandish gaiety.

Military uniforms and the glittering *charro* may be viewed side by side with the sombre European dress; ladies in delicate black with airy *mantillas* vie with the *mestiza* women in flaunting hues and *rebozos;* the poorly clad *Indio*, bending under his heavy load, pushes his groping path through a crowd of sauntering idlers; while hard by perhaps copper-skinned flower-girls exhibit their magnificent bouquets, which they offer for a few *reales*, spread out temptingly on a wide part of the pavement; *aguadores* cased in their leather garments with huge water-jars (*chochocol*) on their backs, suspended by straps from their foreheads, and a smaller jar (*cantaro*) hanging in front, attached to a string round their necks, patiently plod along under their burden; *carboneros*, men and women, bending under their dingy *huacalitos*, wander from house to house; whilst countless hawkers of confectionary, *dulces, agua fresca, tamales*,* and a hundred other dainties, carry their wares on their heads, and make the air ring with their motley cries. Imagine the bustle and the noise of the Neapolitan *vicoli* a hundred-fold increased, and you have a faint idea of a Mexican street-scene.

The capital numbers 200,000 inhabitants, more oddly mixed than in any other community in the Republic. Indians and *mestizos* constitute the bulk of the population, whilst by far the great majority of Mexican creoles reside here. There is also a considerable contingent of foreigners of all nationalities, as large in proportion to the size of the city as that of London or Paris. Frenchmen, I believe, are most numerous; next rank Germans, Italians, Spaniards, Americans, English,

* A species of savoury roll, made of maize-dough and meat.

Swiss, and Austrians. For many years past Mexico has been popular with the French, and long before the late war they flourished as *perruquiers, chefs de cuisine,* barbers, and small shopkeepers. Since their army visited the country their numbers have much increased; but, as may be expected from their antecedents, they have not risen to any prominent position. In their own sphere, however, they are prospering, and the sons of the small French town Barcellonette have lately struck terror among the other traders in calicoes and muslins by their power to undersell their competitors. The latter maliciously ascribe their superior mercantile ability to their low origin, and remark that a man who lives on six *reales* a week can easily outdo the aristocrats of the trade who spend six *pesos*. The Mexicans prefer the French to all other nationalities; it is an old liking, which the late war has not destroyed, and hardly even diminished. The reasons for this are many. There exists a certain similarity of character between them; they have been reared in the same religion; and last, but not least, the gushing, ceremonious politeness of the Frenchman fascinates the Mexican, whose vanity is easily tickled by these demonstrative though insincere formalities. When questioned as to their fondness for the French, Mexicans will tell you repeatedly that *un Frances tiene educacion*, which by no means implies that a Frenchman is educated, for in that respect they and Mexicans rank much alike, but that the Gaul knows how to embrace *à la Mexicana*, *i.e.*, fall into his friend's arms as if he were about to wrestle with him, and actively pat his back with the right hand of affectionate acquaintance.

The Germans in the city of Mexico are the chief merchants, and although they do not monopolise the trade of the capital, as they do that of the ports and interior towns, their firms are notwithstanding among the most important. Besides, almost every watchmaker, tailor, and hatter will be found to be of Teuton or Swiss origin. It is to the Germans likewise that the Mexicans owe the introduction of European beer, and throughout the country the signboards with their placards of *cerveceria aleman* recall memories of *baierisch* or *lager-bier*. The few English residents are nearly all connected with the principal banks and the Mexico and Vera Cruz Railway. They with the Americans (their courteous and hospitable Minister, the Hon. John W. Foster, at their head) and a very few Germans form the *élite* of foreign society in the capital.

The Spaniards and Italians are so intermixed with the native population, that it is difficult to disassociate them from the general mass; but not a few of the Austrians, Belgians, and Swiss, remnants of Maximilian's heterogeneous army, are frequently encountered among the *leperos** and *pordioseros* † of the *portales*, the Indian birdseller on the *plaza*, or the inmates of the prisons.

* The *leperos* of the city of Mexico are that peculiar nondescript class which in Europe is only to be found in the *lazzaroni* of Naples. Clad in rags, with no fixed abode, they earn their livelihood in the most mysterious manner, and ever cheerful in temperament, they combine unusual shrewdness with a remarkable ability for repartee.

† The *pordiosero* is the Mexican beggar. His custom to ask alms in the name of God—*por Dios*—has given him this appellation, which has become a perfectly recognised expression.

CHAPTER XI.

ON SOCIETY AND POLITICS.

General ignorance about Mexico—Causes of the civil wars—The Laws of Reform—The intervention—Maximilian's death—Measures against the priests and religious societies—Custom-house malpractices—Inheritance from the Spaniards—Population of the Republic—Creoles—*Mestizos*—Indians—Climate and productiveness of the country—The future.

FEW countries among those classed within the pale of civilisation are so imperfectly known to the world as the Republic of Mexico. To the historian its name is fraught with little else but the prowess of Cortez; to the journalist it is synonymous with internal struggles and convulsing *pronunciamientos;* whilst the financier regards it with contempt as a faithless and obdurate debtor.

In later years, the unfortunate attempt of the Hapsburg Archduke to transform it into an Empire has added another dark stain to its already tarnished name, and the mere mention of the country will evoke remarks upon the "horrible assassination" of the Emperor Maximilian.

The public at large learn little more than certain isolated facts, from which they draw hasty conclusions — nearly always erroneous, because based upon utterly imperfect data. The vilest epithets are lavishly showered upon the people, and it is rare that allowances are made for the peculiar condition of the country and its history for the last fifty years.

Until 1821, Mexico formed part of the Spanish Empire, and from that year dates its first breath of independent life. At that time, the two great parties in the country—the Republicans or Liberals, and the Church party or Conservatives — had already commenced their embryo struggles, which for half a century since have changed the beautiful land into a perpetual battlefield, causing progress and civilisation to halt at its frontiers, and educating the people in strife and crime. Viewed in their entirety, the continued civil wars present a terrible illustration of the iniquity and influence of the Roman Catholic priesthood, for every ghastly blot on the chronicle of modern Mexico is associated with the devastating machinations of the clergy. From time immemorial they have been contending for the mastership with the Liberals; from time immemorial their resources and energies have been husbanded to send armed legions into the field against the men who were struggling to endow their country with the treasures of instruction and knowledge. The Roman Curia, with all the wealth at their command, have fought fiercely to enforce their reign of corruption and ignorance against that of liberty and enlightenment; and now, after half a century of upheaval and awful bloodshed, the Republic is commencing to purge itself of this social gangrene, and the country already glimmers with the first dawn of regeneration.

The task of the Liberals has been gigantic, and whatever may be the faults of the Mexicans—and they are numerous—this great honour must be conceded them, that they have been in the van of the great contest of modern times—the fight of liberty against Ultramontanism. The curse of Spain was left indelibly branded upon her colony even when its independence was accomplished: the population were thoroughly priest-ridden, fanatic, ignorant, and ever ready to rise against the power in authority; the clergy corrupt, debased, and utterly criminal, shrinking from no deed, however vile, when an iota of their power was endangered. What wonder that revolutions were easily fomented, and that hordes could be rallied by the thousand, eager to rush madly, with crucifix in hand, against any champion of emancipation from the priest. In the general confusion, small chiefs, often neutrals, would gather adherents, and prowl about the country for the sake of plunder, and a state of hopeless tumult was the inevitable result.

This reign of terror continued until, in 1855, Comonfort became President and inaugurated reforms, which were improved and completed by his successor, Juarez, who in July 1859 at Vera Cruz (where he resided, owing to the occupation of the metropolis by the clerical counter-president Zuloaga) promulgated his celebrated Laws of Reform, which enacted the suppression of monastic orders, the nationalisation of all church property, and civil as well as religious liberty throughout the Republic. Against this Magna Charta the clergy opposed the most violent intrigues, which, failing in Mexico, spread to Europe, where they ultimately succeeded in organising the intervention of 1861, which commenced with the landing of the combined forces of France, England, and Spain, and ended in the execution of the Archduke Maximilian. France alone (for luckily England and Spain withdrew when the real state of affairs became apparent) is responsible for this iniquitous intervention, which has been more baneful to Mexico than all those internal dissensions which it professed to terminate. The Napoleonic interference not only protracted the most bloody civil war that the country had ever experienced, but brought a third and foreign power on to the field, which, although siding with one party, was in reality opposed to both, and ultimately forsook its partisans in an ignoble and treacherous manner.

The French had no sooner quitted the country when Juarez easily overcame Maximilian's army, and the latter expiated by his death, not his own faults, but those of his advisers committed under his name. The so-called Black Decree signed by him two years previously, and by which many Liberal officers of rank were shot without trial, was the main reason why mercy was refused to a prince who was suspected by the Republicans (not without some cause from their standpoint) as an impostor and an usurper.

A regular trial was accorded to Maximilian, and his cause was advocated by able and indefatigable defenders; and although it would perhaps have been a more politic and certainly a more humane act on the part of the Mexicans to have allowed him to return to Austria, yet it is only utter ignorance or prejudice that can stigmatise his execution as a "murder" or an "assassination."*

Since the termination of Maximilian's Empire, the country has continued comparatively undisturbed under the rule of Liberal Presidents. There have been *pronunciamientos*, it is true, but they have been confined to isolated localities; and the

* Compare the official documents on this subject contained in "The Fall of Maximilian," by W. H. Chynoweth. London, 1872. Trübner & Co.

priests, though still immensely powerful, have not ventured to coalesce, or, if they have, have not succeeded in organising any formidable opposition to the Government. The ecclesiastical source of the intervention, and the consequent anomaly of a foreign prince on the *throne* of the Republic, opened the eyes of many who had hitherto been their adherents, and made them cognisant of their real object. This increase to the strength of their party prompted the Government to propose to Congress the incorporation with the Constitution of the Laws of Reform above mentioned, and that measure was duly passed in December 1873.

For the last eight years the Government has been vigorous in executing these laws to the very letter. No monk, no nun, no Jesuit as such, is permitted to reside in the Republic; no priest is allowed to range the streets in the garb of his order; cloisters and monasteries have been converted into reformatories and schools; and the levying of taxes for clerical purposes is prohibited. The masses are being afforded the means of instruction, and the aim of the Government is to rescue the youth of the land from the hands of the priest, and entrust him to those of the schoolmaster. The clergy are naturally bitter and violent in their sermons and newspapers, complain of oppression, and endeavour to ridicule the principle of liberty which the Government claims to embody.

There are not a few in our own country who, although thoroughly opposed to the principles of Roman Catholicism, yet consider interference with its malpractices, such as has been the policy of Mexico for years, and has recently become that of Prussia, as an infringement on the *liberty* of the citizen or the subject. They thus hold the same opinions in this matter as the Mexican clergy. But would these lovers of unconditional freedom wish to repeal the various enactments against *license* in betting, gambling, prize-fighting, and duelling? And what else are these various prohibitions but so many curbs on the free will of the individual, enacted for the good of the community? They are, one and all, restrictions against a class, intended to preserve the people at large from immorality, which in its development might become dangerous to the State;

they are precautions taken to prevent a subtle poison from being instilled into the minds of weak individuals, who, too ignorant to keep aloof of their own accord, would without the supervision of the State cause the ruin of themselves and others. What but this mean the laws directed against scheming priests? What else is compassed by the expulsion of monks, nuns, and Jesuits? Nothing more far-reaching than to deliver the community from a class of parasites, who, while monopolising the wealth of the people, extinguish every spark of independent thought, and under the disguise of religion make mind and body servile to their interests. What is there more dangerous to the welfare of the commonwealth? what more blighting to the growth of true morality?

A nation aroused from such spiritual stagnation is apt to relapse into apathy or to be frenzied into atheism.

But it may be urged that his religion is the birthright of each individual, and that to meddle with it is not the part of any but a "paternal" government. This is an important truth, but religious conviction does not embrace the abuse of religious ritual.

The life of the soul, as of the mind, cannot be healthy under a despotism, though, too, it can rarely thrive without guidance. It is surely better that the earnest laity should lop off the mouldering branch than that a degenerate priesthood should sap the vital roots.

There is no sway more disastrous than that of an effete and heartless Pharisaism. If to restrain the encroachments of the clergy be intolerant, to be enslaved by them is intolerable.

The few countries that, since the time of the Reformation, have cast off the yoke of Rome can hardly appreciate the monstrous aggressions of the priesthood of Roman Catholic countries; and it thus happens that while the latter are one by one taking measures against the clergy, and ridding themselves of religious societies, the Protestant countries, such as England and the United States, are quietly harbouring the refugees, who in time will doubtless illustrate afresh the fable of the husbandman and the viper. Mexicans who wish to join the Jesuits or become monks, or Mexican women who desire to enter a convent, cannot now do so in their own country, and they are strangely enough compelled to go to the United States or Europe if they would enroll themselves in a religious order.

But whatever the exertions of the Liberals in this direction, they can progress but slowly. That which has taken more than three centuries to construct cannot be demolished or counterbalanced in a decade; and however vigorous the present administration in Mexico, and the feeling of the minority that constitutes the educated classes, the mass of the population is still entirely in the grasp of the priests, and the confessional can still muster more adherents than the schools. The lower ranks, say three-fourths of the entire population, are still partisans of the clergy; and although interest may at times induce or force, urge them to join the standing army, yet they would more readily obey the priest than the officer if circumstances were to place the former at their head.

Notwithstanding the most strenuous efforts of the Central Government, the influence of the capital cannot affect the remote provinces very rapidly, in a country so devoid of ready means of communication. In the distant States, despite the suspension of church taxes, and the other reforms, the church is the only building that is in repair amid misery, filth, and ignorance; the church alone flourishes in the wretched *pueblo*, and deriving nourishment from the surrounding poverty, is like the gigantic *maguey* which grows fat and succulent upon the arid sand. Of all the States through which my route lay, I found this fact most striking in Jalisco. There, energetic as have been the labours of the federal administration, the priests are still too much in the ascendant to admit of a rapid or wide-spread amendment; and though they conform outwardly to the regulations of Government, they work their silent way secretly and surely into the homes and hearts of the people, like the canker that gnaws the core of the outwardly spotless fruit. Their attentions are directed towards the poor on the one hand, and the wealthy on the other: they care less comparatively about the *bourgoisie*, who are sufficiently rich to dispense with their alms, and intelligent enough to discover their plans. They thus secure the support of the masses and the money of the opulent—the most valuable machinery for their designs. The war that was formerly waged everywhere with steel and powder, is now a battle of words in private dwellings; and instead of provinces and capitals, it is the control of the rising generation for which Liberals and Ultramontanes are contending. There can be no doubt as to the ultimate result, but who can tell what time must first transpire?

I could scarcely believe all that had been told me with regard to the power exercised by the clergy in the most aristocratic society, until I had some conversation with a scion of one of the best and richest families in Guadalajara.

I had spoken to him about railways, and what a national blessing it would prove if they were generally introduced; he answered me very earnestly that, although he would have no objection to the construction of a line between the capital and Guanajuato, he should be sorry to see his own native town Guadalajara connected by rail with the rest of the Republic. It would, he said, "disturb the quiet of our city, and by bringing us in contact with the outer world, introduce modern customs and destroy our holy religion!"

Too much praise cannot be bestowed upon the present Government for their activity and sagacity in grappling with this momentous question of the priesthood; and their tactics, so far thoroughly successful, promise to be of the greatest benefit to the country. Other internal evils, however, of equal importance and difficulty, are not so energetically tackled; but this is not so much owing to indolence on the part of the federal administration, as to a deficiency in the governments of the several States. It is only in certain matters that the central authorities can interfere in the different sovereign departments; in most dilemmas the latter are their own masters, and as their governors are elected by the citizens of the State, they are often not exactly qualified for the high position which they occupy.

In quelling rebellions, and especially during the war of the intervention, the Republicans have been forced to employ chiefs of *guerrilleros,* whose anterior career fitted them rather for the treadmill than for the important commands they not unfrequently obtained. This was an act of sheer necessity on the part of the Liberal leaders. These bands existed, and had to be dealt with. The alternative lay between recruiting the ranks from their numbers, and thus strengthening the constitutional cause, or allowing them to enlist in the service of the enemy, which would have proved a double disadvantage. A class of officers thus sprang up who, criminals in their antecedents, were nevertheless most useful to the Republicans, and were thus, after the wished-for object had been attained, entitled to the gratitude of the victorious Government. These "Bohemians," dangerous and turbulent in themselves, were, and still are, employed of necessity, partly to reward them for past services, but mainly to make them forget insurrection and *pronunciamientos*. All the privileges of the Central Government in a time of State election are therefore frequently applied to the benefit of such nominees, and it thus often happens that State Governors are the offshoots of a somewhat dubious society.

It is impossible to form a correct idea of Mexican affairs by a mere stay in the capital and the adjoining towns.

There, all is modelled to a higher standard, and the vigilance of the reformers is observable in every particular. It is most probable that, with a prolonged period of tranquillity, this lofty tone will permeate the Republic, but the distant States are at present far from imitating the example of the capital. The reins of office are there mostly held by unprincipled adventurers who, during their brief period of sunshine, do their utmost to make hay at the expense of the State. This, too, is the result of favouring *parvenus* solely because they have assisted in the time of rebellion, and are too formidable to be ignored. As there are many more of this clique than there are offices at the disposal of the administration, the limit to emolument is fixed at between six and twelve months, when the possessor is recalled without any reason being assigned, only to make room for another of the same stamp. As this is well known, their pillage, during their ephemeral tenure, of the public revenues is easily explained.

This is especially the case with the Customhouse officials, and more particularly with those stationed on the Pacific coast, who enter into regular contracts with the merchants in order to defraud the Government and enrich themselves. It is customary for captains of merchantmen, when arrived off the port, to send a boat ashore with the manifest to the merchant, so as to enable him to negotiate with the Custom-house officer about the terms on which the goods are to be admitted. Until an arrangement has been effected, the vessel cruises in the vicinity; and should a satisfactory settlement not be granted, the captain proceeds to the next port, and so on until a sufficiently compliant official is discovered. As a rule, the first harbour essayed is found to answer the purpose!

This practice is fostered by the very severe tariff (almost as high as that of the United States), which in some instances imposes an *ad valorem* duty of 150 per cent., and I have heard merchants in Manzanillo, Colima, and Guadalajara, openly declare that if it were not for the habitual " arrangement " with the Custom-house officer, it would not pay them to import goods. The usual " contract " stipulates for payment of half the legal duty into the Government coffers, whilst the other half is equally apportioned between the official and the merchants. By this transaction, the latter gain a quarter of the lawful tax, which, if their own statement is to be trusted, constitutes all their profit on the importation.

I do not recount these circumstances for the sake of gossip, or to cast a slur on either the authorities or the merchants, but because I consider the knowledge of these facts essential to a thorough comprehension of Mexican commerce. There is not the slightest doubt that only a comparatively short period of quiet is needed to enable the country to shake off abuses, the most detrimental effect of which is not the pecuniary loss which they occasion to the treasury, but the demoralising effect they exercise on the population.

The finances of the Republic, as may be imagined, have for a long time been in a deplorable state, principally owing to the enormous sums which the Government have constantly been forced to expend upon the maintenance of the army. Half, and at times more than half, the entire revenue has for years been consigned to the War

Department, and until the entire country has attained that degree of stability at which the present administration are aiming, the exchequer must continue to languish.

The constant fiscal embarrassments have at times forced the Government to measures which nothing short of the utmost pressure can palliate. Thus, for instance, the most urgent considerations only could have compelled the authorities to sanction a direct breach of the Constitution such as is perpetually committed by the exaction of duty on goods passing from one State of the federation to another. Such duties are specially prohibited by the Constitution, but they are nevertheless levied in almost all States, special custom-houses and officials existing for the purpose. In this instance the Central Government not only does not interfere, but legalises as it were the unlawful practice, by themselves receiving 25 per cent. of all the duties so levied. This suicidal policy will also, doubtless, very soon be a bugbear of the past.

The Mexicans, although generally very different from the Spaniards, have yet retained many qualities of their former masters. Thus the incomprehensible and absurd pride of Castillians clings to the Mexican in a lamentable degree. He is proud beyond anything, though he may be a criminal, or a pauper; he is proud for pride's sake, without any other justification for his pet vice. With this extraordinary temperament he combines the most tender susceptibility, and is as easily offended as pleased.

These peculiarities characterise alike individuals and the national Government, and however efficient they may be in dealing with their internal affairs, these qualities seriously impede their relations with other countries. They are of opinion that their friendship ought to be solicited by others, little regarding the fact that foreign alliance is by far more important to themselves than it can ever be to other nations. Discoursing on this topic Mexicans will assume a haughty attitude, and tell you that their country is sufficiently rich and productive to dispense with all foreign aid, and that if other nations did not seek for relations with Mexico, Mexico would certainly not trouble about it herself. This feeling is doubtless one of the causes which have prevented the country from keeping pace with other nations on the path of progress.

The Republic numbers over nine millions of inhabitants. Of these, over two-thirds are pure Indians, the descendants of the tribes found by Cortez in the country. Of the remaining three millions, two and a half are *mestizos*, whilst the pure creoles hardly amount to 500,000. There are no official statistics upon which to rely for these figures. It is impossible to draw the line between half-castes and descendants of pure Spanish blood, but this much is certain, that there are by far fewer genuine creoles than the Mexicans themselves believe, and if the truth were known, the above estimate of half a million would still considerably dwindle.

The whites are the aristocrats of the land; so far, they have represented the intelligence of the nation, and the majority of its leaders, both political and scientific, belong to their ranks; they consider themselves, and are generally considered, the natural superiors of their fellow-citizens. Thus there exists a craving to be classed as belonging to the undoubted Spanish race, and when the *mestizo* is not conspicuously marked with a brown or yellow skin, he will repudiate affinity with other blood, and in spite of his physiognomy endeavour to pass for a creole.

The *mestizos* naturally comprise a class of various elements, owing to the multifarious grades of intermixture between the white and indigenous races. Thus a portion would, in their characteristics, rank with the whites, whilst another and a more considerable class border on the pale of Indian society. As a race, however, the *mestizos* are unmistakeable; they, although numerically much less important than the Indians, are the Mexicans *par excellence*, combining, as they do, the character of the Spaniards with that of the aborigines. Unfortunately they possess neither the best traits of the whites, nor the loftiest instincts of the *Indios;* they have inherited much of the arrogance and unmeaning pride of the one, as well as a considerable measure of the indolence and callousness of the other. As is natural in a mongrel race, there are numerous exceptions to this rule, which must be taken more as a verdict on most than a sweeping judgment on all. The severity of this definition, however, is justified in a certain measure by the fact that most of the disturbances for the last half century, and much of the misery caused by the civil wars, is due to *mestizos*. Whites, as a rule, were the instigators and ringleaders, but in the majority of cases the combatants were of the half-caste breed, for the Indians rarely joined any party of their own free will. The *mestizos*, although in times of quiet industrious and orderly, are easily inflamed to revolt, and it is they that form the turbulent element in Mexican society. Individually they are affable and amiable, like most people of easy-going habits; and, ever prone to a love of amusement, they will abandon any occupation for a dance or dissipation.

The Indians are the bulk of the population, and that class on which the future of the country chiefly depends. There were at the time of the conquest, and there are now, more than thirty different races, speaking as many different languages, and stamped by distinctive peculiarities. They are all, however, infinitely superior to the other aboriginal races on the North American continent. They had acquired a by no means trivial civilisation before the Spaniards conquered them, and the great majority have, in spite of the awful oppression and ill-treatment experienced at the hands of the white discoverers, preserved their sterling virtues to this day. Three centuries of slavery have certainly not conduced to an amelioration of their condition, and as regards the Aztecs and their neighbours whom history has painted in such heroic proportions, this protracted period of servitude has obliterated the energy and enterprise they could once undoubtedly claim. Since the independence of Mexico the former *peones* of the Spaniards have been free citizens of the Republic, but the unsettled state of the country has not, until quite lately, allowed the Government to take measures for their instruction and elevation from the ignorance and darkness into which slavery and the priesthood have plunged them. Considering the capricious treatment they have received, the *Indios* must be admired for the way in which they have preserved a certain cheerfulness of spirit, and constant willingness to work if only encouraged. The genial climate and their subordinate position have rendered them indolent when left to their own devices, but when superintended they are excellent artisans, operatives, and servants ; and, indeed, it is they that perform all the labour in the country. The ignorance and degradation in which they have been nurtured have naturally deadened in them the very idea of a luxurious affluence—an idea which, if history is to be believed, they certainly possessed in the olden time ; their wants are exceedingly few, and thoughts of accumulating property or bettering their condition are as yet entirely foreign to them. To judge, however, from isolated examples, it appears fairly established that education will awake the nation from their sloth and torpor, and that although long years will be needed to redeem the stupefaction of the past, yet there seems no cause to doubt that ultimately this Indian population of Mexico will prove an illustrous family in the community of nations.

Those who stigmatise the population of the Republic as beyond hope of improvement, and who deem its future a hopeless blank, cannot have seriously weighed the wonderful career of Juarez, one of Mexico's noblest presidents, who was a pure Indian, as well as the services of many others, who, like him, have sprung from the unadulterated and indigenous race.

It is well known that Mexico is a surpassingly rich country, and it has been repeatedly said, that there is no product that the land cannot be made to yield. This is no exaggeration. Its geographical position and topographical configuration combine to render it unique in its climate. The tropical temperature belonging to its latitude is moderated by the elevation of the ground, and all the climates of the globe, from intense heat to eternal snow, are found on its surface.

From the Pacific coast the country slopes gently to an altitude of 8000 feet, whilst on the Atlantic side the acclivity is more abrupt and the decline precipitous. The central district forms a vast table-land, undulating in its general features; it enjoys the most perfect climate imaginable, and is for the greater part composed of arable soil. The mountains conceal minerals of all descriptions, amongst which silver ore is by no means the rarest, and competent authorities assert that coal is not unknown in different parts of the Republic.

The *tierra caliente* admits of all tropical products; the *tierra templada* furnishes cereals of all kinds in unsurpassed quality; whilst the *tierra fria* abounds in timber and much indigenous produce.

When it is possible to speak in such general terms, it is unnecessary to particularise: the land only requires the requisite labour to be bestowed upon it, and there exists but little that cannot be grown in one part of the Republic or the other.

From these premises it is not difficult to infer that Mexico has a great future before her; but that future is entirely dependent on the action of the Government, and the support that the population will lend them to uproot Ultramontanism, diffuse instruction, and improve the means of communication. With regard to the two former measures, the administration are as assiduous as could be desired; but although the importance of the latter question is thoroughly acknowledged, there does not exist the same energy in solving it. If the means of easy transport were once established, the capacity of the country would increase in enormous proportions; and if, finally, by adopting a just and conciliatory policy, the Government should induce foreign capital to seek employment in Mexico, an era of unparalleled commercial prosperity and national greatness would open before her.

CHAPTER XII.

FROM MEXICO TO THE GULF.

Departure from the capital—*Buena vista* station—The Mexico and Vera Cruz Railway—A cold night—Apizaco and the branch line to Puebla—Pico de Orizaba—Boca del Monte—Maltrata—Escorts—Barranca del Infiernillo—Arrival at Orizaba—Fertility around the town—Cotton factory—Resume journey—Barranca de Metlac—Córdoba — Atoyác—Chiquihuite Falls—Luxuriant vegetation of *tierra caliente*—Barrenness of the country near the coast—Arrival at Vera Cruz—Hotel de las Diligencias—Peculiar hotel arrangements —The *norte*—Baths—Embarkation on board the *Floride* and departure.

On the evening of Wednesday, 14th January 1874, I witnessed the assemblage of a numerous party in the hospitable house of Dr S———; but whilst in the full swing of enjoyment, I was reminded that the train which was to take me away from the capital was appointed to leave at midnight. Hurrying from the brilliant ball-room and charming partners, I repaired to the Hotel Iturbide, where two rickety hackney-coaches and at least half-a-dozen busybodies were waiting to transport my own person and luggage to the *Buena vista* railway station. The latter is but a large wooden shed, and whatever the ultimate intentions of the Railway Company may be, both building and arrangements are as yet most primitive. Mexicans, whose experience of these matters can be but quite recent, are employed in the various duties of the station, and the confusion in the luggage department I have rarely seen equalled. In spite of all these minor discomforts, however, my spirits were at their highest; for it was a railway train in which I was about to travel, and not a diligence, and that fact proved in itself sufficient to dispel all predispositions for discontent. I was fortunate enough to journey in company with an American gentleman, by whose thorough acquaintance with the country I had already benefited during my sojourn in Mexico, and who, until I embarked at Vera Cruz, most considerately acted as my informant and guide. Mr P—— and myself were soon ensconced in the old-fashioned English carriages here employed for first-class accommodation, and punctually at twelve o'clock the locomotive's shrill signal whistled adieu to the city of Montezuma.

The Mexico and Vera Cruz Railway is, as regards the time occupied and the various difficulties encountered in its construction, perhaps the most remarkable of all similar enterprises.

It was commenced in 1852, but the company had to battle with the chimerical ideas of one of the then directors, who, among other whims, cherished that of constructing a line from the capital towards the coast, simultaneously with that from the sea up-country. This measure necessitated the carriage of rails and other materials from Vera Cruz to Mexico over a track of country presenting the greatest possible obstacles to transport, thus, at least, doubling the expense. Want of funds, revolutions, and the like, prevented the progress of the undertaking; and when the French invaded the Republic in 1861, the line was only completed a few miles inland from the coast, and a short distance from the capital on the plateau. The French generals, and subsequently the Emperor Maximilian, materially aided the company with funds, and the works advanced fairly, when the overthrow of the Empire again put a stop to their exertions.

This time, however, their idleness was not of long duration, for the Liberals took up the railway question with vigour. Congress considerably increased the subsidy, and finally, on the 1st of January 1873, the line from Mexico to Vera Cruz, 263 miles, was inaugurated by President Lerdo and his ministers.

The line may be divided into three sections: the first from Mexico over the plateau of the *tierra fria* to *Boca del Monte*, a distance of 156 miles; thence down the steep descent of the *cumbres*, to *Paso del Macho*, 60 miles; and finally thence along the gently sloping *tierra caliente* to Vera Cruz, 47 miles. The two end sections presented no difficulties of note, but the centre portion is one of the greatest feats of engineering skill; and it is doubtful whether the marvellous line between Callao and Oroya in Peru, which is to scale an altitude of more than 15,000 feet, will present much greater obstacles than did the short portion of this Mexican enterprise that lies between Boca del Monte and Orizaba, where, in a distance of only 25 miles, the road descends almost 4000 feet, where curves of 300 feet radius, and gradients of three and four per cent. often over loose and yielding ground, follow one another in quick succession.

For more than a hundred and fifty miles after leaving the city, we travelled over the undulating plateau of the *tierra fria*, an appellation which coincided entirely with the temperature that prevailed. The elevation of nigh 8000 feet is disagreeably perceptible when the sun is not shining, and in respect of the cold, it might have been Siberia that we were traversing instead of the tropics. This part of the country is described as one continuous *maguey* plantation, slightly varied by crops and meadows where the soil permits. Large quantities of *pulque* are the staple of this *mesa*, and especially of the seventy miles nearest the capital. This industry has greatly augmented since the construction of the railway, as its transport has been so much accelerated. Formerly, the city's supply came solely from places distant ten or fifteen miles; now, a considerable portion is received from Soltepec and the seven intermediate stations, and the company run a train daily called the "*pulque* train," which brings up the day's provision in the early morning.

At Apizaco, where we arrived at five A.M., the branch line to Puebla joins the main line. This part has been completed for several years, and is twenty-nine miles in length.

When daylight appeared, we were still spinning along the wavy table-land thickly overgrown with its prickly mat of cacti, stubbly trees, and *magueys* of enormous dimensions—many with their slim blossom-stem springing from the centre.

This indeed seems to be the home of the aloe; it thrives nowhere else so well. At times *rancho* buildings would seem to flit past us, and cattle might be seen browsing on the scanty pasture; above all, as if conscious of his eternal sovereignty, Orizaba reared unabashed his snowy front to meet the piercing blue of the cloudless heavens.

This majestic cone, 17,400 feet in height, is an extinct volcano, and the characteristic landmark of a wide range of country. Until we reached the coast, the white, tapering colossus was never lost to view.

At eight o'clock the train stopped at *Boca del Monte*—the Mouth of the Mount—a station, or, more truly speaking, half-a-dozen wooden sheds, on one of which we descried the welcome words, *Hotel Restaurant del Ferro Carril;* and wondering why a mere long "lumber hut," as they say in the States, was dignified with so pretentious a name, we sat down to a very tolerable *potage au riz* and *poulet sauté*, for "mine host" happened to be a Gaul.

At this spot, 7800 feet above sea-level, the plateau suddenly terminates, and the steep decline of the *cumbres* begins. The train was piloted by a double-headed monster engine—a Fairlie locomotive; and immediately after leaving the station, we entered on our downward path. From here, for the next twenty-five miles, the train makes tardy progress—about eight miles an hour—and twines like some serpent down its wavering course, skirting mountain steeps on passes cut into the rock or earth, turning sharp curves that caused the carriages to lean perceptibly to one side, crossing giddy ravines and clefts over slender bridges, and penetrating into the heart of hills and rocks through many tunnels. It was difficult to trust the eye when a survey was made; on one side a perpendicular mass of massive stone, on the other a yawning abyss, and ahead a glistening line that marks the track as it clings to the battlements of a chasmed height.

After whizzing through the first tunnel, the charming valley of *Maltrata* appeared in sight, a soft and glossy sward separating the giant mountains 2000 feet below us, with its chessboard of trim fields, its fruitful gardens and white houses, which seemed, from our altitude, like so many specks; whilst the monarch of the region, the glacier-capped Orizaba, lowered over the many ranges of the *Sierra* in distant and paramount grandeur.

As we proceeded down the slanting line, field and fell, gardens and houses grew larger, the waving crops clearer, and the inhabitants of this snug retreat were descried plying their rustic avocations. Although only thirteen miles of railway lie between Boca del Monte and Maltrata (a distance much in excess of the straight line), the climate is totally different; and cacti, maguey, and dwarf trees are superseded by all the fruitage of the *tierra templada*, for the altitude of Maltrata is but 5500 feet. Thus a descent of 2300 feet is accomplished in thirteen

VIEW ON THE MEXICAN RAILWAY: THE VALLEY OF MALTRATA AND THE PICO DE ORIZABA

miles, establishing an average gradient of three and a half per cent. The engineering works along this portion of the line, and indeed the whole way to Paso del Macho, are stupendous; and the traveller along this wonderful country divides his attention and admiration almost equally between nature's awe-inspiring creation and man's skilful work. Chasms and precipices are gracefully spanned by viaducts and bridges, indestructibly founded of iron, on massive supports of solid masonry; and though apparently slender and almost hazardous, are nevertheless more than efficient for the requisite purpose.*
Six tunnels in quick succession are passed before arrival at Maltrata, which is at length reached by an enormous detour, necessitated by a steep mountain interposing between it and the direct route. The track winds here along the uncertain tracery of the mountain ridges like a stream through a serpentine valley: now it will run due north, then a sharp curve turns it due south, and at length, on the

* On the entire railway, including the branch line to Puebla, there are ten viaducts, fifty-five iron bridges, and ninety-three wooden bridges; the latter are being gradually replaced by works of iron. There are in all fifteen tunnels, the longest of which is about 350 feet. The longest bridge is the Puente de Soledad, measuring 742 feet.

opposite side of a ravine, the road-bed over which we have just glided is discerned slanting down the incline, which towers far above our heads.

At a little before eleven o'clock we stopped at the station, and looked up the rugged *cumbres* behind us, wondering how we had passed their perpendicular and seemingly insurmountable barriers. At Maltrata, the up and down trains pass one another. The train from Vera Cruz happened to be behind time that morning, and the delay afforded us an opportunity to inspect the station, and the convoy by which we had come.

The small station is erected on an artificial plateau levelled out of the continuous declivity, and through which the line runs in a curve. The descent on leaving Maltrata is even steeper than the gradient immediately before, being fully four per cent. The carriages of our train were well filled, especially those of the second and third class, and attached to it there was a large American car tenanted by a company of soldiers. A similar escort is provided for every train. The *ladrones* of this region (especially between Boca del Monte and Paso del Macho), were wont, in the times of the

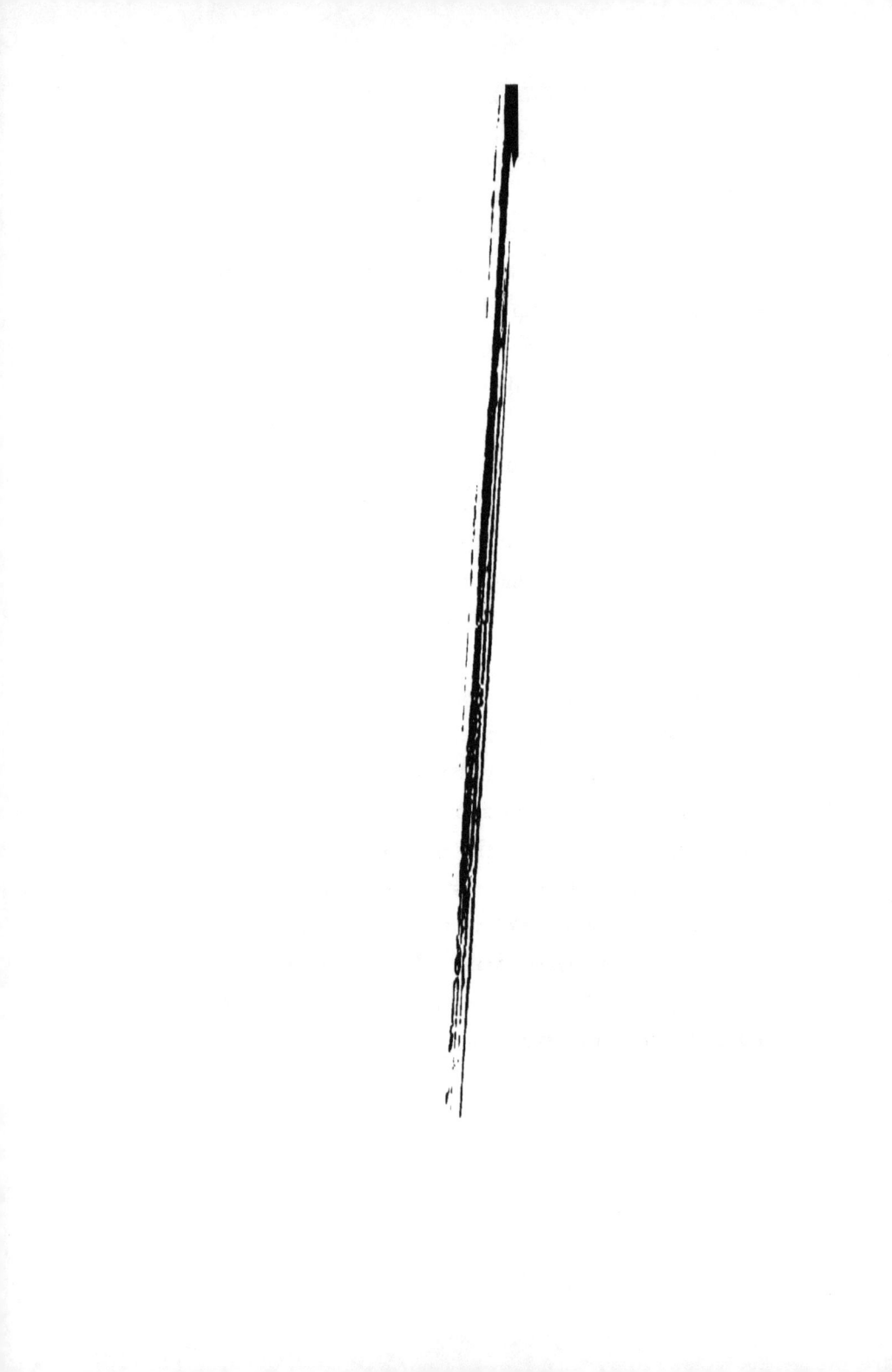

VIEW OF THE RAILWAY SKIRTING THE SIDE OF THE BARRANCA DEL INFIERNILLO.

diligences, to be the most successful of all their *confrères* in the Republic. When the railway first commenced to travel, these worthies, unwilling to relinquish a profitable and hereditary profession, endeavoured to attack the trains as they slackened speed up or down the *cumbres*, but their depredations were nipped in the bud by the Governmental provision of regular escorts.

At length the expected train came puffing up the incline, and we were again *en route*. The powerful Fairlie locomotive, in addition to the efficacious Westinghouse break, restrained the string of carriages from undue speed down the dangerous declivities, as we followed the wayward configuration of the glorious mountains into whose encircling parapets the road has been hewn with astounding skill. Immediately after quitting Maltrata, the line enters the *Barranca del Infiernillo*, a chasm that divides two craggy steeps, and whose dizzy depths the eye can scarcely measure. Bridges across gulfs follow tunnels through rocky promontories; views majestically pencilled succeed one another with surprising rapidity, as we carefully and slowly descend: the mammoth engine hugs its iron path and guides us in safety over the seeming peril. As we progress the vegetation gradually changes, and the signs of lower altitude are observable in bush and brake. Calm weald and wold below us were rich with their dewy green, so different from the dusty growth of the arid plateau, and so gladdening to an eye wearied by cacti and *maguey*.

After passing the *Infiernillo* precipice, ever memorable for its awful beauty, the gradient became less severe, but curves and countercurves caused the train to twist and twirl in an almost incredible manner, until, a few miles before Orizaba, the ground appeared more even and the line less complicated. The twelve miles from Maltrata to the latter station occupied an hour more, and we arrived at noon.

Mr P—— and I had arranged to spend a day at Orizaba, and therefore quitted the train, and repaired to the Hotel de las Diligencias (in this case happily a solecism), where we found the usual provincial accommodation.

Orizaba is 181 miles distant from the capital, and rises 4000 feet above the level of the sea,

VIEW NEAR ORIZABA

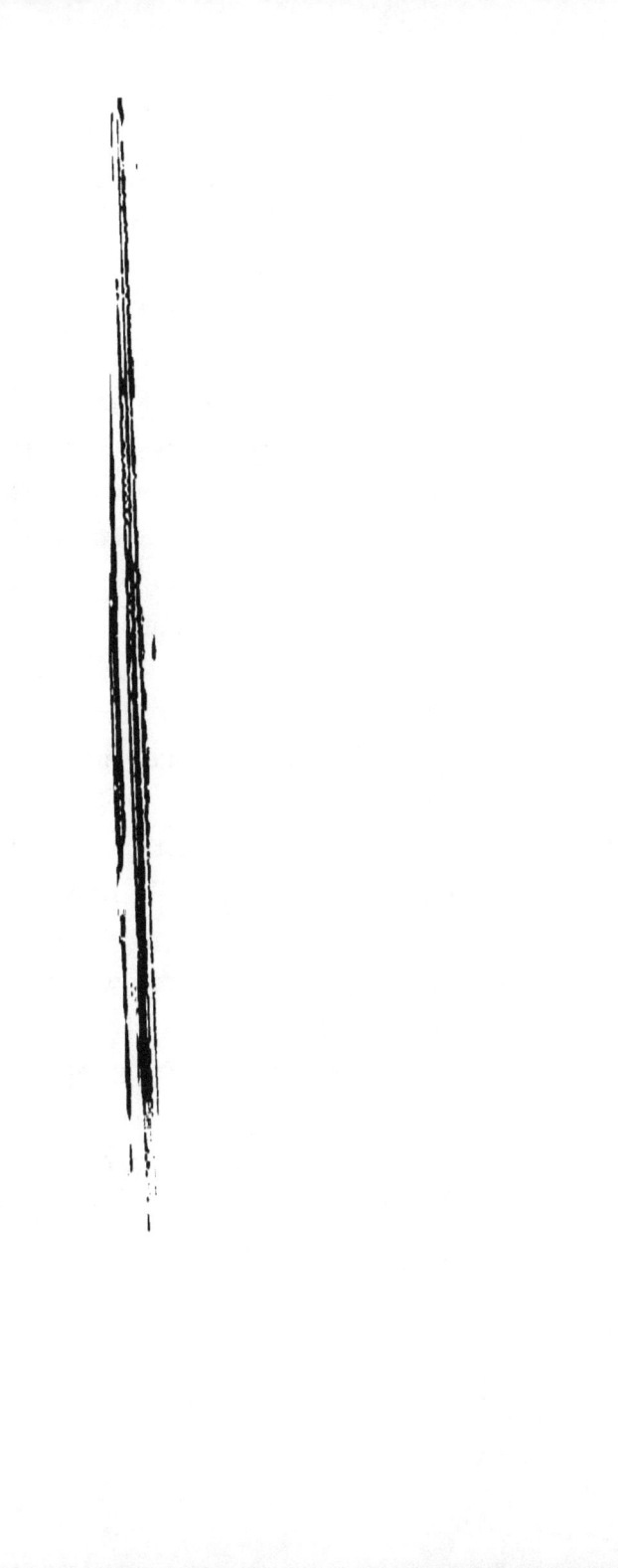

thus being 3600 feet lower than the valley of Mexico. This difference, and its comparative proximity to the sea-shore, have of course a marked influence on the climate and vegetation. It is embosomed in a lovely valley wreathed with mountains, whose summits were enshrouded by curling mists, the leaden blackness of which called to memory the normal state of the west coast of Ireland. Unlike the plateau, where the wet and dry seasons are strictly divided, this part of the Atlantic slope is in its climate exceedingly damp. Whenever the wind blows from the north on the coast (and we were informed that such was the case at the time of our stay), clouds and moisture are wafted across to the *cumbres*, which, too lofty to allow of their passage, arrest and absorb them. This naturally renders the soil extraordinarily fertile, and although the altitude precludes the possibility of ultra-tropical plants, yet we saw flourishing bananas and billowy fields of sugar-cane, cotton plantations, and gardens of glowing fruit.

The town itself is an old, noiseless place, with straight but rather irregular streets, and simple houses, tiled, with sloping and overhanging roofs.

The roadways are badly and unevenly paved, and wide gutters, almost like open sewers, run down their centre. The buildings are mostly low and one-storied, and innocent of any attempt at decoration. Gardens are numerous, especially in the neighbourhood, where the houses are curtained with mellow foliage—bananas, orange, oleander, and coffee trees—which lends to that portion of the town a tangled and straggling appearance. A fine cathedral graces the *plaza*, and the lofty towers and domes of many other churches rise from the low streets. A rivulet waters Orizaba in a deep and rocky valley, and is spanned in several places by curious ancient bridges, one of which is in ruins, and now obsolete. The steep banks of this stream are partially dammed by old walls, from whose cracks and crevices creepers and parasites spring in fantastic luxuriance, draping the masonry with a magnificent carpet of verdure. From the margin of the stream large-leaved weeds and huge ferns shoot up in lavish profusion, and show the thousand different gradations of green; at the brink of this rivulet men and women, scantily clad, were performing the mysterious rites of the laun-

ORIZABA.

dry for the town—rites not too conscientiously cultivated. When the washing and rubbing were accomplished, the linen would be spread on the dry patches of stone or sand which the stream had left untouched in its course, or be suspended from a rock or the twigs of a neighbouring shrub, for the purpose of drying.

This Homeric scene was exceeded in interest by that which awaited us in the market-place, thronged, as it was, with Indians and dark *mestizos*, who had mustered in great numbers, for it was the principal market-day of the week. The animation and bustle reminded me instantly of similar occasions at Colima, and when the difference in the physiognomy of the natives is excepted, there is little to distinguish the one from the other. The market is held in a large open space, and the multifarious products were mostly exhibited on the ground, under fragile stands of sticks and matting, or the characteristic umbrella-shaped *tendajes* or *sombrajos*, suspended on centre-poles, and constantly shifted to shut out the sun. It would be but useless repetition to enumerate the various articles which crowded every stall; suffice it to say, that all conceivable fruits and vegetables of the *tierra caliente* and *tierra templada* were represented, as well as the butcher's supply of flesh and dried meats, and the confectioner's numberless choice of *pan dulce*. Salt and various spices, as well as cold *tortillas* and sausages, were there to attract the hungry, while their vendors substituted large tough leaves for paper, and strips of the fibry palmetto leaf for string, to wrap their delicacies in their neat parcels. The solemn Indians were droning their strange musical language as they sold their own produce and bought supplies, whilst the cheerful and frolicsome *mestizos* were sustaining a loud and lively palaver, accompanied by merry peals of laughter. The *Indios*, whom they pleased to treat as children, would at one time offer scope for their sportive raillery; at another their banter would be directed against one of their own number, or the scrutinising *estranjeros* whose eyes examined them and their wares.

We were much amused by the frequent bartering transactions between the neighbouring stall-keepers; thus we saw two hands-full of salt exchanged for half the quantity of *chile*, and a huge water-melon given in payment for a couple of sausages; but a *tortilla* and a radish vendor could not come to terms. They were both young *mestizos* of sturdy build, and whilst the owner of the radishes, on the principle of "measure for measure," demanded a *tortilla* for every root, the lady who sold the former would only part with four maize cakes for five of the pungent vegetables, and the bargain was unhappily left uncompleted.

Orizaba numbers about 20,000 inhabitants, and since the railway has made it its principal station for stores and repairs, it has gained in importance. In spite of the clammy atmosphere, its climate is very salubrious, for its altitude ensures it against the spread of epidemics; and although a few cases of yellow fever are annually carried into the town by fugitives from Vera Cruz, that terrible malady has never yet assumed alarming proportions.

We visited the *Cocoalapan* cotton factory, a large and admirably-arranged establishment. It is under English management, but owned by a wealthy Mexican. A paper-mill and some smaller manufactories are in the vicinity, where water power is to be found in abundance. We also minutely inspected the railway workshops, where we saw a number of engines of various mechanisms and nationalities. The Fairlie, as the engineer in charge informed us, is as yet the only one that can be used with safety over the *cumbres*, but experiments were just then being undertaken with a very powerful locomotive of American manufacture.

The clouds that had been gathering in the evening dissolved the next morning in a gentle but obstinate drizzle; the icy minaret of Orizaba was perfectly invisible, and its pinnacles thickly veiled in scud and mist. Towards noon the sun began to burst its shroud of moisture, and the fields and orchards were deliciously fragrant when we proceeded to the station to continue our route. The train from Mexico happened to be two hours behind time, and it was not before two P.M. that we were again seated in the train.

The line quits Orizaba, as it enters it, on a gradient of about two per cent.; this is maintained for the next seven miles without any remarkable curves or other difficulties, the railway running almost parallel with the old waggon highroad. The country through which we travelled was an absolute hothouse of fertility; *haciendas, huertas,* and wild patches of delicate leafage succeeded one another, and the more we advanced the more tropical became plants and climate. In half-an-hour we reached the *Barranca de Metlac,* a chasm very similar to those of Beltran and Atenquique on the Pacific side, but considerably smaller in its dimensions. The depth of Metlac is about 200 feet (its eastern side is considerably higher than the western), and not more than about 130 yards across, measurements, however, which proved immense obstacles to the construction of the railway. It was at first contemplated to span the depth by a bridge across the top, but supports of 200 feet in height proved impracticable. The roadway, which, when it strikes the *barranca,* turns to the northward, is cut into its perpendicular wall, sloping at a gradient of three per cent., until it descends half-way, when it crosses to the other side on a bridge, and scales the opposite steep in a similar manner, the two slopes running for some distance parallel to one another. The descent in the severe decline takes the train through no fewer than five tunnels, which perforate as many rocky promontories; and when the level of the bridge is attained, another tunnel into the mountain-side winds in a considerable curve to enable the train to enter the bridge, which stands at right angles to the previous direction of the line. This bridge, which is 445 feet long and 92 high, is one of the most remarkable structures of its kind. It is shaped in a curve from one side to the other, and is certainly one of the most extraordinary works on this railway, so replete with the triumphs of engineering art. When the opposite end of the bridge is gained, a tunnel similar to the one just quitted is entered, so as to allow the train to resume the direction of the *barranca's* course, and the ascent is at once commenced.* The scenery throughout this

---

* I am informed that these skilful engineering operations are due to the ability of Mr William Cross Buchanan, now consulting engineer to the Mexican Railway Company.

CURVED RAILWAY BRIDGE OVER THE BARRANCA DI METLAC

barranca is exquisite. The vegetation closely resembles that described on the Pacific side, giant labyrinths of leafy luxuriance, with here and there a bold rock glaring from its prison-bars of green, and the *Rio de Metlac*, clear as crystal, speeding over its pebbly bed at the base. It is worth a sea-voyage of thousands of miles, if only to see this ravine and the line that traverses it.

Arrived at the eastern *mesa*, a few miles over almost level ground brought us to Fortin, a small place, which, till the end of 1872, was the terminal station of the Vera Cruz section of the railway.

Five miles more over a regular gradient of more than two per cent., and through the most enchanting country, brought us to Córdoba, the Colima of the east. Although Córdoba is 2690 feet above sea-level, and thus more than a thousand feet higher than the western town, its climate is very similar to that of the latter, and what flourishes in Colima may also be found there, with the sole exception of the cocoa-palm, which never grows at a higher altitude than 1500 feet. The *huertas* and plantations of Córdoba enjoy no mean reputation, and had I not been forced to hurry on board the steamer, I should not have passed this spot as hastily as I did.

Córdoba is especially famed for its coffee, which is said to equal that of Colima and Mocha; extensive *haciendas* are exclusively employed with its growth, and through the instrumentality of the railway a considerable export trade in this product to the United States has been inaugurated, as well as in many others. Foreigners have bought estates here, and the place promises to increase in size and importance.

From here, for the next seventeen miles, our route traversed a continuous track of tropical forest, which seems, by its deep shade and shining flowers, to unite the charms of night and morning; and this wood might well realise the most fanciful ideal. My experience of the Pacific coast was entirely eclipsed by the indescribable splendour of this region. It seemed as if we were gliding over an ocean of teeming herbage, in which the shadowy hills formed the waves and the millions of brilliant blossoms the foam and spray. Both sides of the line are securely embanked by

THE ATOYAC RAILWAY BRIDGE

this impregnable fastness of interlaced vegetation, and it is rarely that a small clearing affords room for an Indian hut (little else but a high and steep gable-roof of heavy thatch), or a stream, embowered among matted arches of brushwood, ferns, and creepers, bubbles up from the prolific soil.

Three-quarters of an hour after leaving Córdoba, we crossed the Atoyác river on a fine iron bridge, and reached the little town of the same name, sleeping softly in its narrow valley, amid the whispers of bananas and orange-trees, with an air of such ethereal and suggestive laziness that it might prompt the beholder to assign it as the very birthplace of *"dolce far niente."* Proceeding, we arrived at the last barriers that intervene between the interior and the coast, the *Chiquihuite* mountains, famed for the most enchanting and superb scenery. The line for two miles follows the winding course of the Atoyác river, until it quits its valley and plunges into a tunnel through a gigantic rock. Emerging from the latter, a sharp curve suddenly discloses the remarkable *Rio de Chiquihuite*, where it bounds in a lovely cascade from a rift in the sheer cliff, sixty feet into the gorge below.

The vesture of greenery which drapes every inch of this wonderful region thoroughly screens the fissure whence the water springs. It rushes forth between beaded leaves and quivering branches, and precipitates its volume unobstructed into thin spray and irised mist beneath. It was but a glance that I caught of this sublime picture; for as the remorseless train moved on, an obtrusive rock cruelly interposed between it and the longing eye, and it was seen no more.

The next station was Paso del Macho, where we arrived at a quarter past four. From there (1550 feet above sea-level) the ground slopes gently down to the coast, a distance of forty-seven miles, and there is nothing to distinguish the railway from any ordinary work of the same kind. A great change now takes place in the country. The hitherto superabundant vegetation gradually becomes thinner, the soil becomes thirsty and gritty, and is at times sprinkled with gaunt shapes of rock. Stumpy trees and stunted bushes take the place of the netted undergrowth on the mountains, and it is only where a river refreshes the cracki g soil that the monotony is relieved by coverts of succulent green. Such spots are invariably chosen as the sites of small towns or Indian villages, whose unsymmetrical cabins, with their downy roofs, impart a whimsical beauty to the lawn-like banks.

It is said that this track of country is too low to come in contact with the vapours wafted inland from the sea, which, attracted by the heights, float over the coast-land without fertilising it.

We crossed the *Rio Jamapa* over the longest iron bridge on the line, and arrived at *La Soledad* situate on its eastern bank, and memorable as the spot where the Convention between the invading powers and Mexico was signed on the 19th of February 1862.

The perfectly flat country shows, now and then, a strip of swamp, but it is mostly a cheerless waste of sand, with only the scantiest of vegetation. Palms and bananas, so luscious on the Pacific coast, are here conspicuous only for their absence; there is nothing but low jungle on the patches of marsh, and a few deformed cacti peering between the rough masses of rock and shingle.

We stopped at two stations, *La Purga* and *Tejería*, and finally at seven o'clock passed through a break in the crumbling walls of the ancient fortifications of Vera Cruz, and entered the wooden shed which at present forms the terminus.

As a matter of course, the house to which we repaired was the *Hotel de las Diligencias*—an establishment bearing this appellation being as material a part of every Mexican town as its *plaza* or its *catedral*. This hotel was the reverse of agreeable. The narrow yard at its entrance was redolent of more than the orthodox "two and seventy" odours attributed by the poet to Cologne, and the slatternly French hostess ushered us into the only room vacant, to reach which we were obliged to pass through the apartment of a Havanese family, consisting of husband, wife, infant, and nurse! With evident risk to the comfort of this happy quartette we ventured upon an evening excursion, after partaking of *comida* in the gallery overlooking the above-mentioned delightful court. The sky was overcast, whilst a "norther" or *norte* was howling melancholily, and on arrival at the Custom-house gate, we saw the waves dashing over the stone landing-stage and into the streets. Of the proverbial heat of Vera Cruz I could discover nothing; indeed, the prevailing gale rendered the atmosphere cool and pleasant.

The next morning broke with a clear blue sky, a blazing sun, and not a breath of wind, illustrative of the sudden changes in the weather, more frequent here than even *pronunciamientos*. The "knowing ones," however, prognosticated a speedy return of the hurricane, for this was the season for *nortes*. Although inconvenient to the shipping, and obstructive to the landing of merchandise, they are welcome guests, as they temporarily free the town from the scourge of *vomito* —that most malignant type of yellow fever, for which Vera Cruz enjoys an unenviable reputation.

The town is the chief port of the Republic, and the receipts of its customs amount to more than half the national revenue from this source. It thus seems hardly credible that

Vera Cruz should lack a harbour, or, with the exception of a short stone pier, any other arrangement to facilitate the shipping traffic. But such is the case. Its topography is most unfavourable to the construction of a harbour, but the English Railway Company intend to erect a mole, which promises to be a great improvement. At present, vessels must anchor between the shore and a small island about half a mile to seaward, on which is built the fort of *San Juan de Uloa*. At the back of this island, and parallel with the coast, coral reefs extend for a considerable distance, so that the town can only be approached from the north or south. When a *norte* is blowing, communication between vessels in the roadstead and the shore is impossible; and when the wind becomes very violent, as is frequently the case in January and February, ships often make their way towards the sea to prevent inevitable destruction, in the event of dragging their anchors.

Vera Cruz was founded by the Viceroy Count Monterey at the end of the sixteenth century, and until the declaration of independence its port had the privilege of alone being open to foreign commerce on the Atlantic seaboard of Mexico.

This of course was a source of great wealth to the town, which, as far as its buildings are concerned, retains ample tokens of past grandeur. Originally a fortress, it is still entirely surrounded by massive walls and ramparts; and as the neighbouring country is nothing but a desert, and offers little temptation to use it for building sites, the habitations are mainly confined to the limited space within the walls.

The latter stretch about a quarter of a mile along the sea-shore, and are flanked on both sides by ancient forts, whilst on the land side the ramparts are curved in the form of an arc, and entered by a number of quaint gateways, on which other enemies besides time and tempest have left their ineffaceable marks. The countless ancient cupolas and towers look hoar and venerable, whilst the houses generally are kept in good repair, and notwithstanding their age are carefully coated with paint to conceal their deficiencies.

The streets, though ill-paved, appeared neat

and clean, and made me wonder how the notorious scavengers of the town—the sombre *zopilotes*—could manage to thrive, especially as they seemed to be in the reverse of a starving condition. The open sewer running along the centre of the thoroughfare resembled a clear stream; and with the exception of the hotel-yard, I encountered none of the balmy fragrance for which Vera Cruz is widely famed.

But it must not be forgotten that my visit was in January, perhaps the coolest and healthiest month in the year.

Our first errand on Saturday, January 17th, 1874 (my last day in Mexico), was to patronise the bathing establishment, which I mention on account of its comfort and excellence. Successive compartments, furnished with every necessary appliance, run round three sides of a large *patio*, which is a complete nursery of beautiful plants bedewed by the ever-trickling fountain in the centre.

Facing the hotel is the *plaza*, a capital specimen of this national institution, tesselated with a most curious and artistic pavement

THE ALAMEDA, VERA CRUZ

of marble. Here and in the *alameda*, which is outside the walls, I spied the only palms in Vera Cruz.

But the time for embarkation had arrived. The *Société Transatlantique's* steamer *Floride* had hoisted the "Blue Peter," and a short row through the rolling surf soon brought me on board. At three o'clock the good ship quietly moved from her anchorage near San Juan de Uloa, and an hour later the faint outlines of Montezuma's receding shores had mingled with the hazy horizon.

THE END.

www.ingramcontent.com/pod-product-compliance
Lightning Source LLC
Chambersburg PA
CBHW031959300426
44117CB00008B/829